Nikon D7000

Simon Stafford

MAGIC LANTERN GUIDES®

Nikon
D7000

Simon Stafford

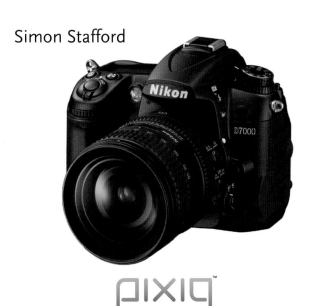

∏IXIⓆ™

An Imprint of Sterling Publishing Co., Inc.
New York

For more information,
visit our website at www.pixiq.com

Book Design: Michael Robertson
Cover Design: Thom Gaines, Electron Graphics

Stafford, Simon.
  Nikon D7000 / Simon Stafford. -- 1st ed.
    p. cm. -- (Magic lantern guides)
  ISBN 978-1-4547-0131-6
  1. Nikon digital cameras--Handbooks, manuals, etc. 2. Photography--Digital techniques--Handbooks,
manuals, etc. 3. Single-lens reflex cameras--Handbooks, manuals, etc. I. Title. II. Series.
  TR263.N5S74 2011
  771.3'2--dc22

                                        2011000543

10 9 8 7 6 5 4 3 2 1

First Edition

Published by Pixiq, An Imprint of
Sterling Publishing Co., Inc.
387 Park Avenue South, New York, N.Y. 10016

Text © 2011, Simon Stafford
Photography © 2011, Simon Stafford unless otherwise specified

Distributed in Canada by Sterling Publishing,
c/o Canadian Manda Group, 165 Dufferin Street
Toronto, Ontario, Canada M6K 3H6
Distributed in the United Kingdom by GMC Distribution Services,
Castle Place, 166 High Street, Lewes, East Sussex, England BN7 1XU

Distributed in Australia by Capricorn Link (Australia) Pty Ltd.,
P.O. Box 704, Windsor, NSW 2756 Australia

This book is not sponsored by Nikon.

Every effort has been made to ensure that all the information in this book is accurate. However, due to
differing conditions, tools, and individual skills, the publisher cannot be responsible for any injuries,
losses, and other damages that may result from the use of the information in this book. Because
specifications may be changed by manufacturers without notice, the contents of this book may not
necessarily agree with software and equipment changes made after publication.

If you have questions or comments about this book, please contact:
Lark Books
67 Broadway
Asheville, NC 28801
(828) 253-0467

Manufactured in Canada

ISBN 13: 978-1-4547-0131-6

For information about custom editions, special sales, premium and corporate purchases, please
contact Sterling Special Sales Department at 800-805-5489 or specialsales@sterlingpub.com.

For information about desk and examination copies available to college and university professors,
requests must be submitted to academic@larkbooks.com. Our complete policy can be found at
www.larkbooks.com.

To learn more about digital photography, go to www.pixiq.com.

Contents

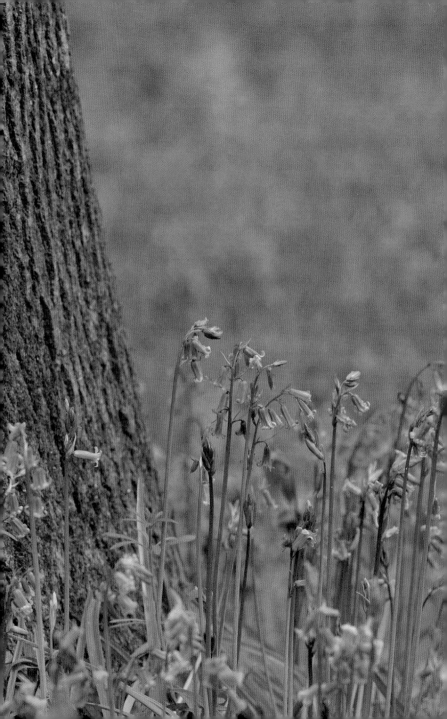

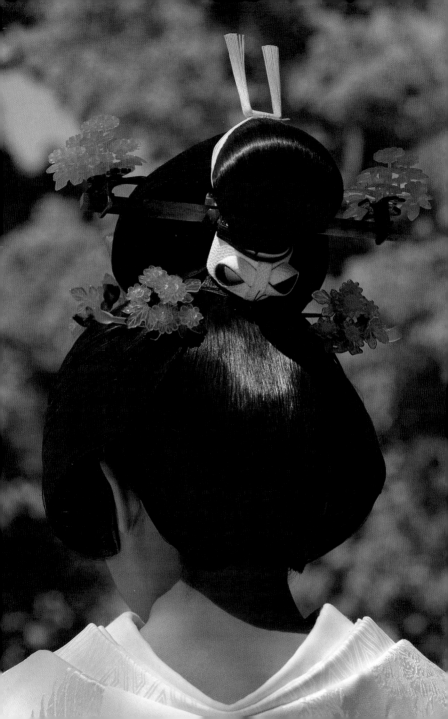

Introducing
the Nikon D7000

Nikon has a long heritage of building fine cameras with urbane qualities born of innovative engineering and progressive design, setting them apart from the rest of the pack, and the D7000 is no exception. It represents a natural evolution of the Nikon DX-format cameras, such as the D300 series, including a video-recording system that has been refined considerably from the one seen in the Nikon D90, which was released in late 2008 and was the first DSLR camera to feature video capability. In terms of its specification, the D7000 usurps the position of the D300s in a number of ways as the flagship of the Nikon DX-format cameras. All these models share cutting-edge technology and many advanced features—so much so that this synergy of design enables them to be used naturally side by side. As a consequence of this design philosophy, the D7000 possesses a meld of qualities that allow it to be used proficiently at any level, from the relatively inexperienced hobby photographer who seeks nothing more than point-and-shoot convenience, all the way up the scale to the demanding requirements of professional photography.

⟩ The Fisheye-Nikkor DX 10.5mm f/2.8G is one of a number of special lenses, including the Micro-Nikkor and PC-E Tilt / Shift lenses, which can be used with the D7000.

Much of the exterior design of the D7000 is very similar to that of other contemporary Nikon DSLR cameras, both in the DX and FX formats. On closer inspection, some external control buttons have been relocated, and there is a new 'flick'-style dedicated button for the Live View feature. The D7000 is built around a sturdy chassis made of polycarbonate with top and rear body panels constructed from a lightweight magnesium alloy. The camera body has extensive sealing against the ingress of moisture and dust, which encases its newly developed 16.2MP (effective) CMOS sensor. Nikon has long been trumpeting that image quality in the digital world rests on three pillars: optical quality of the lens, sensor technology, and internal camera processing. The D7000 epitomizes this in respect of the latter two aspects as its sensor supports a multi-channel output to an in-built, 14-bit analog-to-digital converter (ADC); thereafter, all internal camera processing is handled at a 16-bit depth by a single ASIC. Nikon has dubbed this image-processing regime "Expeed 2." It is at the heart of the camera's ability to record, process, and output high-quality images at a rapid rate.

This fast data processing is combined with a fully mechanical shutter unit that enables the D7000 to cycle at a maximum of 6 frames per second (fps); adding the new dedicated MB-D11 battery pack, which can take one Nikon rechargeable Li-ion EN-EL15 battery or six AA / LR6-sized batteries, extends the shooting capacity but does not increase the frame rate. It also has the **Q** (Quiet) shutter release mode that separates the actions of lifting the reflex mirror and opening and closing the shutter from the actions of re-cocking the shutter mechanism and lowering the reflex mirror. The shutter unit is tested to perform at least 150,000 actuations.

The other principal new features of the D7000 include: a new 2,016-pixel RGB sensor for TTL metering, a new Nikon Multi-CAM 4500DX autofocus sensor, with an array of 39 AF points, and a video-recording feature that operates at 24 fps with full-HD resolution of 1920 x 1080 (1080p). This feature has been enhanced from previous Nikon DSLR models, as it has the ability to perform contrast-detect AF during recording. It also supports a wide range of aperture settings down to a minimum of f/16, and an external stereo microphone. Thus, the D7000 represents a meld of the best qualities of its esteemed stablemates together with some innovative new features, which result from an uncompromising design criteria harnessed to cutting-edge technology and many years of experience accrued by Nikon in the manufacture of digital SLR cameras.

The D7000 is an interchangeable-lens, digital, single-lens-reflex camera that offers complete automation of exposure and focusing, as well as full manual control of all its features and functions. The camera body is built around a very sturdy chassis with all-metal top and rear panels that impart a solid, rugged feel to the camera. It has approximate dimensions (W x H x D) of 5.2 x 4.1 x 3.0 inches (132 x 105 x 77 mm) and weighs approximately 24 oz (690 g) without battery or memory card. It has a Nikon F lens mount with an automatic focusing (AF) coupling and electrical contacts. The origins of this lens-mount design can be traced back to the Nikon F 35mm SLR introduced in 1959, which means that many earlier Nikkor lenses can be used with the D7000. The greatest level of compatibility is achieved with either AF-D or AF-G type Nikkor lenses.

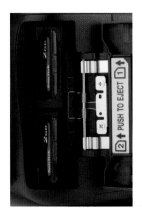

‹ The D7000 has two memory card slots that support SD, SDHC, and the latest SDXC card standards.

Other lenses can be used but provide a variable level of compatibility dependent on their design; AF and Ai-P type Nikkor lenses offer a slightly reduced functionality in terms of the camera's TTL metering system, as its Matrix metering defaults to Color Matrix in place of 3D Color Matrix metering. Even manual focus Ai, Ai-s, Ai-converted, and E-series Nikkor lenses can be used with the D7000, although neither 3D Color Matrix metering nor Programmed-Auto or Shutter-Priority exposure modes are supported.

The basic structure of the Complimentary Metal Oxide Semi-Conductor (CMOS) sensor used in the D7000 is the same as the CMOS sensor used in many other makes of camera. However, the sensor in the D7000 is unique, with a Nikon design specification incorporated in it during manufacture. There are total of 16.9 million photodiodes (pixels), of which 16.2 million are effective for the purpose of recording an image. Each photodiode on the sensor is just 4.78 microns (µm) square. This gives the camera a maximum resolution of 4,928 x 3,264 pixels, sufficient to produce 13.5 x 20-inch (34 x 50 cm) prints at a resolution of 240 ppi without interpolation (re-sizing).

The imaging area is 0.66 x 1 inch (15.6 x 23.6 mm), which is smaller than a 35mm film frame that measures 1 x 1.5 inch (24 x 36 mm) but retains the same 2:3 aspect ratio. Nikon calls this their DX format (elsewhere, it is often referred to as the APS-C format) and uses the same "DX" designation to identify those lenses that have been optimized for use with their digital SLR cameras. Due to the smaller size of the DX-format digital sensor, the angle of view offered by any focal length is reduced compared with a lens of the same focal length used on a 35mm film camera. To estimate the angle of view for a particular focal length in comparison with the coverage offered by the same focal length on a 35mm film camera, multiply the focal length by 1.5x (see pages 27-29 for a full explanation), and you will get the "effective" focal length of that lens when used on a DX camera.

THE PARTS OF THE SENSOR

The CMOS sensor of the D7000 is actually a sandwich of several layers, each with a specific purpose:

Photosite Layer: The photosite layer is responsible for the collection and conversion of light striking the CMOS sensor. Each photosite comprises a photodiode that collects photons of light during the exposure and then converts them into electrons before storing them in an "electron well." As soon as the exposure ends and no more light strikes the sensor, the well is emptied via an amplifier circuit, and the electrical signal is passed to the analog-to-digital converter (ADC), where the electrical signal is converted to a digital value.

Bayer-Pattern Filter: Above the photosite layer is a colored filter layer. The photodiodes on the CMOS sensor do not record color—they can only detect a level of brightness. To impart color to the image formed by the light that falls on the sensor, a series of minute red, green, and blue filters are arranged over the photodiodes in a Bayer pattern, which takes its name from the Kodak engineer who invented the system. These filters are arranged in an alternating pattern of red / green on the odd-numbered rows, and green / blue on the even-numbered rows. The Bayer pattern comprises 50% green, 25% red, and 25% blue filters. The intensity of light detected by each photodiode located beneath its single, dedicated color filter according to the Bayer pattern is converted into an electrical signal before being converted to a digital value by the ADC. If the camera is set to record an NEF (RAW) file, the value for each photodiode is simply saved. When you open this file in an appropriate RAW file converter, the software will interpret the value from each photodiode to produce a red-green-blue (RGB) value, which in turn is converted into an image that can be viewed. However, if the camera is set to record JPEG files, then the value from each photodiode is processed in the camera by comparing it with the values from a block of surrounding photodiodes, using a process called interpolation. The interpolation process produces a "best guess" for the RGB value for each sampling point (photodiode) on the sensor.

Micro-Lens Layer: Immediately above the Bayer pattern filter there is a layer of micro lenses. Since the photodiodes on the sensor are most efficient when the light falling on them is perpendicular, each photodiode has a miniature lens located above it to channel the light into its well to help maximize its light gathering ability; each micro-lens occupies an area larger than the photodiode well below it, and there is virtually no gap between neighboring micro-lenses. This effective ability to gather light, coupled with the relatively large 4.78-micron pixel pitch of the camera's sensor, allows it to scoop up photons very efficiently and contributes to the amazing image quality that can be attained at ISO 1600 or even ISO 3200.

Optical Low-Pass Filter: Positioned in front of the CMOS sensor but not connected to it is an optical low-pass filter (OLPF), sometimes called an anti-aliasing filter.

When the frequency of detail in an image—particularly a small, regular repeating pattern, such as the weave pattern in a fabric—alters at or close to the pitch of the photodiodes on the sensor, there is sometimes a side effect that produces unwanted data (often referred to as artifacts) due to the way the in-camera processing converts the electrical signal from the sensor to a digital value via the ADC. This additional data is manifest in the final image as a color pattern known as a moiré. Furthermore, the same in-camera processing can also result in a color-fringing effect, known as color aliasing, which causes a halo of one or more separate colors to appear along the edges of fine detail in the image.

The OLPF is used to reduce the unwanted effects of color aliasing and moiré. However, the OLPF reduces the resolution of detail, so the camera designers must strike a balance between its beneficial effect and the loss of acuity in fine detail, which increases as the strength of the filter is increased. The OLPF also incorporates a number of important coating layers to help improve image quality:

- To help prevent dust and other foreign material from adhering to the surface of the OLPF, it has an anti-static coating made from Indium Tin Oxide.
- To reduce the risk of light being reflected from the front surface of the OLPF onto the rear element of the lens, which could then result in flare effects or ghost images, the filter has an anti-reflective coating.
- The CMOS sensor is sensitive to wavelengths of light outside the spectrum visible to the human eye. This light, which can be either in the infrared (IR) or ultraviolet (UV) parts of the spectrum, will pollute image files and cause unwanted color shifts and a loss of image sharpness, so the OLPF has both an IR-blocking and UV-blocking coat. These IR- and UV-blocking coatings are very efficient; consequently, the D7000 cannot be recommended for any form of IR or UV light photography, which was possible with some earlier Nikon DSLR cameras, such as the D1 and D100.

The D7000 has inherited the same self-cleaning feature for the OLPF as used in the D90 and D300s. It is used to vibrate the OLPF to help reduce the presence of dust and other unwanted particles on the front surface of the OLPF. This surface, closest to the rear of the lens, is the bane of all digital photographers, because it causes dark shadow spots to appear in the final image; therefore, keeping the OLPF clean is fundamental to maintaining image quality and avoiding the necessity for time-consuming post-processing (see pages 354-360 for more details on OLPF cleaning options).

THE DX FORMAT

Nikon has used DX-format (APS-C) sensors in all of their digital SLR camera models with the exception of the D700 and D3-series, which have an FX-format sensor that is approximately the same size as a regular frame of 35mm film (24 x 36 mm).

At 15.6 x 23.6 mm, the DX format of the D7000 is considerably smaller than the FX format (23.9 x 36 mm). As a consequence, regardless of the focal length of the lens mounted on the camera, the field of view covered by its sensor is narrower than the field of view produced by a lens of the same focal length on an FX-format sensor.

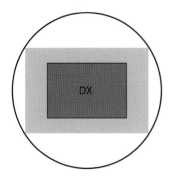

The circle represents the total area covered by the image circle projected from a lens designed to cover the FX / 35mm format. The pale gray rectangle is the image area for the FX-format (23.9 x 36 mm) sensor used in the D700 and D3-series cameras, while the dark gray rectangle represents the area covered by the DX format (15.6 x 23.6 mm) of the D7000.

Through their shooting experience with DX-format Nikon cameras, many photographers have become familiar with the reduced angle of view caused by the smaller format sensor, while others still find the issue confusing. Furthermore, misconceptions persist as to what causes the altered field of view. Use of phrases such as, "it's like getting a free 1.4x teleconverter," or "the focal length is magnified by 1.5x," suggest, as if by magic, that the focal length of a lens somehow increases by 1.5x when mounted on a camera that records pictures in the DX format. This is completely false—the focal length of any lens will remain constant, regardless of the size of the sensor or part of the sensor it projects an image onto; it is the field of view that changes.

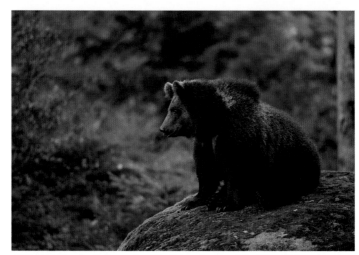

^ The reduced angle of view produced by the smaller size of the Nikon DX-format sensor can be an advantage when you cannot approach your subject closely.

To clarify this concept, consider that a lens with a focal length of 200mm will produce a specific field of view on an FX-format sensor / 35mm film frame; however, when the same focal length is used with the DX format, the field of view is reduced, rendering a view equivalent to that produced on the FX-format frame when a lens with a focal length of 300mm is used. In other words, if you are accustomed to choosing a focal length based on the field of view it produces on the FX / 35mm film frame, you will want to multiply that focal length by 1.5x (the actual factor is closer to 1.52x) in order to estimate the coverage it will provide with the DX format. Using the example of the 200mm focal length discussed above, 200mm x 1.5 = 300mm.

If you still find it easier to think in terms of the angle of view that a particular focal length would give on an FX-format frame because you are familiar with using a 35mm film camera, the following table provides an approximate effective focal length you can use to estimate the field of view with the DX format in the D7000:

FOCAL LENGTH EQUIVALENTS									
Actual	12	14	17	18	20	24	28	35	50	60
Effective	18	21	25.5	27	30	36	42	52.5	75	90

Actual	70	85	105	135	180	200	300	400	500	600
Effective	105	127.5	157.5	202.5	270	300	450	600	750	900

PROS AND CONS OF THE DX FORMAT

While this narrower field of view may seem to be an advantage in some shooting situations because it allows an image to fill the frame of the DX-format using a lens with a shorter focal length than would be required to fill the FX-format frame, it has the reverse effect when you want to achieve a very wide angle of view; consequently, it is necessary to use a much shorter focal length.

There is another beneficial side effect to the reduced angle of view of the DX format. Since the D7000 only uses the central portion of the image circle projected by the many Nikkor lenses designed for the FX / 35mm format, the effects of optical aberrations and defects are kept to a minimum, as these are generally more prevalent toward the edges of the image circle. Using such a lens will often significantly reduce or eliminate some or all of the following:

O Light fall-off (vignetting) toward the edges and corners of the image area, which can be particularly troublesome at large lens apertures

O Appearance of chromatic aberration

O Linear distortion—both barrel and pin-cushion

O Effects of field curvature (i.e., center and corners of frame are not in the same plane of focus)

O Light fall-off (vignetting) when using filters

Nikon also produces a range of Nikkor lenses designed specifically for use on their DX-format DSLR cameras, known as DX lenses. These lenses only need to project an image circle that covers the DX-format sensor enabling them to be made smaller and lighter than their counterparts designed for the FX-format / 35mm cameras (see pages 315-321 for further information on Nikkor lens compatibility).

THE VIEWFINDER

The D7000 has a fixed, optical pentaprism, eye-level viewfinder that shows approximately 100% (vertical and horizontal) of the full frame coverage. The focusing screen is fixed, and the viewfinder provides a very useful magnification of approximately 0.94x (much better than that of the Nikon D3100 and D90 cameras). The viewfinder display includes all the essential information about exposure and focus, including shutter speed, lens aperture, Exposure Compensation factor, ISO value, metering pattern, focus confirmation, battery status indicator, and flash-ready signal. The focusing screen is marked with a pair of arcs to define the autofocus (AF) area covered by the 39 individual AF points. The D7000 employs an LED projection system to display and illuminate the markings on its focusing screen. The screen only shows the bracket markings for the active focus area, which makes the rest of the viewfinder image far less cluttered and easier to see. There is a user-selectable reference grid pattern that can also be displayed, which is very useful for aligning critical compositions and for keeping horizons level.

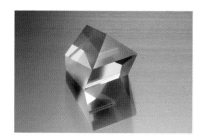

> **The D7000's viewfinder has a solid glass prism.**

ADJUSTING VIEWFINDER FOCUS

The viewfinder has an eye-point of 19.5mm ($-1.0m^{-1}$), which should provide a reasonably good view of the focusing screen and viewfinder information for users who wear eyeglasses. Plus there is a built-in diopter adjustment between -3.0 and $+1.0m^{-1}$. To set the diopter, mount a lens on the camera and leave it set to its infinity focus mark. Switch the camera on and point it at a plain surface that fills the frame. Rotate the diopter adjustment dial to the right of the viewfinder eyepiece until the AF sensor brackets appear sharp. It is essential to do this to ensure you see the sharpest view of the focusing screen. Since the built-in correction is not particularly strong, optional eyepiece correction lenses are available between −5 and +3m⁻¹. These are attached by slotting them onto the eyepiece frame (note: the rubber eyecup must be removed first). Similarly, the viewfinder eyepiece does not have an internal shutter to prevent light from entering when the D7000 is used remotely, so the camera is supplied with the DK-5 eyepiece cap that must be fitted, using the same method as the eyepiece correction lenses, whenever the camera is used remotely in any of the automatic exposure modes.

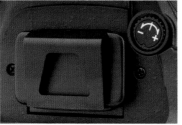

‹ **The viewfinder eyepiece is shown covered with the DK-5. Note that to fit the DK-5, the DK-21 rubber eyecup must be removed. The diopter control dial for the viewfinder eyepiece is located to its right side.**

FOCUS SCREEN DISPLAYS

The viewfinder, which provides a magnification of approximately 0.94x, displays all the essential information about exposure and focus. The camera is supplied with the Nikon B-type clear matte focusing screen, which is marked with bracket lines to define the AF area; Nikon offers no alternative interchangeable focusing screen for the D7000.

As mentioned previously, the D7000 employs an LCD projection system to display and illuminate the AF point markings, viewfinder warnings, and grid lines over its focusing screen, which draws a very low level of power from the camera, even when the camera is switched off. If you remove the battery from the camera, the focus screen will dim and its markings will no longer be visible.

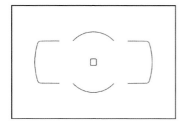

^ **This is the focus screen display of the D7000 with the central AF point marked.**

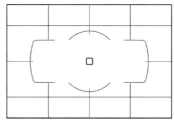

^ **This is the focus screen display of the D7000 with the optional grid lines shown.**

THE MULTI SELECTOR BUTTON

The Multi Selector button, located on the rear of the camera, is used to navigate the Information Display and the menu system of the D7000, plus select the AF point. Its center button can also be assigned certain roles via the Custom Settings menu (see page 231). It has a separate lock switch to prevent inadvertent selection of an alternative AF point. The function of the Multi Selector button is as shown below:

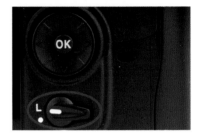

> **The Multi Selector lock is set to its locked position. To unlock it, simply rotate the switch so that the white index mark on the switch lines up with the white dot.**

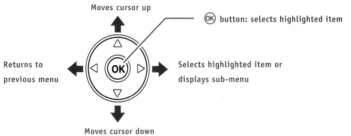

Moves cursor up

button: selects highlighted item

Returns to previous menu

Selects highlighted item or displays sub-menu

Moves cursor down

CONTROL PANEL

This large, monochrome LCD display on the top plate of the D7000—not to be confused with the color LCD monitor on the rear—is called the Control Panel. If the power is switched off, the only information shown is the number of remaining frames available with the installed memory card(s) and which of the two card slots is occupied. If no card is inserted in the camera, the display shows (-E-) to indicate "empty." As soon as the camera is powered on, the display shows a wide range of camera control settings, including battery status, shutter speed, aperture, shooting mode, active focus sensor and focus mode, White Balance, and audible warning, together with Image Quality and Size. Other controls will be indicated as and when they are activated.

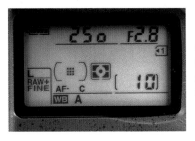

< The control panel of the D7000 is located on the top of the camera, right side, behind the shutter release button.

INFORMATION DISPLAY

The Information Display (ID) shows all the essential information about camera settings and controls on the LCD monitor of the camera. Due to its size, the display is large and clear. The format of the display can be altered using the CS-d9 [Information display] item in the Custom Settings menu (see pages 224-225 for further details).

To open the ID, press the 🎞 button once. It is located near the bottom right-hand corner of the LCD monitor screen. To change a setting for an item shown in the display, press the 🎞 button again to highlight one of the items that can be selected; the item selected most recently will be highlighted in yellow. To shift the yellow cursor, use the Multi Selector button. Once the required item is highlighted, press the ⊛ button to show the options available for that item.

To clear the ID from the screen, press the 🎞 button or press the shutter release button down halfway. The duration of the ID is selected via CS-c4 [Monitor off delay] > [Information display]; the default is 10 seconds.

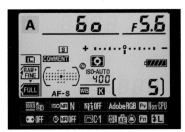

< The Information Display (ID) provides information about camera settings. The style of the display can be set via CS-d9 in the Custom Settings menu.

In line with the stated aim of Nikon to make the D7000 appeal to a very broad range of users with an equally wide range of skill levels, the specification of the D7000 includes the simplicity of the fully automated $\overset{\text{AUTO}}{\square}$ mode, or fully automated control without flash in the $\textcircled{2}$ mode. In addition to these point-and-shoot modes, there are no less than 19 subject / style-specific Scene modes. If you wish to exercise more control over the camera, there is the Programmed autoexposure mode, although this is little more than a point-and-shoot solution. The two semi-automatic exposure modes (Aperture-Priority and Shutter-Priority), plus a fully manual exposure mode, extend user involvement in the picture-shooting process considerably. This section is intended to assist those less experienced users who are eager to take some pictures with their new D7000 but are either unable or reluctant to spend the time at this point to learn how to take control of the camera.

O Charge the EN-EL15 battery in the MH-25 charger until the charge lamp stops blinking. Switch off the charger, remove the battery, and open the battery door on the base of the D7000. Insert the battery as per the diagram on the inside of the door, and then close it.

O When the camera is switched on for the first time, it will display a language-selection menu. Use ▲ or ▼ to select the required language and then press ⓞ.

O Next, a time zone display will be shown. Use ◄ or ► to select the required time zone, and then press ⓞ. Highlight [Date and time]; use ◄ or ► to select an item, and use ▲ or ▼ to change it. Finally, press ⓞ to set the camera clock. Highlight [Date format]; use ▲ or ▼ to select the required date format, and then press ⓞ. Then, highlight [Daylight saving time]; if daylight saving is in effect in the current time zone, press ▲ or ▼ to highlight [On], and then press ⓞ.

O Attach a lens to the D7000. If the lens has an A-M, or M / A-M switch, set A for autofocus, or M/A for autofocus with manual override.

O Adjust the viewfinder focus by rotating the diopter dial beside the eyepiece until the viewfinder display and AF point(s) appear sharp.

O Now, open the memory card port on the right side of the camera, and insert an appropriate SD-type memory card into the top slot (slot 1); ensure that the main label of the card is facing toward the back of the camera.

O Format the memory card by opening the Setup menu and highlighting **[Format memory card]**, press ▶, and then highlight the **[Yes]** option. To complete the format process, press the ⊗ button.

O To set the camera to its Programmed autoexposure mode, rotate the Mode dial until 'P' is aligned with the white index mark on the left side of the viewfinder head.

O Set the focus mode selector switch on the front of the camera to AF. Then, press and hold the AF-mode button, which is located in the center of the focus mode selector switch. Now, rotate the Main Command dial until AF-S is displayed in the top control panel. Next, rotate the Sub-Command dial until a single AF point is shown in the AF area brackets displayed in the top control panel. Finally, compose a picture, making sure that an AF point covers an area of the subject required to be in focus. Press lightly on the shutter release button, activating the focusing system. If the camera can acquire focus, the focus indicator ● will appear in the viewfinder. If ● is shown blinking in the viewfinder, the camera has not been able to acquire focus; re-compose the picture, place the selected AF point over an alternative part of the subject, and press lightly on the shutter release button again.

O Release Shutter: The shutter button has a two-stage release mechanism; pressing it down halfway activates the AF and TTL metering systems, while pressing it down all the way operates the shutter. Avoid stabbing your index finger down on the shutter release button, as this will increase the risk of camera shake. Simply roll the tip of your index finger smoothly over the edge of the shutter release button to take the picture. The green access lamp on the back of the camera will illuminate as soon as an exposure has been made, indicating the camera is saving the image. To make another exposure, lift your index finger clear of the shutter release button and repeat the process described above.

O To review a picture, press the ▶ button. Use ◀ or ▶ to review other pictures stored on the memory card. To view additional shooting information about the displayed picture, press either ▲ or ▼. To return the camera to the shooting mode, press the shutter release button lightly.

O To delete a picture, display it on the monitor as just described and press the 🗑 button. A confirmation dialog will be displayed. Press the 🗑 button again to complete the process.

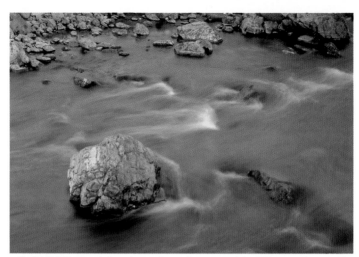

∧ The EN-EL15 battery delivers impressive performance and should be more than capable of powering the D7000 for a full day in the field.

POWERING THE D7000

The D7000 can be powered by a variety of sources. The main battery is the rechargeable lithium-ion EN-EL15 (7.0V, 1900mAh, 4Wh) that weighs approximately 3.1 oz (88g). The profile of the battery ensures that it can only be inserted the correct way into the camera. It is charged with the dedicated MH-25 Quick Charger (supplied with the camera), which supports both AC and DC power supplies. A fully discharged EN-EL15 can be completely recharged in approximately 2 hours and 35 minutes using the MH-25. Unlike some other types of rechargeable batteries, the EN-EL15 does not require conditioning prior to its first use (it is supplied partially charged).

USING THE EN-EL15 BATTERY

Whenever you insert or remove an EN-EL15, it is essential that you set the power switch of the D7000 to the off position. To insert an EN-EL15 into the D7000:

1. Invert the camera and push the small button on the battery chamber lid toward the tripod socket. Turn the camera over, and the battery chamber lid should swing open.

2. Open the lid fully and slide the battery into the camera, observing the diagram on the inside of the chamber lid. The small yellow battery-retaining clip will lock into place once the battery is fully inserted.

3. Press the lid down (you will feel a slight resistance) until it locks (you will hear a slight click as the latch closes).

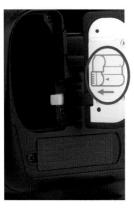

‹ **Note the diagram on the inside of the battery chamber door indicating how the EN-EL15 should be inserted.**

NOTE: If you are in the process of making any changes to the camera settings and the battery is removed while the power switch is still set to the on position, or the power supply from the EH-5A is interrupted, the camera may not retain the new settings. Likewise, if the camera is still in the process of transferring data from the buffer memory to the storage media when the battery is removed, image files are likely to be corrupted or data lost.

To remove an EN-EL15 from the D7000:

1. Repeat Step 1 (above).

2. Hold the lid open, turn the camera upright, and push the battery retaining clip toward the center of the camera, and then allow the battery to slide out, taking care that it does not drop.

3. Close the battery chamber lid.

To charge an EN-EL15:

1. Connect the MH-25 to an AC power supply.
2. Hold the EN-EL15 battery so its main label is facing downward and the battery terminals are to the left; now slide the battery in through the opening on the side of the MH-25 until is clicks into place. The charge lamp should begin to flash immediately, indicating that charging has commenced. Fully recharging a completely discharged battery will take approximately 2 hours and 35 minutes.

NOTE: The MH-25 can be used worldwide, connected to any AC supply, at any voltage from 100V to 250V, via an appropriate power socket adapter.

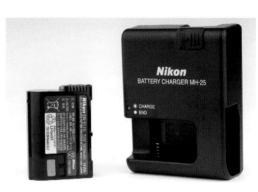

> The MH-25 (right) is the dedicated AC charger for the EN-EL15 battery (left).

Lithium-ion batteries do not exhibit the same charge memory effects associated with certain types of rechargeable batteries. Therefore a partially discharged EN-EL15 can take a top-up charge without any adverse consequences to battery life or performance. However, I do recommend that you avoid giving a battery a top-up charge when its charge level is at 90% or more, and likewise, do not repeatedly run a battery down to a charge level of 10% or less before recharging it. In the former case, there is a risk of reducing overall battery capacity; in the latter, successive charging of a battery from near exhaustion to full charge will likely reduce its life expectancy.

HINT: To ensure the battery has recharged fully, do not remove it from the charger as soon as the charge lamp stops flashing, which is intended to indicate that charging is complete. I recommend leaving the battery in place a little longer until it has cooled to the ambient room temperature, as the battery is unlikely to have reached a full 100% charge.

HINT: If you carry a spare EN-EL15, always make sure that you keep the plastic terminal cover in place. Without it, there is a risk that the battery terminals may short and cause damage to the battery.

The EN-EL15 rechargeable battery has an electronic chip in its circuitry that allows the D7000 to report detailed information regarding the status of the battery. To access this information, select **[Battery info]** from the Setup menu, and three parameters concerning the battery will be displayed on the monitor (see the table below).

PARAMETER	DESCRIPTION
Bat. Meter	Current level of battery charge expressed as a percentage
Pic. Meter	Number of times the shutter has been released with the current battery since it was last charged. This number will include shutter release actions when no picture is recorded (e.g., to record an Image Dust Off reference frame, or to measure color temperature for a Preset White Balance value)
Battery age	Displays the condition of the battery as one of five levels (0 - 4); level 0 indicates the battery is new, and level 4 indicates the battery has reached the end of its charging life and should be replaced.

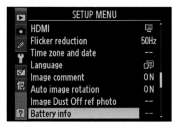
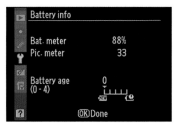

∧ **Select the** [Battery info] **item in the Setup menu to see information about the battery's capacity and condition.**

USING THE MB-D11 BATTERY PACK

The MB-D11 is a battery pack / grip that attaches to the base of the D7000 body via the tripod socket. In addition to providing extra battery capacity, the MB-D11 has a shutter release button, Main and Sub-Command dials, a miniature version of the Multi Selector button, and an AE / AF lock button, which can be assigned a variety of roles to improve handling when the camera is held in the vertical (portrait) orientation. Also, the additional bulk and weight the MB-D11 adds to the D7000 helps to balance the camera, especially when using longer, heavier lenses.

The battery pack can accept either one EN-EL15 battery, or six AA / LR6-sized batteries that must be fitted in the MS-D11 battery holder (included with the MB-D11). There are three compatible battery types: LR6 (Alkaline), HR6 (Nickel Metal Hydride), and FR6 (Lithium). It is important that, whichever type of AA / LR6-size battery is installed, the [MB-D11 Battery Type] option at CS-d13 is set to match it (there is no requirement to select this Custom Setting when using the EN-EL15 battery).

HINT: If you use AA batteries, I strongly recommend that you avoid the LR6 (Alkaline) types unless there is no alternative. It is important to be aware that in cooler ambient temperatures (i.e., below 20° C / 68° F), the performance of these batteries is impaired significantly, and they may even cease to function in cold conditions.

The electrical contacts for the MB-D11 are located beneath a rubber contacts cover in the base of the D7000. This cover must be removed before fitting the battery pack. To keep from losing it, stow the contacts cover in the holder set in the top plate of the MB-D11. Once it's attached and the camera is switched on, you can use CS-d14 [Battery order] to determine the order in which the battery in the camera and the battery in the MB-D11 will be used. At the default setting, the battery installed in the MB-D11 is used first; the [BP] icon that appears next to the battery charge level indicator in the camera's control panel confirms this.

HINT: If you use the battery installed in the MB-D11 first, you can swap it out once it becomes discharged without interrupting the power supply to the camera, as the battery installed in the camera becomes the active battery. As soon as you insert a charged battery back in the MB-D11, the camera reverts to drawing power from the battery pack (assuming CS-d14 is set to its default value).

The status of the installed batteries can be checked using the **[Battery Info]** item of the Setup menu (as described previously). Using either the EN-EL15 battery or the MD-11, the values for the battery meter (charge level expressed as a percentage), picture meter, and charging life are shown. The information for the EN-EL15 battery installed in the camera is displayed at the left of the monitor, while the status of the MB-D11 battery is shown on the right side.

EXTERNAL POWER SUPPLY - EH-5A AC ADAPTER

The Nikon EH-5A AC adapter and EP-5B power connector, which are optional accessories, can also power the D7000. (The EH-5, which was originally made available for cameras such as the D100, D70 series, and D40, but has since been replaced by the EH-5a can also be used.) Either version of this AC adapter, both of which are rated for an input of 100 – 240V / AC 50-60Hz, is particularly useful for extended periods of shooting, such as time-lapse photography, image playback, or data transfer directly from the camera to a computer. The cord of the EH-5A AC adapter must be connected to the cord of the EP-5B, which is then inserted in either the battery chamber of the D7000, or the MB-D11 if it is fitted to the camera. The EH-5a is also useful for preventing the camera from powering off while the reflex mirror is raised using the mirror lock-up facility for inspection or cleaning of the optical low-pass filter.

HINT: Always ensure that the power switch is set to the off position before connecting or disconnecting the EH-5A / EP-5B to the camera. There is a risk that the camera's circuitry could be damaged if you plug or unplug the AC adapter while the power switch is set to the on position.

INTERNAL CLOCK / CALENDAR BATTERY

The D7000 has an internal clock and calendar that are powered by a fixed, internal rechargeable battery; fully charged, it will power the clock and calendar for approximately three months. It requires charging for approximately 48 hours by the camera's main power supply: either a single EN-EL15 inserted in the camera body, an EN-EL15 battery in the MB-D11 battery pack, or six AA / LR6 batteries in the MS-D11 battery holder within the MB-D11 battery pack. Alternatively, the clock / calendar battery will be charged whenever the D7000 is switched on and powered by the EH-5a AC adapter.

Should the clock battery become exhausted, CLOCK will flash in the control panel, and the clock is reset to a date and time of 2010.01.01 00:00:00. If this occurs, insert a fully charged battery and leave it in place for a few days. The clock and calendar will need to be reset to the correct time via the [Time zone and date] option in the Setup menu.

NOTE: Since the user cannot exchange the internal clock and calendar battery, the camera must be returned to a service center for a replacement battery to be fitted should it not hold a charge.

BATTERY PERFORMANCE

Operation of the D7000 is totally dependent on an adequate electrical power supply. Obviously, the more functions the camera has to perform, the greater the demand on its battery, so reducing the number of functions and the duration for which they are active is fundamental to reducing power consumption. This can be an important consideration, especially if you are traveling with your camera or expect to spend any extended period away from an AC electrical supply.

On the following pages, I have set out some of the principal causes of battery power drain together with a few suggestions as to how you can conserve battery power.

O Using the camera's color LCD monitor increases power consumption significantly. Unless you need it, turn the monitor off. Consider setting the [Image review] option in the Playback menu to off (the default setting is on). Alternatively, consider selecting shorter durations for the

CS-c2 **[Auto meter-off display]** and CS-c4 **[Monitor off Delay]** items in the Custom Settings menu in place of the default durations. To help reduce time spent scrolling through the camera's menu system, I recommend consolidating those menu items you use frequently within the My menu option, so you only need to consult a single menu list.

O Recording NEF (RAW) draws far more power compared with recording JPEG files. There is nothing that can be done to mitigate this issue other than carrying at least one spare battery if you habitually shoot using the NEF format. In my experience, shooting in an average ambient temperature range of 61–75° F (16–24° C), using autofocus, and with Vibration Reduction active on my lenses, I can expect a fully charged EN-EL15 to last for approximately 500 exposures when recording compressed NEF files at a 14-bit depth.

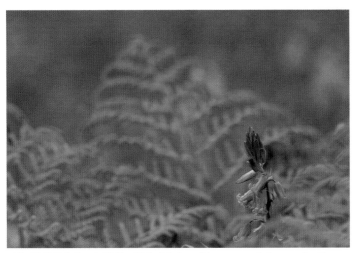

⌃ The EN-EL15 battery is highly efficient, but careful management of camera functions, especially Vibration Reduction, Live View, and D-Movie mode, will help extend battery life.

O Driving the autofocus function of lenses draws relatively little power, as the demand on the battery is delivered in peaks of very short duration, but the Vibration Reduction (VR) feature available with some Nikkor lenses is another matter. The VR function of all Nikkor lenses draws power from the camera battery, and it tends to be active for far longer periods compared with AF operation. Consequently, VR can reduce battery life by approximately 10-15% when active.

O The video-recording function (D-Movie mode) places the highest demand for power on the camera battery, since both the sensor and monitor screen are powered continuously, often for protracted periods, and the camera has a large amount of data to process accordingly. If you expect to make frequent use of this function, I advise you to carry at least one and probably two or three spare EN-EL15 batteries.

O Using the built-in Speedlight flash unit will place a significant demand on the battery and shorten the duration of any shooting session considerably.

Low temperatures cause a change to the internal resistance of a battery regardless of its type, which impairs performance. Lithium-ion batteries are fairly resilient to cold conditions. However, to ensure you can keep shooting, particularly in freezing conditions, keep at least one spare battery in a warm place, such as an inside pocket, and as the performance of the battery in the camera dwindles, exchange it with the warm one. Allow the used battery time to warm up again and keep rotating between the batteries to maximize the shooting capacity.

BATTERY STORAGE

A fully charged Nikon Lithium-ion EN-EL15 battery in good condition will retain its full capacity over a short period; however, if the battery is left dormant for a number of weeks or more, regardless of whether it is installed in a camera or not, expect it to suffer a perceptible loss of charge, so ensure it is recharged fully before use (for earlier comments concerning top-up charging, see page 38). If you expect to store a camera battery for an extended period, avoid leaving it fully charged or heavily discharged. Storing a fully charged battery can have a long-term effect on its overall capacity, while storing a heavily discharged battery can risk it shifting to a deeply discharged state, which can damage it. The optimum charge level for a battery that will be stored for a month or longer is 20 – 80%. Always store your camera and batteries in a well-ventilated, cool, dry place.

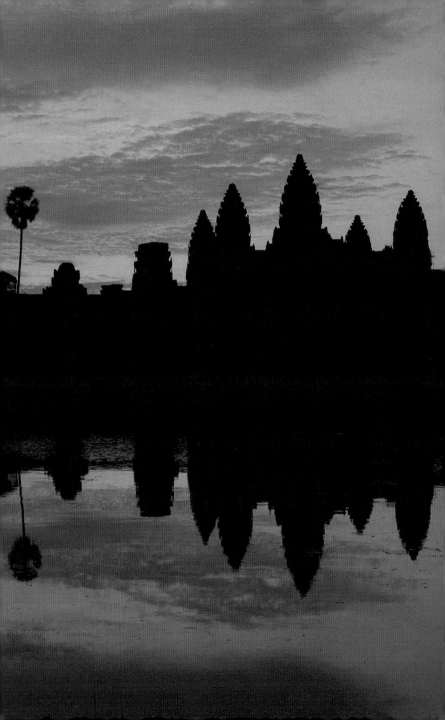

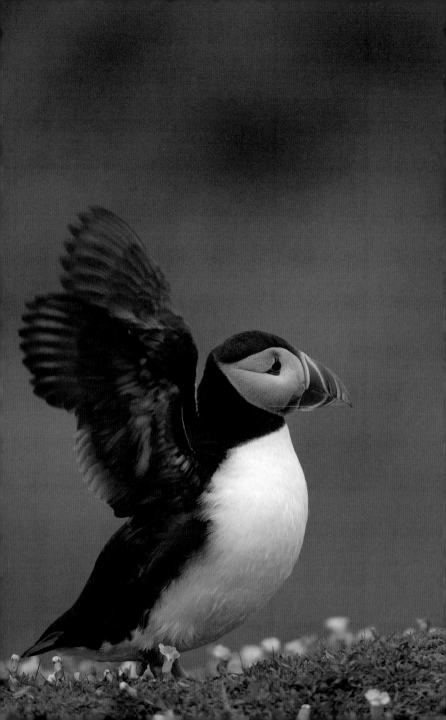

The Exposure and Focusing Systems

EXPOSURE

Regardless of whether you are content to let the D7000 make decisions about exposure settings, or you want to take control of the camera and make them for yourself, it is essential to understand how the camera sees, evaluates, and processes light.

ISO SENSITIVITY

Film requires you to make a decision about which ISO (sensitivity) rating to use in order to cope with the prevailing or expected lighting conditions, and the entire roll must be exposed at the same ISO value. One of the great advantages of digital photography, on the other hand, is that it allows you to adjust the ISO sensitivity from picture to picture.

The ISO sensitivity rating used by Nikon DSLR cameras follows the guidelines set by the International Organization for Standardization for rating film speed (sensitivity) using the ISO scale; therefore, where the sensitivity setting on a camera complies with these guidelines, it is referred to as being ISO equivalent.

The D7000 offers ISO sensitivity settings within its normal ISO range from 100 to 6400 that can be adjusted in steps of 0.3, 0.5, or 1 EV, plus the option to increase it by 1 EV above ISO 6400 (ISO equivalent 12,800), in steps of 0.3, 0.5, 0.7, and 1 EV, and by 2 EV above ISO 6400 (ISO equivalent 25,600) in a further single step. The ISO sensitivities in this expanded range are expressed as values prefixed with "Hi" followed by the size of the EV step; for example, a setting of Hi 0.3 corresponds to an ISO sensitivity of 8000 (1/3 stop faster than 6400).

The "base ISO" is the ISO value at which the sensor delivers optimal performance, and in the case of the D7000, that is ISO 100. So, as a general rule of thumb, I recommend you shoot at the lowest ISO setting appropriate for the subject / shooting conditions to get the very best in terms of image quality out of your camera.

> The ISO button is located to the left of the LCD screen, second button from the bottom.

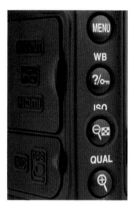

To adjust the ISO sensitivity, press the **ISO** button and rotate the Main Command dial until the desired value is displayed in the control panel and viewfinder. Alternatively, the ISO can be adjusted via the **[ISO sensitivity settings]** item in the Shooting menu. Among the choices in the **[ISO sensitivity settings]** submenu is the option to have the camera set ISO automatically according to lighting conditions. To set the step value for the adjustment of ISO sensitivity, use CS-b1 **[ISO sensitivity step value]**.

ISO Noise: The analogy with film ISO continues insomuch as, at higher ISO settings, digital images will show increasing amounts of electronic "noise," characterized by a grainy, sometimes muddy look, often associated with blotchy color patterns. For digitally captured photos, this often manifests as blue and red pixels scattered throughout the image, especially in shadow or dark areas. Generally, as the ISO sensitivity value is hiked higher and higher, the color saturation and image contrast are reduced correspondingly.

The ISO noise performance of the D7000 is without doubt the best of any Nikon DX-format DSLR produced to date, but you can still expect to see noise in any image that comprises mostly dark tones or has distinct areas of dark tone at higher ISO settings, especially if the exposure is not spot-on. Although the D7000 may not be a match for the professional grade Nikon D3s, or even the D700 FX-format cameras, its high ISO performance is so good that it opens up real potential for low-light photography for the DX-format shooter.

Setting ISO sensitivity to 200 presents no problem, as image quality at 200 is virtually indistinguishable from that at ISO 100. At ISO 400, there is a very slight increase in the noise level, but the noise pattern is random (rather like a film grain pattern) and thus not intrusive. Even at this elevated ISO level, the color saturation and contrast remain remarkably good, as they do all the way out to ISO 6400. Beyond ISO 400, however, noise does become clearly perceptible (albeit well controlled). The point at which ISO noise becomes unacceptable will be a matter of personal opinion, but I suspect that for most users looking for excellent to good image quality, this is likely to be around ISO 3200. That is not to say that ISO sensitivity settings above 3200 should not be used if the shooting conditions dictate that there is no other option—after all, a noisy image is usually better than no image.

Furthermore, the noise at ISO 1600 to 6400 can be used for creative purposes and is particularly effective with the black-and-white options available on the D7000, emulating the qualities of high-speed, grainy black-and-white film. Moving on up the ISO scale into the Hi setting territory, the image quality remains very usable at ISO 12,800 (equivalent) and is acceptable at ISO 25,600. At these settings, the noise is prevalent but images produced by the D7000 do not show the characteristic banding or other artifacts associated with other cameras that offer an equivalent ISO level.

To help reduce the effects of noise at higher ISO settings, there is the High ISO Noise Reduction feature, which is set via the Shooting menu (see page 209 for more details). While this can be quite effective, it will

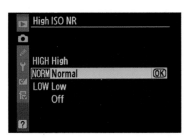

‹ Select [Normal] for [High ISO NR] in the Shooting menu for moderate Noise Reduction without much loss of detail.

result in some loss of definition in very fine detail, especially at its High setting. Unless you have good reason to try and deal with ISO noise in-camera, it is usually preferable to use either the Noise Reduction feature of an NEF (RAW) file converter or a dedicated noise reduction application, such as Noise Ninja (visit: www.picturecode.com) or Neat Image (visit: www.neatimage.com).

ISO Sensitivity Auto Control: It is important to understand how this feature works, because it may not be quite what you expect. In the **P** (Programmed) and **A** (Aperture-Priority) autoexposure modes, the ISO sensitivity will not be altered unless underexposure would occur at the value specified for the **[Minimum shutter speed]** in **[Auto ISO sensitivity control]** under the **[ISO sensitivity settings]** item in the Shooting menu. The range of shutter speeds for **[Minimum shutter speed]** extends from 1 second to 1/4000 second. However, if the camera cannot achieve a proper exposure at the ISO sensitivity specified as the **[Maximum sensitivity]** value, which covers the range from ISO 400 to Hi 2 (ISO 25,600), the D7000 will then begin to select slower shutter speeds.

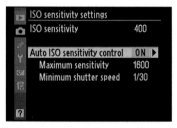

∧ The [ISO sensitivity settings] display in the Shooting menu

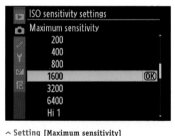

∧ Setting [Maximum sensitivity]

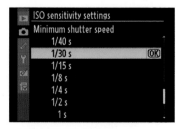

∧ Setting [Minimum shutter speed]

In **S** (Shutter-Priority autoexposure) mode, the ISO sensitivity is shifted when the exposure reaches the maximum aperture available on the lens. Indeed, this is probably the exposure mode that is most useful with this feature because it will raise the sensitivity setting and thus maintain the selected shutter speed, which is usually critical to the success of the picture. In **M** (Manual) exposure mode, the sensitivity is shifted if the selected shutter speed and aperture cannot attain a correct exposure (as indicated by the display in the viewfinder). When the ISO Sensitivity Auto Control feature is active, ISO-AUTO is displayed in the viewfinder, control panel, and the Information Display; if the camera alters the ISO sensitivity from what you've set, ISO-AUTO will blink as a warning.

TTL METERING

The D7000 has three metering pattern options that will be familiar if you have used a Nikon AF camera before: Matrix, Center-Weighted, and Spot. To select a metering mode, press and hold the ☒ (metering mode) button, which is located just behind and to the left of the shutter release button on top of the camera, and then rotate the Main Command dial until the appropriate icon is displayed in the control panel and Information Display.

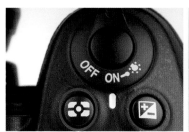

∧ The ☒ button is located on the top of the D7000, behind the shutter release button.

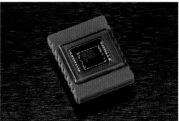

∧ The D7000 has a newly developed, 2016-pixel RGB sensor for TTL metering; it is located inside the top of the viewfinder head, just above the viewfinder eyepiece.

NOTE: Matrix metering is the only metering pattern option available when shooting in the fully automated, point-and-shoot 🅰, ⚡, and **SCENE** modes.

⊡ Matrix metering: The metering pattern for this mode covers virtually the entire frame area. Each of the 2016 pixels (segments) on the RGB metering sensor, which is located the viewfinder head of the camera just above the eyepiece, acts as a sampling point. This newly developed sensor takes over from the long-established 1005-pixel sensor that has been used in many mid- and upper-range Nikon SLR and DSLR cameras since it appeared first in the Nikon F5 camera, introduced during 1995. The new sensor in the D7000 also benefits from the addition of a small diffraction grating placed immediately in front of it, which separates the light falling on the sensor into its component colors to improve the efficiency and accuracy with which it assesses both the nature and the color of the light from the scene being photographed; it is the core of the Scene Recognition System that assesses the distribution of color within the frame and uses this information to improve metering accuracy, especially for skin tones.

⟩ The coverage of the Matrix metering pattern extends virtually to the edges of the full frame area, as shown by the yellow shading.

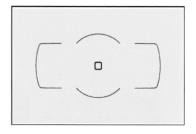

To derive the most from the Matrix metering capabilities of the D7000, it is necessary to use a D- or G-type Nikkor lens, since these provide additional focus distance information that assists the camera in estimating how far away it is from the subject. The metering system also knows which AF point is selected and uses this information to estimate the position of the subject within the frame. Nikon calls this system 3D Color Matrix metering II. If an AF Nikkor lens that does not communicate distance information to the camera is used, the system simply defaults to standard Color Matrix metering II (i.e., the distance information is not integrated in the exposure computations). This also applies to the use of a non-CPU type lens, provided the focal length and maximum aperture value are specified using the **[Non-CPU lens data]** item in the Setup menu.

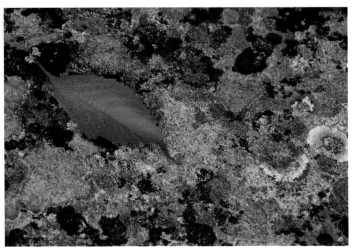

^ 3D Color Matrix metering II is the most sophisticated of the three TTL metering patterns available on the D7000, and the only one that is sensitive to color.

In the automated exposure modes, the Matrix metering (and i-TTL flash control) also benefits from the enhanced analysis of highlights within the frame performed by the Scene Recognition System. By assessing the distribution of contrast (brightness pattern), as well as the overall level of scene illumination and color, then comparing the results against a database of brightness patterns derived from over 30,000 sample images that cover an enormous range of lighting conditions, the D7000 offers the most advanced TTL metering available in a Nikon camera to date. Matrix metering uses five principle factors when calculating an exposure value:

○ The overall level of illumination in the scene
○ The ratio of brightness between the 2016 pixels (brightness pattern)
○ Distribution of color within the scene
○ The focused distance provided by the lens (D- or G-type only)
○ The location of the active AF point

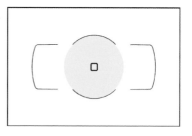

HINT: Shooting an evenly illuminated scene with moderate contrast with the active AF point covering a midtone, the D7000 produces consistently good exposures via its Matrix metering; however, the Matrix metering does appear to be influenced into producing greater variability in results when the active AF point covers a very light or very dark tone. In these situations, it is advisable to check the histogram display. (See pages 139-142 for more information.)

⌂ **Center-Weighted Metering:** The Center-Weighted metering pattern is derived from the TTL metering systems used by early Nikon SLR film cameras. In these cameras, the frame area was usually divided in a 60:40 ratio with the bias placed on the central portion of the frame. The principle benefit of this system in those cameras was it reduced the effect of lens vignetting, which causes the periphery of the frame area to not be illuminated as brightly as the center of the image field. The D7000 uses a higher ratio of 75:25, with 75% of the exposure reading based on the central circular area of the frame and the remaining 25% based on the outer area (it is also possible to select an option that alters the size of the central circular area or sets an average reading for the entire frame area via CS-b4). Unlike Matrix metering, no color information is assessed when the Center-Weighted pattern is selected, so metering is performed using a grayscale.

> The coverage of the Center-Weighted metering pattern can be adjusted via CS-b4 [Center-weighted area]. At its default settings, it covers an 8-mm-diameter circle at the middle of the frame (the yellow shading is for illustrative purposes only).

HINT: Center-Weighted metering offers nowhere near the level of sophistication of 3D Color Matrix metering, but for some subjects, its simplicity can be an advantage for photographers who like to control exposure and understand how it works.

⊡ **Spot metering:** Spot metering is extremely useful for metering from a highly specific area of a scene. For example, faced with a subject against a virtually black background, which might cause the Matrix metering system to overexpose the subject, the Spot meter allows you to take a reading from the subject without it being influenced by the background. The sensing area for the Spot-metering pattern is a circle, approximately 0.14 inch (3.5 mm) in diameter, which represents about 2.5% of the total frame area. This circle is centered on the active AF point, unless Auto-Area AF is selected or a non-CPU lens is used, in which case, the central AF point is the only area to perform metering. Again, as with the Center-Weighted pattern, no color information is assessed when the Spot-metering pattern is selected, so metering is performed using a grayscale.

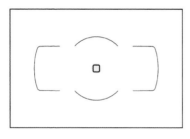

‹ The coverage of the Spot-metering pattern extends over a 3.5-mm-diameter circle centered on the active AF point, which represents approx. 2.5% of the total frame area.

HINT: It is essential to remember that in Center-Weighted and Spot metering, the TTL metering system measures reflected light, and is calibrated to give a correct exposure for a midtone (both options using a grayscale). When using either of these two patterns you must make sure that the part of the scene you meter from represents a midtone, otherwise you will need to compensate the exposure value.

HINT: In Dynamic-Area AF, the D7000 will attempt to follow a moving subject by shifting focus control between different AF points. If this occurs, the Spot metering remains centered on the AF point selected initially.

AUTO AND THE SCENE MODES

The AUTO, ⊕, and **SCENE** modes represent the most automated level of control available on the D7000. The camera manages many key controls and features in an attempt to select a combination of shutter speed and aperture that will be appropriate for the current scene. It does this by using information from the through-the-lens (TTL) metering system in the camera, which assesses the overall level of illumination, contrast, and color quality of the prevailing light, together with information from the autofocus system used to estimate the location of the subject in the frame area and its distance from the camera. The user has very limited scope to intervene and override them; for example, the metering pattern, White Balance, and Picture Controls cannot be adjusted from their default settings. This is unlikely to be of any concern to the novice who is content to let the D7000 make decisions on their behalf, but the for more seasoned user, I would recommend avoiding these modes and suggest working in either Aperture-Priority, Shutter-Priority, or the Manual shooting mode.

To select any one of these modes, simply turn the Mode dial so that the icon representing the desired mode lines up with the mark to the right of the Mode dial (between it and the accessory shoe).

HINT: AUTO, ⊕, **SCENE** modes, and **P, S, A,** and **M** exposure modes are all selected from the Mode dial. I have found that, due to the high profile of the D7000's Mode dial, it can be dislodged from its intended position very easily when carrying or handling the camera, so always double check its position be fore you begin shooting.

> The Mode dial is located on the camera's top left-hand corner. Select AUTO for fully automated control of virtually all camera settings.

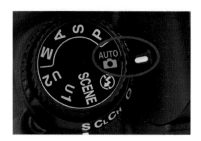

AUTO **AUTO:** The AUTO mode is designed as a universal point-and-shoot mode and is most effective for general-purpose snapshot photography, such as family events or vacations.

AUTO (Flash Off): This mode is essentially the same as the AUTO mode, with the exception that the built-in flash is turned off and will not operate regardless of the level of ambient illumination, even if it is very low. It is useful in situations where the use of flash is undesirable—for example, when shooting in a museum where flash may be prohibited or in natural low-light conditions where you do not want to spoil the atmosphere by using flash. Although the operation of the built-in flash is cancelled, the AF-Assist Illuminator lamp will still function to assist autofocus operation in poor lighting conditions.

> **HINT:** Since the camera can set slow shutter speeds in this mode, always check the viewfinder information to ensure that the selected shutter speed will allow the camera to be held without risk of camera shake affecting the picture. At slow shutter speeds, consider using a camera support like a tripod.

The following **SCENE** modes are selected by setting the Mode dial to **SCENE**, opening the Information Display by pressing the Info button, and then rotating the Main Command dial. The respective icon and title of each mode is displayed in the Information Display.

Portrait: The mode is designed to select a wide aperture (low f/number) in order to produce a picture with a shallow depth of field. Generally, this renders the background out of focus so it does not detract from the subject, although the effect is also dependent on the distance between the subject and the background, and the focal length of the lens used. This mode is most effective with focal lengths of 100mm or more and when the subject is relatively far away from the background.

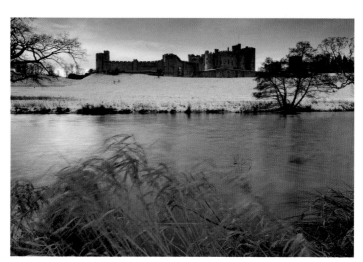

^ It is often important to include an element with strong visual interest in the foreground of a picture taken with a wide-angle lens, as this will add impact to the shot.

Landscape: The mode is designed to select a small aperture in order to produce a picture with an extended depth of field. Generally, this renders everything from the foreground to the horizon in focus, although this will depend to some degree how close the lens is to the nearest subject. This mode is most effective with wide-angle or wide-angle zoom lenses, and when the scene is well lit.

HINT: When using a wide-angle focal length (i.e., a focal length less than 35mm), try to include an element of interest in the foreground of the scene, as well as the middle distance, to help produce a balanced composition and a way of leading the viewer's eye into the picture.

Child: The parameters are similar to the mode, except the Picture Control is ⬛SD Standard to give a more vibrant rendition of color.

HINT: One of the simplest ways to improve pictures of children is to lower the camera to your subject's eye level.

☆ **Sports:** The ☆ mode is designed to select a wide aperture in order to maintain the highest possible shutter speed to "freeze" motion in fast-paced action. Furthermore, this combination produces a picture with a very shallow depth of field that helps to isolate the subject from the background. This mode is most effective with telephoto or telephoto-zoom lenses, and when there are no obstructions between the camera and the subject that may cause the lens to focus on something other than the subject.

HINT: There is always a slight delay between pressing the shutter release button and the shutter opening; therefore, it is important to anticipate the peak moment of the action and press the shutter just before it occurs. The decisive moment will be missed if you wait to see it in the viewfinder before pressing the shutter release.

❀ **Close-Up:** The ❀ mode is for taking pictures at short shooting distances of subjects such as flowers and insects. It is designed to select a small aperture in order to produce a picture with an extended depth of field. Generally, depth of field is limited when working at very short focus distances, even when using small apertures, so this program tries to render as much of the subject in focus as possible. The final effect will also be dependent on how close the camera is to the subject and the focal length of the lens used.

▣ **Night Portrait:** The ▣ mode is designed to capture properly exposed pictures of people against a background that is dimly lit. It is useful when you want to include background detail like a cityscape or sunset in the photo and is most effective when the background is in low light, as opposed to totally dark conditions. The built-in Speedlight will activate automatically in low light, or an external Speedlight such as the SB-400 or SB-700 can be used.

▤ **Night Landscape:** The parameters are similar to the ▣ mode, except the Picture Control is ▤SD Standard to give more vibrant colors, while the built-in flash and AF-Assist Illuminator are disabled; it is optimized for shooting cityscapes by improving the rendition of artificial lighting and reducing image noise.

> **HINT:** Do not wait for the sky to turn a featureless, inky black, but try to shoot in the twilight period when there is still color in the sky.

⚡ **Party / Indoor:** It is optimized for using flash to take photos of people, as the Red-Eye Reduction feature is activated. Auto ISO is set in an effort to capture as much ambient light as possible.

🏖 **Beach / Snow:** The parameters are similar to the 🏔 mode, except the exposure is optimized to account for the very light tones of sand and snow, and prevent them from causing underexposure.

🌅 **Sunset:** Designed to ensure that the rich red / orange hues of a sunset are retained, the White Balance is set to Direct Sunlight. Exposure is biased toward using larger aperture values to compensate for the relatively low light condition that is likely to be encountered.

🌆 **Dusk / Dawn:** The parameters are similar to the 🌅 mode, except the White Balance is set to a color temperature of 4550K to help preserve the colors of a pre-dawn or post-sunset sky. Exposure is biased toward using larger aperture values to compensate for relatively low light conditions.

🐕 **Pet Portrait:** The parameters are similar to the 🏃 mode, except the built-in flash can be used (although the AF-Assist Illuminator is turned off). Exposure is biased toward using fast shutter speeds to capture a moving subject with crisp definition.

🕯 **Candlelight:** The White Balance is set to 4350K to help achieve accurate rendition of color in conditions where the only light source is candlelight. Exposure is biased toward using larger aperture values to compensate for the relatively low light condition that is likely to be encountered. Use of a tripod is recommended, as shutter speeds are likely to be very slow. Flash is set to off to preserve the atmosphere of the scene.

🌸 **Blossom:** Color rendition is optimized for the bright colors of flowers and blossoms, but without causing them to become oversaturated.

☘ **Autumn Colors:** Similar to ☘ except the Picture Control is set to 🖻VI Vivid to boost the color saturation and contrast levels to produce a very vibrant rendition of typical autumn leaves.

🍴 **Food:** Very similar to ✿, except the flash mode is set to 🔲 Fill flash. The built-in flash will not pop up automatically in conditions of low light, so you must press the ⚡ button to pop it up if you want to use it.

🏔 **Silhouette:** Very similar to ⛰ except the Active D-Lighting is switched off to prevent the camera from adjusting the highlight and shadow tones like it normally would for a backlit subject. This ensures the maximum silhouette effect between a bright background and dark subject.

🖽 **High Key:** Exposure is biased to provide a full exposure to make light tones appear very bright; it best suited to scenes filled with very light tones in good lighting conditions.

🖽 **Low Key:** Exposure is biased to provide a very restrained exposure to make dark tones appear very dense and to preserve detail in bright highlights; it best suited to scenes filled with very dark tones and lit by high-contrast lighting.

SETTINGS IN 🔲 *AND SCENE MODES*

When using the 🔲 and **SCENE** modes, the level of user control is very restricted:

- O The following controls can be adjusted from their default settings: Image Quality, Image Size (JPEG only), ISO, Release mode, AF mode, AF-Area mode, and flash mode. If you alter any default setting, it is only retained while the camera remains in the current shooting mode. If you turn the Mode dial to another shooting mode, the default setting is restored.
- O The following controls cannot be adjusted from their default settings: White Balance, metering, Active D-Lighting, and Picture Control (contrast and sharpening are applied automatically).
- O The following controls are not available: Bracketing, Exposure Compensation, Flash Compensation.

The 🅰 AUTO, 🚫 (Flash off), and **SCENE** mode default settings:

MODE / CONTROL	WHITE BALANCE	PICTURE CONTROL	FLASH MODE	ACTIVE D-LIGHTING	AF-AREA MODE
Auto	Auto	Standard	Auto	Auto	Auto Area
Flash Off	Auto	Standard	Flash Off	Auto	Auto Area
Portrait	Auto	Portrait	Auto	Auto	Auto Area
Landscape	Auto	Landscape	Flash Off	Auto	Auto Area
Child	Auto	Portrait	Auto	Auto	Auto Area
Sport	Auto	Standard	Flash Off	Auto	Dynamic Area
Close-Up	Auto	Standard	Auto	Auto	Single Point
Night Portrait	Auto	Portrait	Auto Slow	Auto	Auto Area
Night Landscape	Auto	Standard	Flash Off	Auto	Single Point
Party / Indoor	Auto	Standard	Auto + Redeye	Auto	Auto Area
Beach / Snow	Auto	Landscape	Flash Off	Auto	Single Point
Sunset	Direct Sun	Landscape	Flash Off	Auto	Single Point
Dawn / Dusk	4550K	Landscape	Flash Off	Auto	Single Point
Pet Portrait	Auto	Standard	Auto	Auto	Dynamic Area
Candlelight	4350K	Standard	Flash Off	Auto	Single Point
Blossom	Auto	Landscape	Flash Off	Auto	Single Point
Autumn Colors	Auto	Vivid	Flash Off	Auto	Single Point
Food	Auto	Standard	Fill flash	Auto	Single Point
Silhouette	Auto	Landscape	Flash Off	Off	Single Point
High Key	Auto	Standard	Flash Off	Off	Single Point
Low Key	Auto	Standard	Flash Off	Off	Single Point

P, S, A, AND M EXPOSURE MODES

The D7000 offers four other, more user-control-oriented exposure modes; to select them rotate the Mode dial until the required mode, **P**, **A**, **S**, or **M**, is aligned with the white index mark.

NOTE: For **P** or **S** mode to operate, you must have a CPU lens attached to the camera; if you attach a non-CPU-type lens, the shutter release will be disabled.

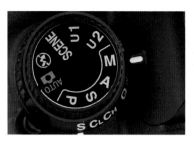

< Always check the position of the Mode dial before you take a picture, as it can be easily moved by mistake due to its high profile.

NOTE: If you use a non-CPU lens when shooting in A or M mode, ensure the focal length and maximum aperture value are specified using the [Non-CPU lens data] item in the Setup menu.

NOTE: If you use a CPU-type lens with an aperture ring, ensure it is set and locked to the minimum aperture value (i.e., the highest f/number).

Programmed Auto (P): Programmed autoexposure (Program) mode automatically adjusts both the shutter speed and the lens aperture to produce a properly exposed image, as determined by the selected metering mode.

If you decide that a particular combination of the shutter speed and aperture chosen by the camera is not suitable, you can override the P mode settings by turning the Main Command dial when the camera meter is activated. This is called Flexible Program mode and P* appears in the control panel when it is in use; however, there is no indication in the viewfinder that you have overridden P mode, aside from the altered shutter speed and aperture values. The two values change in tandem, so the overall exposure level remains the same (i.e., increasing the shutter speed decreases the aperture). If you override the Program mode, it will remain locked to its new settings for shutter speed and aperture, even if the meter powers off automatically and is then switched on again by pressing the shutter release halfway. To cancel the override, you must rotate the Main Command dial until the asterisk next to the P is no longer displayed, change exposure mode, turn the power off, or perform a Two-Button Reset. (See pages126-128.)

HINT: In my opinion, Program mode is little better than the point-and-shoot exposure control options on many entry-level cameras, because you relinquish control of exposure to the camera. If you want to make informed decisions about shutter speed and aperture for creative photography, do not use **P** mode!

Aperture-Priority Auto (A): In this mode, you select an aperture value and the D7000 will choose a shutter speed to produce an appropriate exposure, as determined by the selected metering mode. The aperture is controlled by the Sub-Command dial (default) and is changed in steps of 0.3 EV (default). The shutter speed the camera selects will also change in increments of 0.3 EV (default). The EV step level can be adjusted using CS-b2 [EV steps for exposure cntrl].

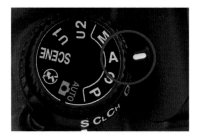

NOTE: If a non-CPU lens is attached to the camera and its maximum aperture value is specified using the [Non-CPU lens data] item in the Setup menu, the f/number is displayed in the viewfinder and control panel, rounded to the nearest whole stop value. Otherwise, the aperture displays in the viewfinder and control panel will only show the total number of stops from the maximum aperture value of the lens.

Shutter-Priority Auto (S): In this mode, you select a shutter speed between 30 seconds and 1/8000 second, and the D7000 will choose an aperture value to produce an appropriate exposure, as determined by the selected metering mode. The shutter speed is controlled by the Main Command dial (default) and is changed in steps of 0.3 EV (default). The aperture value the D7000 selects will also change in steps of 0.3 EV (default). The EV step level can be adjusted using CS-b2 [EV steps for exposure cntrl].

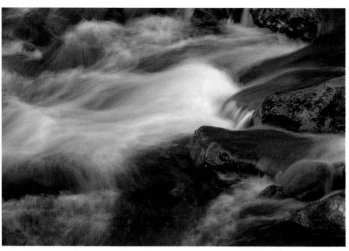

^ The shutter speed is not merely a method of controlling the exposure level, but it offers creative possibilities too, especially with a moving subject. Here, a slow shutter speed (1/4s) was used to capture motion blur in the water.

NOTE: In P, A, and S modes, if the subject or scene is too bright, the D7000 will display the warning, ⌘ ⁝, in the viewfinder and control panel. Likewise, if the subject or scene is too dark, it will display the warning, ᴸ ▨, in the viewfinder and control panel.

Manual (M): Manual mode offers the photographer total control over exposure, and is probably the most useful if you want to learn more about the relationship between shutter speed and aperture and how they affect the final appearance of your pictures. You choose and control both the shutter speed (via the Main Command dial) and lens aperture (via the Sub-Command dial). (If required, the priority of the two command dials can be changed via CS-f6.) An analog display shown in the control panel and viewfinder indicates the level of exposure your settings would produce. If the camera determines the exposure values are set for a proper exposure, a single indent mark appears below the central '0.' If the camera determines that the settings would produce an underexposed result, the degree of underexposure is indicated by the number of indent marks that appear to the right (minus) side of the central '0.' Conversely, if the chosen settings would create an overexposed result, the degree of overexposure is indicated by the number of indent marks to the left (plus) side of the central '0.' The more indent marks that appear, the greater the degree of exposure "error."

ADVANCED EXPOSURE TOPICS

LONG TIME EXPOSURES (M MODE ONLY)

To shoot at exposure durations of more than 30 seconds, select the ᏏuᏝᏏ setting from the range of shutter speeds. It can be useful when shooting in very low-light conditions or for creating special effects like photographing fireworks or moving traffic at night. Using a tripod or some other form of stable camera support in conjunction with the MC-DC2 remote release cord is highly recommended, as is checking that the installed EN-EL15 battery is fully charged. I also strongly recommend that you use the Long Exposure Noise Reduction feature, which can be found in the Shooting menu.

Select **M** exposure mode and rotate the Main Command dial until the shutter speed is displayed as ᏏuᏝᏏ in the viewfinder, control panel, and Information Display. After selecting the ᏏuᏝᏏ option, focus the camera and then press and hold the shutter release button down all the way to begin the exposure. To end the exposure, let go of the shutter release button. If you use the MC-DC2 remote cord, press and lock its release button to start the exposure, and then unlock its release button and let go of it to end the exposure.

Alternatively, the ML-L3 IR remote release can be used in conjunction with the ▣))) Remote Control mode, which is selected by rotating to the Release Mode dial to the ▣))) position. Now select the - - setting in the shutter speed range. To start the exposure, press the release button on the ML-L3 while pointing it at either the front or rear receiver window; the exposure will end after a maximum duration of 30 minutes, or sooner if the ML-L3 release button is pressed again.

AUTOEXPOSURE (AE) LOCK

If you take a meter reading in **P**, **A**, or **S** mode and recompose the picture after taking a reading, it is likely—particularly with Spot metering—that the metered area will now fall on a different part of the scene and probably produce a different exposure value.

The D7000 allows you to lock the initial exposure reading in Center-Weighted or Spot metering before you reframe and shoot. Start by positioning the part of the scene you want to meter within the appropriate metering area, press the shutter release halfway to acquire focus and an exposure reading, and then press and hold the ᴬᴱ⁻ᴸ AF-L button (when set to its default setting of **[AE/AF lock]** under CS-f5) to lock the exposure (and focus, except in Manual focus mode). You can now recompose and take the picture at the metered value. "AE-L" will appear in the viewfinder display while this function is active. While the exposure lock function is active, it is possible to alter the shutter speed and / or aperture value in **P**, **A**, and **S** modes without altering the metered exposure level. In **P** mode, shutter speed and aperture can be changed (in tandem); in **S** mode, the shutter speed can be changed; and in **A** mode, the aperture can be changed.

HINT: It is possible to use the shutter release button to perform the auto-exposure lock function; select **[On]** at CS-c1 **[Shutter-release button AE-L]**, and the exposure will lock any time the shutter release button is held down halfway.

HINT: Use of the exposure lock function is not recommend when the camera is set to perform Matrix metering, as it may produce inconsistent results.

EXPOSURE COMPENSATION

Exposure Compensation can be applied regardless of the TTL metering pattern in use, but the most consistent results are achieved with either Center-Weighted or Spot metering. As mentioned previously, in these two TTL metering patterns, the D7000 uses simple grayscale metering with no color information or influence of the Scene Recognition System to affect the meter reading. Working on the assumption that the camera is pointed at a scene with a reflectivity that averages out to that of a

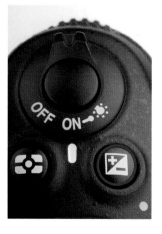

midtone, it appears Nikon has calibrated the TTL metering against a reference that has a reflectivity value of approximately 15 – 18%; hence, if you use an 18% gray photographic card to estimate exposure, you should find your results will be both accurate and consistent.

Many scenes you encounter will not reflect 15 – 18% of the light falling on them. For example, a landscape under a blanket of fresh snowfall is going to reflect far more light, while an animal with a very dark brown coat will reflect far less than an average midtone. Unless you compensate your exposure accordingly for these extremes, the camera will attempt to render them as midtones, causing a light tone to appear underexposed and a dark tone to be overexposed.

> The Exposure Compensation button allows you to alter the exposure value metered by the D7000 in order to counter likely over- or underexposure situations.

To set Exposure Compensation in **P**, **S**, and **A** exposure modes, hold down the ⊞ button, located behind and to the right of the shutter release button. Turn the Main Command dial until the required value is shown in the control panel. The numerical value is also displayed in the viewfinder while the button is held down and also displayed on an analog scale of ±2 EV. The degree of compensation will change +/- in steps of 0.3 or 0.5 EV depending on which step size is selected at CS-b2 **[EV steps for exposure cntrl]**.

In **M** exposure mode, the exposure is set according to the value suggested by the camera's TTL meter if the analog display shows no deviance either side of the '0' midpoint. If an Exposure Compensation factor is applied in **M** exposure mode, the display shifts either to the left (+ compensation) or right (– compensation) of the '0' midpoint on the analog scale displayed in the viewfinder and control panel, by the amount of compensation applied. As you dial in the compensation, you will see a small + or – icon displayed to the right of the analog scale along the bottom of the viewfinder display (the ⊞ button must be depressed to see this). As soon as you release the ⊞ button, a ⊞ icon appears in place of the + or – icon (it is also shown in the control panel), and the numerical value of the compensation amount is no longer displayed. To put the Exposure Compensation into effect, you must now adjust the shutter speed and / or aperture so that the analog scale display is shifted back so that no indent marks are shown either side of the '0' midpoint. Once you have made these adjustments and the analog scale is centered on '0' again, if you press the Exposure Compensation button, the analog scale shifts to show the amount of compensation applied and the icon to the right of the scale indicates whether it is a plus or minus value. This is a useful and quick way to check how much compensation you have applied.

> **NOTE:** Although Exposure Compensation can be applied in **M** exposure mode as described, it is often quicker to simply adjust the shutter speed and / or aperture so the required level of exposure adjustment is displayed on the analog exposure scale.

The ⊞ icon remains visible in the viewfinder and control panel, regardless of the exposure mode in use, as a reminder that you have an Exposure Compensation value applied. Once you have set a compensation factor, it will remain locked until you hold down the ⊞ button and reset the compensation value to 0.

BRACKETING EXPOSURE

It is important when shooting digital pictures to expose as accurately as you can, as overexposure will lose highlight detail, and underexposure tends to degrade image quality due to electronic noise as well as blocked shadow detail. In Exposure Bracketing, the D7000 varies the Exposure Compensation with each exposure in a sequence of a set number. Such bracketing of exposures can be useful in difficult lighting conditions when there is insufficient time to check exposures and / or adjust camera settings appropriately.

Bracketing is also a very useful feature for any photographer shooting high dynamic range (HDR) pictures, which is a technique that uses software to combine a number of shots of the same scene taken at different exposure levels to produce a single image with an extended dynamic range (i.e., a tonal range beyond that which the camera could record in a single exposure).

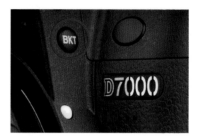

> The **BKT** (bracketing) button is located on the front of the camera, to the left side of the viewfinder head.

The bracketing system in the D7000 allows you to take a sequence of exposures varied in steps of 0.3 or 0.5 EV, subject to the setting selected at CS-b2 **[EV steps for exposure cntrl]** over a range of ±0.3 to ±2 EV. The bracketing sequence can be selected to affect the exposure (AE only), flash output (Flash only), or a combination of the two (AE & Flash), by selecting the appropriate option at CS-e5 **[Auto bracketing set]**. The combinations of number of exposures and Exposure Compensation level are shown in the following table:

NO. OF SHOTS	BRACKETING PROGRESS INDICATOR	BRACKETING ORDER
3F	+◀◀▮▶—	Normal exposure, underexposure, overexposure
+2F	◀▮	Normal exposure, overexposure
--2F	▮	Normal exposure, underexposure

NOTE: Flash Bracketing works similarly to non-Flash Exposure Bracketing: The amount of light from the flash in the exposure is adjusted with each shot, also in steps of 0.3 or 0.5 EV. This function works with both i-TTL flash control and the Auto-Aperture flash control available with the SB-900 and SB-800.

To activate Exposure Bracketing, select the required option under the CS-e5 **[Auto bracketing set]** item. Press and hold the **BKT** button and rotate the Main Command dial to set the number of shots in the bracketing sequence, and then turn the Sub-Command dial to set the step size. **BKT** will be displayed in the control panel, viewfinder and Information Display. While bracketing is active, a progress indicator that shows the number of exposures in the sequence is displayed in the control panel and Information Display. As each exposure is made, the indicator will change to reflect the number of exposure remaining in the bracketing sequence.

To cancel bracketing, press the **BKT** button and rotate the Main Command dial until the number of shots in the bracketing sequence is set to zero (**BKT** is no longer displayed in the control panel, viewfinder, or Information Display).

Bracketing Considerations: The following are some things to keep in mind when using the exposure bracket function on the D7000:

- Using **S** Single Frame release mode, the shutter release button must be depressed to make each exposure in the bracketing sequence.

- If you set the D7000 to one of the continuous release modes, **CL** or **CH**, and then press and hold the shutter release button down, the camera will only take the number of frames specified in the bracketing sequence. The camera stops regardless of whether the shutter release continues to be depressed.

- If you turn the D7000 off or have to change the memory card during a bracketing sequence, the camera remembers which exposure values are outstanding, so when you turn the camera on or insert a new memory card, the sequence will resume from where it stopped.

- You can combine a bracketing sequence with a fixed Exposure Compensation factor. For example, if you apply an Exposure Compensation of +1 EV to deal with a scene containing predominantly light tones, and then set a bracket sequence of three frames with a step size of 1 EV, the actual exposures you make will be at 0, +1, and +2 EV, rather than −1, 0, and +1, which it would be without the +1 Exposure Compensation.

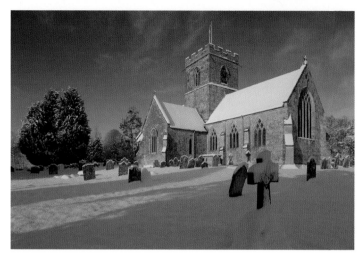

^ In a scene that contains a high level of contrast and areas of very light tone, control of the exposure level is critical. The histogram display will help to ensure a full exposure is captured without highlight detail being compromised.

EXPOSURE CONSIDERATIONS

If the D7000 is your first digital SLR camera, and your previous photography has been with a 35mm camera and color negative film, you may find controlling exposure with the D7000 rather more demanding. Color negative (print) film is very tolerant to exposure errors, particularly overexposure, and the automated processing machines used to produce your prints are capable of correcting exposure errors over a range of –2 to +3 stops and adjust color balance at the same time. Chances are, you will never have noticed your exposure errors when looking at the finished prints!

Controlling exposure with a digital SLR is analogous to shooting on transparency (slide) film: There is virtually no margin for error—even moderate overexposure will "blow out" highlight detail, leaving no usable image data in these areas. Underexposure is little better since it quickly gives rise to noise, which will degrade image quality, particularly in areas of dark tone. Make sure you check the histogram display and pay attention to each of the three individual color channels (see pages 139-142 for more details).

The autofocus system of the D7000 is highly capable, and its 39 AF points provide significant coverage of the total frame area. The 39 points are subdivided in to 15 cross-type sensors plus 18 line-type sensors that are oriented parallel to the long edge of the frame.

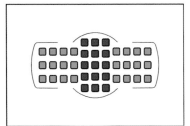

‹ The AF points shown in red are the 15 cross-type sensor, while the remaining 18 points shown in green are line-type sensors (the color shading is for illustrative purposes only).

› The two types of sensor are oriented as shown; the line-type sensors are aligned with long edge of the frame.

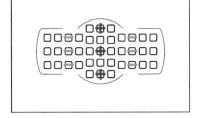

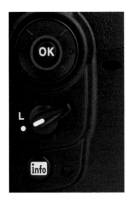

‹ The Multi Selector button's locking switch must be set to this position before you can use it to select an AF point.

The 39-point autofocus (AF) system of the D7000, which includes a 3D-Tracking capability made possible by the innovative Scene Recognition System (SRS), is essentially derived from the 51-point AF system that has won wide acclaim in the D3-series, D700, and D300 series cameras.

In the D7000, however, it benefits from an increase in both speed and accuracy, in part thanks to its new 2016-pixel RGB metering sensor and the brand new Nikon Multi-CAM 4800DX autofocus sensor that has 1300 more sampling points than any previous Nikon AF SLR camera.

THE AUTOFOCUS SENSOR

The new Multi-CAM 4800DX sensor has a total of 4800 photodiodes distributed between the 39 AF points. When normal autofocus operation is initiated, the D7000 uses a phase-detection focusing method (as opposed to the contrast-detection system employed in the Live View autofocus). The phase-detection system uses a beam splitter comprising two optical prisms in a small, semi-transparent area of the main reflex mirror that capture the light rays coming from the opposite sides of the lens. The prisms are coupled with a small secondary mirror located behind the main mirror that directs the light from the prisms to the Multi-CAM 4800DX module, which is located in the base of the mirror box at the bottom of the camera. The double image projected onto the AF module is then analyzed for the patterns of light intensity and the phase difference between them is then calculated to determine whether the subject is in front of or behind the current plane of focus. This not only informs the AF system which way the focus must be adjusted, but also by how much. The focus point is adjusted immediately and the phase difference checked, and as long as it is within the tolerances of the AF system, focus will not be altered again, as the camera has determined that focus has been acquired.

> The distribution of the 39 AF points within the frame area is as shown. Choose the number of points (39 or 11) available for manual AF point selection using CS-a6.

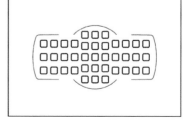

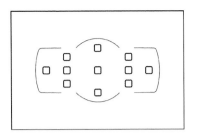

‹ Selecting just 11 points can allow you to work more quickly, because there are fewer points to scroll across; their distribution within the frame area is shown at left.

That the central fifteen AF points are cross-type means they are sensitive to detail in both horizontal and vertical orientation; therefore, they are the most reliable. The remaining 18 AF points are line-type; these are only sensitive to detail in a direction that is perpendicular to their orientation, which is parallel to the long edge of the viewfinder frame.

HINT: One of the most common causes of inaccuracy when using the AF system is the size of the subject relative to the area of the frame occupied by the AF point. If the size of the area of the subject being focused on is small compared to the area covered by the AF point, as is often the case when using a wide-angle lens, the AF system is likely to miss the intended focus point. As a general rule of thumb, make sure that the subject covers at least 50% of the area covered by the AF point.

HINT: Sometimes when using one of the line-type sensing areas, the autofocus system of the D7000 will "hunt" (i.e., the camera will drive the focus of the lens back and forth, but is unable to attain focus). This is often an indication that the detail in the subject is aligned in the same orientation as the focus sensing area under the active AF point, and thus there is insufficient contrast in the subject for the AF system to acquire focus. If this occurs, try twisting the camera slightly (10 – 15°). This slight adjustment is often enough to allow the camera to acquire focus, as the focus sensing area can detect more contrast in the detail of the subject. Once focus is confirmed, lock it (see "Focus Lock" section on pages 89-90) and recompose the picture before releasing the shutter.

The AF point, selected in either Single-Point or Dynamic-Area AF, can have a profound effect on the ability of the camera to achieve autofocus depending on whether it is a cross or line type—the fifteen central cross types are far more reliable in low-light or low-contrast conditions.

Furthermore, the number of AF points selected in Dynamic-Area AF (9, 21, or 39) should be considered with care, and be based on the nature of the subject and scene being photographed. The general rule of thumb is to use as few AF points as possible so the camera has less data to process, so that it can focus more quickly.

HINT: The AF system is designed to work with any Nikkor AF lens that has a maximum aperture of f/5.6 or larger. If an accessory such as a teleconverter or extension tube is used with a lens and reduces its effective maximum aperture to less than f/5.6, autofocus operation is likely to become slow and unreliable.

SCENE RECOGNITION SYSTEM

In addition to the new AF sensor, the autofocus system of the D7000 also benefits from the capabilities of Nikon's Scene Recognition System (SRS), which has been enhanced by the new 2016-pixel RGB-metering sensor. This new metering sensor can recognize a subject by its shape, size, and color. To employ the benefits of the SRS, however, it is necessary to use a D- or G-type Nikkor lens. The SRS requires the focus distance information these lenses provide in order to perform the necessary calculations needed for its two principle features, Subject Identification and Subject Tracking. This pioneering system brings significant benefits to the performance of the autofocus system, and improves autoexposure and Auto White Balance functionality.

The SRS is optimized to recognize skin tones, particularly in any area detected by the 2016-pixel RGB sensor that relates to the average size of a human face; this is why the focus data from a D- or G-type lens is essential, as the camera calculates the size of the area on the metering sensor based on the distance information supplied by the lens. To the human eye, the range of skin tones can look noticeably varied, but a metering system that uses a red-green-blue sensor does not "see" in the same way, and skin tones all appear very similar to such a system. For this reason, Nikon's SRS system is a vast improvement over basic RGB sensors.

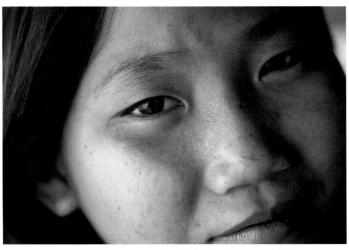

∧ The D7000's Scene Recognition System is optimized for skin tones and helps to improve the accuracy of 3D Color Matrix metering, autofocus, and Automatic White Balance.

FOCUS MODES

The D7000 has three principal focusing modes: Single-Servo AF (AF-S), Continuous-Servo AF (AF-C), and Manual focus (M), plus Auto-Servo AF (AF-A), in which the camera selects either AF-S or AF-C automatically, based on its assessment of whether or not the subject is stationary (AF-S) or moving (AF-C). To select between the Autofocus and Manual focus modes, rotate the Focus-Mode selector located on the side of the lens mount below the lens release button (see picture on page 83), until the white index mark is aligned with the required option. To select the AF mode, set the switch to its AF position and then press and hold the button at the center of the AF mode switch. Now rotate the Main Command dial to select AF-S, AF-C, or AF-A, which will be displayed in the control panel.

NOTE: With most AF-Nikkor lenses, for manual focus to be enabled, the Focus-Mode selector lever must be set to M. However, if the lens you are using has a switch that allows you to select an M/A (manual / autofocus) mode, you need only touch the focusing ring and the lens can be focused manually. As soon as you release the focusing ring and press the shutter release down halfway, the camera will resume autofocus operation. If the lens attached to the camera has an M/A mode option, the Focus-Mode selector on the camera body can be left set to AF.

SINGLE-SERVO (AF-S)

As soon as the shutter release button is pressed down halfway, the D7000 will focus the lens. At the default settings, the shutter can only be released once focus has been acquired; the in-focus indicator (●) is displayed in the viewfinder. Focus will remain locked while the shutter release is half-depressed. No form of focus tracking is performed when the camera is set to AF-S; therefore, this mode is best suited to photographing stationary subjects, where the camera-to-subject distance will remain constant.

In AF-S, at the default setting for CS-a2 [AF-S priority selection], the shutter cannot be released until focus has been acquired; Nikon refers to this mode as having "focus priority." Once focus is acquired in this mode, the focus distance is locked as long as the shutter release button is pressed and held down halfway, or the AF-L button is pressed and held down, assuming CS-f5 is set to its default (see pages 234-235 for more on CS-f5's numerous options). In most shooting conditions, particularly in good light, having to wait for the camera to acquire focus has no practical consequence. However, under certain conditions, such as in low light or with low-contrast subjects, there is often a discernable lag between when you press the shutter release button and when the shutter opens, because it generally takes the camera longer to establish focus in these circumstances, particularly if one of the outer, line-type sensing areas is used. If getting the shot is your first priority, then consider using AF-C.

Using Trap Focus: You can use the AF-S mode to perform a technique very useful in shooting wildlife or sports, called trap focusing. Trap focus allows the camera to be pre-focused at a specific point and have the shutter released automatically as soon as a subject passes through it. Provided you can predict the path of the subject, this technique can be very useful. To set up the D7000 for trap focus, do the following:

1. Set CS-f5 [Assign AF-L button] to [AF-ON Only] (focusing is only performed when the AF-L button is pressed, and not when the shutter release button is pressed).
2. Select AF-S (Single-Servo) AF focus mode.
3. Select Single-Area as the AF-Area mode. (If the lens you are using has a focus mode switch on it, set it to A or M/A.)

Pre-focus the lens on a point the same distance from the camera as the point through which the subject will pass, by pressing the AE-L/AF-L button. Once focus is acquired, release the AE-L/AF-L button (focus is now locked at that distance). Recompose the picture so that the selected AF point covers the point you expect the subject to pass through. Now, fully depress the shutter release (this is necessary to keep the camera activated and enable the shutter to be released as soon as focus is detected). I recommend using a remote shutter release with a lock facility, such as the Nikon MC-DC2. When the subject enters the space covered by the selected AF point the camera will detect focus, and the shutter will be released. The camera will not take a photo until something enters the designated focal plane, because Single-Servo AF is "focus priority."

CONTINUOUS-SERVO (AF-C)

While the shutter release button is pressed down halfway, the D7000 focuses the lens continuously. If the camera-to-subject distance changes—for example, the subject begins to move—the camera will initiate Predictive Focus Tracking to shift focus as it follows the subject. Because focus is monitored constantly, it does not matter whether the subject continues to move or stops and starts periodically, the camera will continue to focus until either the shutter is released or you remove your finger from the shutter release button.

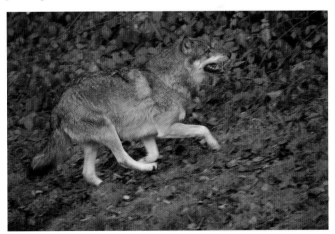

∧ When photographing a moving subject, AF-C (Continuous-Servo) autofocus will use the camera's Predictive Focus Tracking system to help maintain focus accuracy.

In this mode, at the default setting for CS-a1 [AF-C priority selection], the shutter will operate immediately upon pressing the shutter release button all the way down, regardless of whether or not focus has been achieved; Nikon refers to this mode as having "release priority." Some photographers assume (mistakenly) that if the shutter is released before the camera has attained focus in the AF-C mode, the picture will always be out of focus. In fact, in this mode, the combination of constant focus monitoring and Predictive Focus Tracking is normally successful in causing the focus point to be shifted within the split second delay between the reflex mirror lifting and the shutter opening, to obtain a sharp picture. Even if the camera's calculations are slightly off, the depth of field often masks minor focusing errors. To maximize AF performance when using the AF-C mode to photograph a moving subject, it is imperative that the camera be given sufficient time to assimilate information to perform the focusing action. To do this, press and hold the shutter release button halfway (or the AE-L/AF-L button if it is set to perform AF activation) as far in advance of releasing the shutter as possible (see details of CS-f5 [Assign AE-L/AF-L button] for selecting the AF-ON option, pag 234-235). In my opinion, assigning the AF-ON option to the AE-L/AF-L button improves camera handling, as it allows you to keep the camera in AF-C mode, yet control exactly when the AF system is active (see the "Focus Lock" section on pages 89-90 for further details).

NOTE: To increase the chance of attaining sharp focus with a moving subject, I recommend using AF-S-type lenses, because they have internal focusing motors, which provide faster focusing compared with using AF lenses that rely on the focusing motor built-in to the D7000.

Focus Tracking with Lock-On: In an effort to prevent the camera from re-focusing on an object that appears briefly between the intended subject and the camera once the camera has established focus on the subject, the D7000 will deliberately delay shifting focus. The duration of delay before the camera shifts focus can be controlled using CS-a3 [Focus tracking with lock-on]. If you want to photograph a subject where the camera-to-subject distance is changing abruptly during a series of shots, the Lock-On feature can prevent rapid acquisition of focus. In this case, I recommend selecting either [Short] (to reduce the delay to its minimum) or **[Off]** (the camera will re-focus immediately). At a soccer or football game, where a subject may be obscured intermittently and unpredictably by another player coming between the camera and the subject, a slightly longer delay in re-focusing is likely to be preferable, so try the **[Normal]** option, while at a track and field meet, photographing runners in lanes, where the subject may be blocked by another runner for a longer period, a setting of **[Long]** will help maintain focus on the intended subject. Nikon does not publish the specific duration of the various delay periods that can be selected using CS-a3.

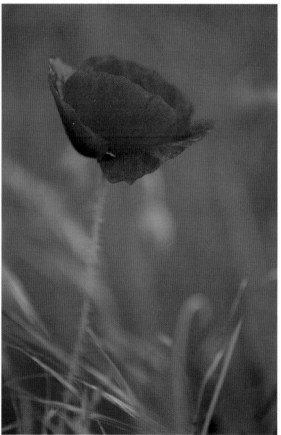

› When shooting at close focusing distances, autofocus may not position the point of focus exactly where you want it to be. I recommend using Manual focus in this situation.

AUTO-SERVO (AF-A)

As soon as the shutter release button is pressed down halfway, the AF system assesses whether the subject is stationary or moving and will select AF-S or AF-C accordingly. The two AF modes operate as described above.

MANUAL FOCUS (M)

You must rotate the focusing ring of the lens to achieve focus. There is no restriction on when the shutter can be operated. With a lens that has a maximum aperture of f/5.6 or larger, the electronic rangefinder feature will display the in-focus confirmation signal (●) when focus is achieved, which can be particularly useful in low-light or low-contrast conditions.

NOTE: The focus and release priority assigned in AF-S (Single-Servo) and AF-C (Continuous-Servo) modes can be reversed using CS-a2 and CS-a1, respectively. I recommend that changes from the default settings should only be made once you understand how the focusing system works, and then only if the specific shooting situation requires the priorities to be reversed.

AUTOFOCUS AREA MODES

The D7000 has four Autofocus-Area modes (not to be confused with the three focusing modes described above) that determine how the 39 AF points are used: Single-Point AF, Dynamic-Area AF, 3D-tracking, and Auto-Area AF.

> The black lines marked on the focus screen define the AF area. Here, a single AF point is selected at the center of the frame.

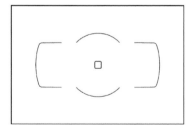

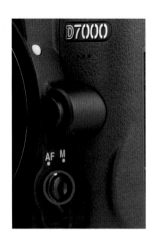

< The center button of the Focus-Mode
selector is used in conjunction with the
Command dials to select the AF-Area modes.

To select the AF-Area mode, set the Focus-Mode selector to its AF position and then press and hold the button at the center of the selector. Now, rotate the Sub-Command dial to select Single-Point AF, Dynamic-Area AF (9, 21, or 39-point), 3D-Tracking, or Auto-Area AF, the selected option will be displayed in the control panel.

[▫] *SINGLE-POINT AF*

The D7000 will use only the single AF point that you manually select for focusing; the camera takes no part in choosing which AF point to use. The selected AF point is highlighted in the control panel and the Information Display.

[▣] *DYNAMIC-AREA AF*

In AF-C and AF-A with Dynamic-Area AF selected, the D7000 also uses the user-selected AF point for focusing; however, if the subject leaves the area covered by this AF point briefly, the camera immediately evaluates information from the other surrounding AF points, and will attempt to maintain focus using these AF points as appropriate until the subject is covered by the originally selected AF point. The number of focus points can be set to 9, 21, or 39. The selected AF point and supporting points is highlighted in the control panel and the Information Display. The AF point you initially selected remains highlighted even if another AF point is used momentarily to maintain focus. In AF-S mode, the camera only uses the AF point you selected; selection of alternative AF points is not performed.

When Dynamic-Area AF is selected, only the Multi-CAM 4800DX AF sensor is used to perform focus tracking. This is different from 3D-Tracking (see below) in that it uses both the Multi-CAM 4800DX AF sensor and the 2016-pixel RGB sensor. Essentially, in Dynamic-Area AF, the camera reverts to the established AF system used by earlier Nikon DSLR cameras. In some situations, this can be an advantage; since the camera has far fewer computations to perform compared with the 3D-Tracking option; therefore, the AF response is faster. The Dynamic-Area option will be more reliable when, for example, you are shooting a moving subject under restricted-spectrum artificial light, (e.g., some types of fluorescent and mercury vapor lighting), as this affects the ability of the 2016-pixel RGB sensor to detect skin tones. This, of course, renders the SRS less effective, which in turn will impinge on the performance of the Auto-Area AF and 3D-Tracking AF.

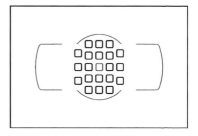

› The diagram shows the normal distribution of AF points in the 21-point configuration for Dynamic-Area AF; only the selected AF point (shown in red) is displayed in the viewfinder.

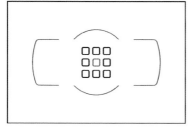

‹ The Dynamic-Area AF, such as the 9-Point option shown here, offers faster AF than the 3D-Tracking option, but the disadvantage is that the selected AF point (marked in red) must be positioned over the subject, so rapid changes to the composition are not possible if focus is to be maintained.

In AF-C and AF-A with 3D-tracking AF selected, the D7000 again uses the AF point that you initially selected for focusing. However, once focus is acquired, selection of the AF point is fully automated and the camera will use its 3D-Tracking feature to track the subject. This mapping of the subject by the 2016-pixel RGB sensor is combined with the focus tracking information from the Multi-CAM 4800DX autofocus sensor, enabling the AF system to predict with speed and precision which AF point(s) to use in order to maintain focus.

Remarkably, the subject mapping by the RGB metering sensor continues to operate if the subject moves momentarily outside the area covered by the 39 AF points; as soon as the subject returns to the AF area (as defined by the bracket lines shown on the viewfinder screen), autofocus resumes, even if the subject is at a different location within the AF area covered by the 39 AF points from the one it occupied immediately before it left the AF area. This combined tracking of the subject by the AF sensor and the RGB metering sensor is only used in the Auto-Area and 3D-Tracking AF-Area modes, and although far from foolproof (the Auto-Area tends to be more reliable than the 3D-Tracking system), they can produce quite amazing results and certainly offer a very advanced form of focus tracking.

The 3D-Tracking mode differs from the Dynamic-area AF mode in that with 3D-Tracking, the camera automatically selects the active focus point as soon as focus is acquired, even if the camera and / or subject move relative to one another. This enables focus to be maintained while rapid and significant changes in composition are made, because it is no longer necessary to maintain tracking by keeping the selected AF point over the subject, which is necessary except for brief lapses in the Dynamic-Area AF mode.

This option is most effective where the camera-to-subject distance remains fairly constant but the subject is moving laterally across the frame, or you wish to make rapid changes to the composition by placing the subject from one side of the frame to the other. If the subject moves out of the viewfinder it will be necessary to reacquire focus by placing the selected AF point over the subject and then activating AF again.

▣ *AUTO-AREA AF*

In Auto-Area AF, the D7000 selects the AF point(s) automatically using information from the Multi-CAM 4800DX autofocus sensor and (as long as a D- or G-type Nikkor lens is used) Subject Identification information established by the Scene Recognition System. It is particularly adept at identifying skin tones and is therefore very useful for photographing people. In AF-S (Single-Servo), the active AF point(s) are highlighted for approximately 1 second; in AF-C (Continuous-Servo), all the active AF points are indicated briefly, and then they turn off, leaving only the main AF point illuminated.

The selected AF-Area mode is displayed in both the control panel and the viewfinder of the D7000, as follows:

AF-AREA MODE	CONTROL PANEL	VIEWFINDER
Single-Point AF	(·)	S
9-Point Dynamic-Area AF	(▦)	d 9
21-Point Dynamic-Area AF	(▦)	d21
39-Point Dynamic-Area AF	(▦)	d39
3D-Tracking AF	(▦) 3D	3d
Auto-Area AF	AUTO (▦)	Auto

NOTE: Single-Point AF mode is selected automatically when the D7000 is set to Manual focus.

NOTE: If either the 9-Point or 21-Point option for Dynamic-Area AF is used and the selected AF point is located at the periphery of the area covered by the 39 AF points, such that the normal symmetrical distribution of the surrounding AF points around the selected AF point cannot be maintained, the camera continues to use the designated number of AF points (i.e., 9 or 21), but they are now arranged around the selected AF point in an asymmetrical pattern; however, this pattern will not be indicated by the camera.

SELECTING THE AF POINT

To manually select the AF point the D7000 will use initially to attain focus in Single-Point or Dynamic-Area AF, perform the following:

1. Rotate the Focus Selector lock (located immediately below the Multi Selector) counter-clockwise so the white index mark is aligned with the white dot.
2. If the camera is not already active, press the shutter release down halfway and release it.
3. Press the Multi Selector up, down, left, right, or diagonally to select the required AF point.
4. You can select the central AF point by pressing the center button of the Multi Selector.
5. To prevent unintentional selection of an alternative AF point, rotate the Focus Selector lock to the "L" position when you are finished.

NOTE: Selection of the autofocus area can be set to wrap around, by selecting the [Wrap] option at CS-a5 [Focus point wrap-around]. If you press and hold the Multi Selector, the selection of the autofocus area will scroll continuously in the direction in which the Multi Selector is pressed, and when it reaches the end of the frame, it will jump to the other side. This enables the selected autofocus area to be shifted rapidly from one side of the frame area to the other.

FOCUS MODE & AF-AREA MODE OVERVIEW

If you are new to Nikon's AF system, it will probably take a while to get used to the functionality of the focus mode and focus-area mode options of the D7000. Therefore, you may wish to re-read these sections and refer to the following chart that summarizes the various autofocus operations.

AF MODE	AF-AREA MODE	SELECTION OF AF POINT
Manual	Single-Point AF	User
AF-S (single-servo)	Single-Point AF	User
AF-S	Dynamic-Area AF	User [1]
AF-S	Auto-Area AF	Camera [2]
AF-S	3D-Tracking	Not available
AF-C (continuous-servo)	Single-Point AF	User [3]
AF- C	Dynamic-Area AF	User [3, 4]
AF-C	Auto-Area AF	Camera [2, 3]
AF-C	39 Point (3D-Tracking)	User [3, 5]

1. Camera will only use the AF point selected by the user; no other AF points are used.
2. Active AF point(s) are highlighted for approximately one second. In AF-C, the main AF point remains highlighted.
3. The camera monitors focus continuously after focus has been acquired, adjusting focus if camera-to-subject distance alters.
4. The camera will use an alternative AF point if the subject momentarily leaves the selected AF point.
5. The camera will shift focus to an alternative AF point if the composition is altered; the subject is tracked automatically, based on color and contrast pattern information.

HINT: As you change the AF-Area mode from Single-Point through Dynamic-Area, 3D-Tracking, and on to Auto-Area, you relinquish more control to the camera in the selection of the AF point. Therefore, you should consider the most appropriate option based on the nature of the subject you are photographing and whether or not it is moving:

○ For static subjects, use AF-S with Single-Point AF.

○ For subjects that move in a predictable direction, use AF-C with its Predictive Focus Tracking in combination with the 9-, 21-, or 39-Point option, using as few points as possible.

○ For a subject that moves unpredictably, or when you need to recompose rapidly while maintaining focus, use the AF-C with the 3D-Tracking option.

○ Finally, for point-and-shoot style photography, especially with people in the scene, consider the Auto-Area AF, but remember that making the most of this feature requires use a D- or G-type Nikkor lens.

FOCUS LOCK

Once the D7000 has acquired focus, it is possible to lock the autofocus system, so the shot can be recomposed and focus distance will be retained, even if an AF point no longer covers the subject.

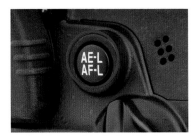

‹ The AE-L/AF-L button is located on the top right of the rear panel of the camera, to the right of the viewfinder eyepiece.

IN AF-S (SINGLE-SERVO)

Pressing the shutter release button halfway will activate autofocus. As soon as focus is acquired, the in-focus indicator (●) is displayed in the viewfinder and focus is locked; it will remain locked as long as the shutter release button is depressed halfway. Alternatively, press and hold the AE-L/AF-L button to lock focus; once focus is locked using the AE-L/AF-L button, it is not necessary to keep the shutter release button depressed.

IN AF-C (CONTINUOUS-SERVO)

The autofocus system remains active, constantly adjusting focus as necessary, as long as the shutter release button is held halfway down. To lock focus in this focus mode, press and hold the AE-L/AF-L button; once focus is locked using the AE-L/AF-L button, it is not necessary to keep the shutter release button depressed.

A popular technique that provides quick and easy control of the AF system, allowing to you shift between having the focus distance locked and using the full capabilities of the D7000 to follow focus on a moving subject, is to use the AF-ON option, which can be assigned to the to the AE-L/AF-L button by selecting it under CS-a5 [Assign AE-L/AF-L button]. In this configuration, the AF system is only active while the AE-L/AF-L button is pressed and held down; the shutter release button is disabled as far as activating the AF system. This allows you to keep the camera in AF-C mode, press the ᴬᴱ⁻ᴸ/ᴬꜰ⁻ᴸ button to acquire focus with the selected AF point and then lock focus by releasing the ᴬᴱ⁻ᴸ/ᴬꜰ⁻ᴸ button. Now you can recompose at will and the focus distance will not alter, even when you half depress the shutter release button. If you need to revert to AF-C with its Predictive Focus-Tracking feature, simply place the selected AF point over the subject and press and hold the ᴬᴱ⁻ᴸ/ᴬꜰ⁻ᴸ button again. Using this technique obviates the need to set AF-S when shooting stationary subjects, where you wish to recompose so the subject is not covered by the active AF point, thereby improving camera handling.

Once focus has been locked in either AF-S or AF-C focus mode, ensure the camera-to-subject distance does not change. If it does, reactivate autofocus and refocus the lens at the new distance before using the autofocus lock options.

AF ASSIST ILLUMINATOR

The D7000 has a small, built-in AF-Assist lamp, which is designed to facilitate autofocusing in low-light conditions. It is located on the front of the camera between the finger grip and the viewfinder head. Whatever the intentions of the camera's design team were, I consider this feature to be largely superfluous! Here are a few reasons why I suggest cancelling its operation under CS-a7 [Built-in AF-assist illuminator]:

○ The lamp only works if you have an autofocus lens attached to the camera, the AF-Area mode is set to either Single-Point AF or Dynamic-Area AF with the center focus point selected, or Auto-Area AF is active.

○ It is only usable with focal lengths of 24mm – 200mm.

○ The operating range is only 1.67 – 9.83 feet (0.5 – 3.0m).

○ Due to its location, many lenses obstruct its output, particularly if they have a lens hood attached.

○ The lamp overheats quite quickly (6 to 8 exposures in rapid succession is usually sufficient) and will automatically shut down to allow it to cool. Plus, at this level of use, it also drains battery power faster.

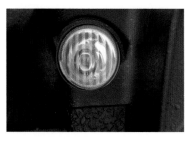

< The AF-Assist lamp: its position and low power limit its usefulness.

HINT: Provided the conditions described are met, it is possible to use the built-in AF-Assist Illuminator lamp of the SB-900, SB-800, SB-700, or SB-600 Speedlight, or the SU-800 Speedlight commander unit—the camera's lamp is disabled in these circumstances. If you want to use either the SB-900, SB-800, SB-700, or SB-600 off-camera, the Nikon SC-29 TTL flash cord also has a built-in AF-Assist lamp that attaches to the camera's accessory shoe.

LIMITATIONS OF THE AF SYSTEM

Although the autofocus system of the D7000 is very sophisticated and highly effective, there are some circumstances or conditions that can impair or limit its performance:

O Low-ambient-light conditions

O Low-contrast ambient light or low subject contrast

O Highly reflective surfaces

O Subject too small within the area covered by the AF point(s)

O The AF point covers a subject comprising very fine detail

O The AF point covers a regular geometric pattern

O The AF point covers a region of high contrast

O The AF point covers objects at different distances from the camera.

If any of these conditions prevent the camera from acquiring focus, either switch to Manual focus mode, or focus on another object at the same distance from the camera as the subject, and use the Focus-Lock feature before recomposing the picture.

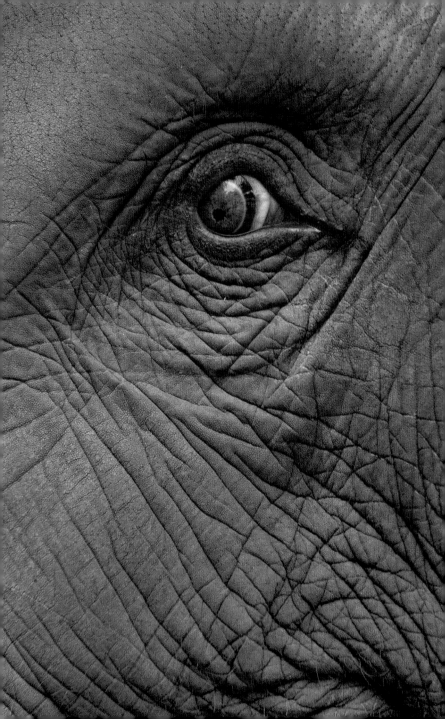

Shoot and Review

THE SHUTTER

The specification of the electronically timed, mechanical shutter used in the D7000 is impressive for a camera in its class. The shutter blades are constructed from a durable composite of Kevlar™ and carbon fiber material, which provides great strength with low mass to ensure both durability and accuracy; the unit is proven to at least 150,000 cycles.

The shutter speed range of the D7000 is 30 seconds to 1/8000 second and can be set in increments of 0.3 or 0.5 EV. The normal flash sync speed is 1/250 second, and there is an option for exposures beyond 30 seconds using the ᏰᏢᏝᏰ setting, plus there is a Long Exposure Noise Reduction feature, which can be used in such circumstances (see pages 208-209 for more details).

SHUTTER RELEASE

The shutter release button of the D7000 is located conventionally on the top, right-hand portion of the camera. If the camera is on, light pressure on the shutter release button—pressing it down halfway—will activate the metering system and initiate autofocus (assuming the camera is not set to Manual focus). If you take your finger off the button, the camera will enter a standby mode after a fixed period, the duration of which depends on the selection made within CS-c2 **[Auto meter-off delay]**; six seconds is the default setting. Simply press the shutter button halfway again to reactivate it.

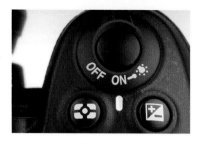

> The shutter release button of the D7000 is located on the top right-hand side of the camera.

If you continue to press the shutter release button, the shutter mechanism will actuate and an exposure will be made. There is a short delay between pressing the button all the way down and the shutter opening that is usually referred to as shutter lag, which for the D7000 is approximately 50 milliseconds when recording NEF (RAW) 12-bit or JPEG files. The mirror blackout time is approximately 90 milliseconds when shooting at a frame rate of 6 fps (frames per second). (1 millisecond = 1/1000 second; and "mirror blackout time" refers to the duration of time the viewfinder is blacked out while the reflex mirror is in the raised position while the shutter is open.)

However, the release of the shutter can be delayed further, and in some cases prevented, if certain features and functions are in operation at the time the release button is pressed. The following are some of the factors that may cause an extended delay in shutter operation:

○ The capacity of the buffer memory is probably the most common cause of shutter delay. It does not matter whether you shoot in Single or one of the Continuous release modes (see pages 96-97 for description); once the buffer memory is full, the camera must write data to the memory card before any more exposures can be made. As soon as sufficient space is available in the buffer memory for another image, the shutter can be released. For this reason, using memory cards with a fast data write speed is recommended. The D7000 supports the fast proprietary data transfer rates of the 30MB/s versions of some SDHC standard memory cards, such as the SanDisk Extreme III cards, as well as the very latest SDXC standard cards, so it is worth using these cards with faster data write speeds.

○ If the camera is set to Single-Servo autofocus mode, the shutter is disabled until the D7000 has acquired focus. In low-light or low-contrast scenes, the autofocus system can often take longer to achieve focus, adding to the delay. CS-a2 [AF-S priority selection] allows this priority to be overridden.

- In low light conditions, the D7000 will activate the AF-Assist lamp, if its operation is selected via CS-a7 and the required camera settings have been made, which introduces a short delay while the lamp illuminates and focus is acquired. The AF-Assist lamp only operates in Single-Servo autofocus mode, and either Auto-Area, Single-Point, or Dynamic-Area AF, and when the center AF point is active.

- The Red-Eye Reduction function, which is one of the flash modes available on the camera, introduces an additional one-second delay between pressing the shutter release button and the exposure being made. This is the time the lamp takes to emit light that causes a subject's pupils to constrict before the shutter opens and the flash unit fires.

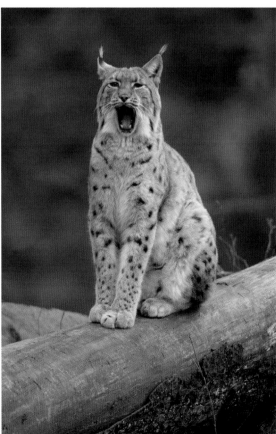

> When shooting to capture a specific moment, it is important to anticipate the action to allow for the slight delay between pressing the shutter release and the shutter opening.

Unlike a 35mm film camera, the D7000 does not have to transport film between exposures; so in that sense, it does not have a motor drive, but the shutter mechanism still has to be cycled. The camera offers a range of release modes: **S** Single-Frame and two Continuous-Frame modes (**CH** and **CL**), **Q** Quiet Shutter-Release mode, a ↻ Self-Timer option, **MUP** Mirror Lock-Up, plus Live View that provides a real-time image on the camera's LCD monitor to enable focusing and composition of a picture.

To set the release mode, hold down the Release Mode dial lock button and rotate the dial to the desired position: **S** Single Frame, **CL** Continuous Low Speed, **CH** Continuous High Speed, **Q** Quiet Shutter Release, ↻ Self-Timer, ▄◗))) Remote Control, and **MUP** Mirror Up.

S SINGLE FRAME

A single image is recorded each time the shutter release button is pressed. To make another exposure, the button must be pressed again; you can continue to do so until its buffer memory is full (in which case, you must wait for data to be written to the memory card), or the memory card becomes full.

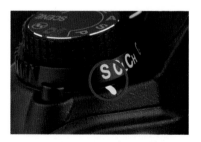

HINT: You do not have to remove your finger from the shutter release button completely between frames; by raising it slightly after each exposure, maintaining a slight downward pressure on the shutter release button, you can keep the camera active and be ready for the next shot.

Cʟ *CONTINUOUS LOW SPEED*

In this mode, if you press and hold the shutter release button down, the D7000 will continue to record images at a frame rate between 1 and 5 fps. The actual frame rate can be set via CS-d6 [CL mode shooting speed].

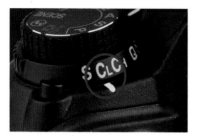

Cʜ *CONTINUOUS HIGH SPEED*

In this mode, if you press and hold the shutter release button down, the D7000 will continue to record images up to a maximum rate of 6 fps.

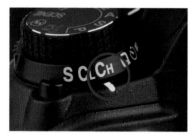

NOTE: The quoted frame rates for the D7000 are based on the camera being set to Continuous-Servo AF, Manual or Shutter-Priority exposure mode, and a shutter speed of 1/250 second or faster. It is important to remember that buffer capacity, other autoexposure modes, and Single-Servo autofocus (particularly in low-light) can reduce the frame rate significantly.

NOTE: The maximum number of exposures that can be made in a single sequence can be set via CS-d7 [Max continuous release] to any number between 1 and 100.

Q *QUIET SHUTTER RELEASE*

In this release mode, the action of raising the reflex mirror and opening the shutter has been separated from the noise of lowering the reflex mirror and recycling the shutter mechanism. This makes the operation of the camera noticeably quieter compared with the Single-Frame release mode. The shutter mechanism has been modified with the addition of an extra damping mechanism to slow the movement of the reflex mirror on its return. This release mode is ideal for shooting discreetly in any environment where the noise of the Single-Frame release mode would be intrusive.

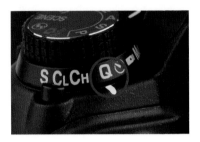

○ *SELF-TIMER*

The Self-Timer option is used to release the shutter after a predetermined delay. The default delay is 10 seconds, but it can be adjusted to 2, 5, or 20 seconds via CS-c3 [Self-timer]. The Self-Timer feature also allows you set a predetermined number of exposure (1-9) to be made, with a selectable delay between each of either 0.5, 1, 2, or 3 seconds.

To use the Self-Timer, the camera should normally be placed on an independent means of support, such as a tripod. Compose the picture and ensure focus is confirmed before depressing the shutter release button (in AF-S focus mode, the shutter release will be disabled unless focus is acquired).

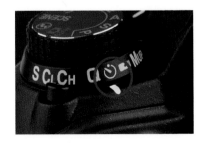

HINT: Make sure you do not pass in front of the lens after setting the Self-Timer, as the autofocus may shift the point of focus and prevent the camera from operating. I recommend setting the camera to manual focus when using the Self-Timer feature.

NOTE: If ⚙, SCENE, **P**, **A**, or **S** automatic exposure mode is used in conjunction with the Self-Timer feature, it is essential to cover the viewfinder eyepiece with the supplied DK-5 eyepiece cap. In normal shooting, the photographer's eye is to the viewfinder, which blocks extraneous light from entering the viewfinder eyepiece and influencing the camera's TTL metering sensor that is located in the viewfinder head above the eyepiece. If you fail to cover the eyepiece, exposures will be inaccurate.

After the shutter release button is pressed, the AF-Assist lamp will begin to blink (the audible warning will also beep if it is activated) until approximately two seconds before the exposure is due to be taken, at which point the light stops blinking and remains on continuously (the frequency of the audible warning beep will increase) until the shutter is released. To cancel the Self-Timer operation during the countdown, turn the Release Mode dial to another release mode.

▬◉))) *REMOTE CONTROL*

The shutter release is controlled using the release button on the optional ML-L3 infrared remote control release. The D7000 offers three options under the **[Remote control mode]** item in the ⚙ Shooting menu, as follows: **[Delayed remote]**, in which the shutter is released 2 seconds after the ML-L3 release button is pressed, **[Quick-response remote]** where the shutter is released immediately when the ML-L3 release button is pressed), or **[Remote mirror-up]**, where pressing the release button of the ML-L3 will cause the reflex mirror to be raised, and pressing it a second time will release the shutter to make the exposure (the shutter will be released after 30 seconds if the ML-L3 release button is not pressed a second time). The latter option is another method of locking up the mirror to reduce the effects of internal camera vibration, which can often reduce image resolution, especially at telephoto focal lengths.

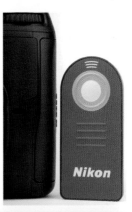

〉 The optional Nikon ML-L3 IR remote release offers a method of reducing camera shake associated with long exposures.

〉 The D7000 has two IR receivers, one of which is located on the rear of the camera to the right of the Multi Selector button for use with the ML-L3. The other one is located on the front of the camera. The presence of two receivers means that it doesn't matter which side of the camera you are on; the camera will "see" the remote either way.

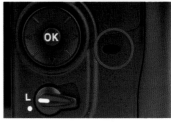

The ML-L3 has an effective range of approximately 16 feet (5 m) and must have line-of-sight with either of the two infrared receivers on the D7000, one located on the front of the camera and the other on the rear of the camera. In [Delayed remote], the Self-timer lamp will light for about 2 seconds before the shutter is released, in [Quick-response remote] the Self-Timer lamp will flash after the shutter has been released, and in [Remote mirror-up] the Self-Timer lamp will flash when the ML-L3 release button is pressed a second time, or after 30 seconds if it is not pressed.

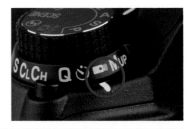

NOTE: To cancel the Self-Timer or Remote modes, select an alternative release mode.

The mirror up **Mᴜᴘ** release mode option should not be confused with the [Lock mirror up for cleaning] option available via the ϒ Setup menu, which is used to facilitate inspection and cleaning of the optical low-pass filter (see pages 358-360 for details).

Locking the reflex mirror into its raised position helps to reduce the vibrations that can often occur, particularly at slow shutter speeds, when the reflex mirror lifts up out of the light path to the camera's sensor. However, once the mirror is locked into the up position, it is not possible to see through the viewfinder; therefore, exposure, composition, and focus must be confirmed before initiating this mode.

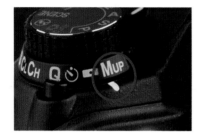

NOTE: Once in the raised position, the reflex mirror prevents light from the lens reaching the 2016-segment RGB metering sensor located in the viewfinder head, so exposure settings will be based on the light reflected from the scene immediately prior to the mirror being raised; if the illumination of the scene changes after the mirror has been raised, exposure will not be accurate. Likewise, autofocus detection is no longer possible, so in autofocus modes, the focus distance is locked at the distance set prior to the mirror being raised.

The Mirror Up feature has two distinct phases; the first press of the shutter release button will cause the mirror to lift and lock into its raised position. The shutter release button must be pressed a second time to operate the shutter and make the exposure. It is important to pause briefly between the two phases to allow any vibration caused by the mirror movement to dissipate. Once the exposure has been completed, the mirror will return to its normal position. Since the purpose of using the Mirror Up feature is to eliminate camera vibrations, it counter-productive to jar the camera by pressing the shutter release button. To reduce any other potential source of vibration, mount the camera on a tripod or other type of rigid camera support, and use a remote shutter release to operate the shutter; the D7000 has a remote accessory terminal for connecting the Nikon MC-DC2 remote release cord for this purpose.

*MULTIPLE EXPOSURE (**P, S, A,** AND **M** MODES ONLY)*

The Multiple Exposure feature is not accessed using the Release-Mode dial, but it is a release mode nonetheless. It enables either 2 or 3 exposures to be shot consecutively and then combined into one image; the images are not saved individually, but as a single combined image. To use Multiple Exposure:

1. Highlight **[Multiple exposure]** in the ◘ Shooting menu, and press ▶.
2. Highlight **[Number of Shots]** and press ▶, and then use ▲ or ▼ to select either 2 or 3.
3. Press ⓞⓚ to confirm the selection and return to the **[Multiple exposure]** menu.
4. Highlight **[Auto gain]** and press ▶, then highlight either **[On]** or **[Off]** and press ⓞⓚ to confirm the selection and return to the Multiple Exposure menu. (See the hint on the opposite page for more information on Auto Gain.)
5. Highlight **[Done]** and finally, press ⓞⓚ.
6. The ▦ icon will be displayed in the control panel. Frame and shoot the images you wish to combine. In either of the Continuous release modes, the camera can record all exposures in a single sequence and will stop once the designated number has been recorded. In Self-Timer mode, the D7000 will take the number of designated pictures automatically, regardless of the number of shots specified under CS-c3. In other release modes, an exposure is made each time the shutter release is pressed, so continue until the designated number has been recorded.
7. To stop the Multiple Exposure feature before the designated number of exposures has been recorded, press the MENU button to highlight the **[Multiple exposure]** item in the ◘ Shooting menu, press ▶ to display the **[Reset]** option, which will have replaced **[Done]** and press ⓞⓚ to confirm the action.

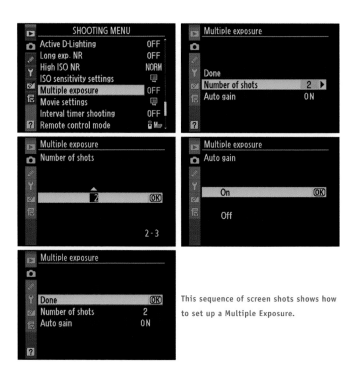

This sequence of screen shots shows how to set up a Multiple Exposure.

HINT: When Auto Gain is activated, the camera will automatically make adjustments to the exposure level of each image recorded in the sequence so that the final cumulative exposure is correct. This useful feature obviates the need to make exposure calculations to compensate for the cumulative effect of combining the individual exposures.

The Multiple Exposure icon will appear in the control panel once the function has been set, and it will blink while the exposures are being made. When the selected number of exposures has been completed, will disappear from the control panel and the [Multiple exposure] feature is turned off automatically. To create another Multiple Exposure sequence at different settings, you will need to repeat steps 1-6 above. However, to shoot another Multiple Exposure sequence using the same settings for [Number of Shots] and [Auto gain], simply select [Done] from the options under the [Multiple exposure] item and press ▶.

INTERVAL TIMER SHOOTING

The Interval Timer shooting feature, like Multiple Exposure, is accessed via the ◙ Shooting menu, not the Release-Mode dial, but it is a release mode. The Interval Timer allows you to take a set number of pictures of the same scene over a specified period of time, at predetermined intervals—a technique often called time-lapse photography, which has applications in both scientific and art photography.

Given a suitable subject or scene, this technique can produce some visually interesting results, especially if you play the images sequentially in a slide show. For example, the opening and closing of a flower blossom during the course of a day or the changes that take place at a busy street corner every few minutes during rush-hour can be fascinating to observe. The D7000 provides you with the ability to capture such changing conditions using the [Interval timer shooting] item in the ◙ Shooting menu.

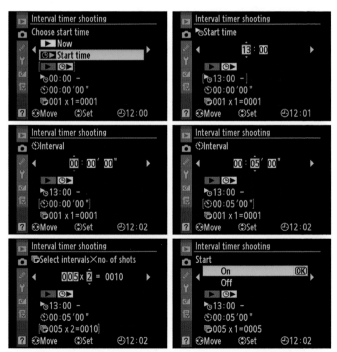

Interval Timer shooting is configured in the camera as shown in this series of screen grabs.

To configure the camera for Interval Timer shooting involves several steps. Due to the protracted duration required for some time-lapse sequences, it may be necessary to use the EH-5a AC adapter; if one is not available, make sure the EN-EL15 battery is fully charged; or better still, use the MB-D11 battery pack to combine the EN-EL15 battery installed in the camera with another one in the battery pack, for an even higher capacity to extend the potential shooting period.

NOTE: Precise and consistent framing is important, so I recommend the use of a tripod or other form of sturdy, rigid camera support.

To configure Interval timer shooting:

1. Highlight **[Interval timer shooting]** in the ◘ Shooting menu and press ▶.
2. Two options are presented in the **[Choose start time]** dialog box:
    - **[Now]**: The camera will initiate the shooting sequence approximately three seconds after settings have been confirmed in the camera.
    - **[Start time]**: The camera will delay the beginning of the shooting sequence until the specified time.
3. If you selected **[Start time]**, press ▶ to set the time when you wish the first image to be taken. Press ◀ or ▶ to highlight hours or minutes and press ▲ or ▼ to adjust setting. The maximum delay is 23 hours, 59 minutes (if you selected **[Now]** for **[Start time]**, skip this step). Once settings have been made, press ▶ to highlight the interval setting options.
4. Press ◀ or ▶ to highlight hours, minutes, or seconds; and press ▲ or ▼ to adjust the time interval between each single exposure, or between each sequence of exposures. The maximum duration is 24 hours. Once settings have been made, press ▶ to highlight the options for number of intervals and shots.
5. Press ◀ or ▶ to highlight the number of intervals and number of shots, and press ▲ or ▼ to adjust the setting for each. The first number to set is that of intervals; use ▶ to select each of its three digits. Next is the number of shots at each interval. The third number to set is the total number of shots that will be fired throughout the duration of the Interval Timer shooting process (the maximum number of intervals is 999, and the maximum number of shots at each interval is 9). Once settings have been made, press ▶ to highlight the **[Start]** options, **[On]**, or **[Off]**.
6. Highlight **[On]** and press ⊗ to initiate the timer sequence. Highlight **[Off]** to save the settings without initiating the timer sequence.

Once Interval Timer shooting has been set correctly and is activated, a message stating "Timer Active" will appear on the monitor momentarily, and "INTVAL" is displayed in the control panel and Information Display, blinking; the number of intervals remaining will be displayed in the shutter speed display, while the number of exposures remaining in the current interval will be displayed in the aperture display just before each interval is shot, until the full shooting sequence has been completed. To view this information at any other time during Interval Timer shooting, press the shutter release button down halfway. Interval Timer shooting can be paused by doing any of the following:

O Highlighting the [Pause] option in the Interval Timer menu and pressing ⊙K
O Turning the camera off and then on again
O Rotating the Release Mode dial or Live View switch

To resume Interval Timer shooting, open the Interval Timer menu and set a new start time: [Now] or [Start time], as described above, and then press ▶. Highlight [Restart] in the displayed options and press ⊙K. Interval Timer shooting can be stopped by doing any of the following:

O Highlighting the [Off] option in the Interval Timer menu and pressing ⊙K
O Performing Two-Button Reset
O Resetting the Shooting menu
O Changing the Bracketing settings
O Terminating Multiple Exposure shooting

NOTE: It is possible to apply Exposure, Flash, Active D-Lighting (ADL), and White Balance Bracketing during Interval Timer shooting. The settings for the bracketing sequence must be set before Interval Timing commences. In Exposure, Flash, and ADL Bracketing, the camera will take the number of exposures specified in the bracketing sequence regardless of the number of shots set in the Interval Timer option. If White Balance Bracketing is set, the camera will make a single exposure at each interval, creating the number of images specified in the bracketing sequence each time.

NOTE: If any automatic exposure mode is used in conjunction with the Interval Timer feature, it is essential to cover the viewfinder eyepiece with the supplied DK-5 eyepiece cap. (See page 31 for more information.)

Essentially, Live View provides a real-time video signal from the camera's sensor to the LCD monitor, which refreshes at 24 frames per second (fps), to show the view of the scene that the lens is pointed toward (it is the same view as the optical viewfinder). This enables pictures to be composed in situations when using the optical viewfinder is difficult, or not desirable—for example, when shooting from a very low position, or when the Live View zoom feature is helpful for composing or for checking focus.

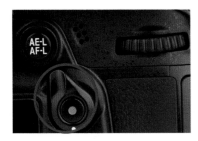

‹ The "flick" style switch to activate Live View makes it simple to go back and forth between normal shooting and Live View.

One fundamental difference between shooting conventionally via the optical viewfinder and using Live View on the D7000 is the method of autofocus; in Live View, the camera uses contrast detection autofocus, which employs information from the CMOS sensor to assess contrast at the selected focus point and adjust focus based on the highest level of contrast. The advantage of this system is that the focus point can be positioned anywhere within the area of the frame and is not restricted to the 39 AF points as used by the phase detection AF system for normal shooting via the optical viewfinder. However, contrast detection AF has the distinct disadvantage of being slower than the phase detection AF used in conventional shooting. To acquire focus, it must focus through the plane of the intended point of focus, so that the system can sense a lower contrast level before re-adjusting focus to the point of maximum contrast. In a nutshell, autofocus for Live View and the D-Movie mode (see pages 110-111) is very good for static subjects, especially where the most accurate focus is required, like in close-up photography, but it is of little use for moving subjects, as it simply is not quick enough.

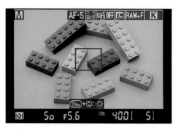

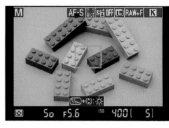

^ The Live View screen is shown here with the Live View Information Display. Note that the AF point is displayed in red to indicate that focus has not yet been acquired.

^ The AF point is displayed in green to indicate that focus has been acquired.

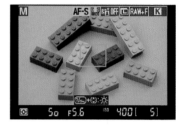

> The AF mode and AF-Area mode (highlighted in yellow) can be altered in Live View by holding down the AF-Mode button and rotating the Command dials.

One very welcome refinement of the D7000 is the single "flick" type switch used to open Live View located on the back of the camera where it can be reached very conveniently with the right thumb. For Live View to operate, the reflex mirror of the D7000 must be raised out of the light path from the lens to the camera's sensor, so the optical viewfinder is always blacked-out when Live View and D-Movie mode are active, plus of course, the normal Information Display is not available. The Live View shooting Information Display shows much of the information you would see in the optical viewfinder display and the Information Display shown on the monitor in normal shooting, yet without this impinging too much on the Live View image area. To scroll through the various pages of the Live View Information Display, press the ⓘⓝⓕⓞ button:

o The information displayed on the [Show photo indicators] page includes: exposure mode, AF mode, AF-Area mode, Active D-Lighting, Image Size, Image Quality, White Balance, metering mode, shutter speed, aperture, ISO, Exposure Compensation, and the number of shots remaining (at current settings).

o The information displayed on the [Show movie indicators] page includes: all the information displayed on the previous page, plus the recording time (minutes and seconds) remaining in D-Movie mode at the current resolution and quality settings, an indicator for the status of the built-in / external microphone, and the video quality setting (resolution).

o There are three more pages: [Hide all indicators] that hides the Information Display and only shows the exposure settings and the 16:9 frame markings for video, the [Framing grid] that overlays the screen with a grid pattern to facilitate framing and composition, and the [Virtual horizon] screen where there is a Virtual Horizon display to assist in leveling the camera.

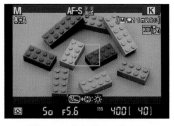

∧ The [Show movie indicators] page

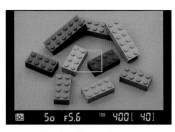

∧ The [Hide all indicators] page

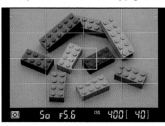

∧ The [Framing grid] page

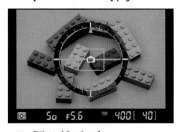

∧ The [Virtual horizon] page

To open Live View, rotate the Ⓛⱽ switch clockwise; the reflex mirror will lift and the view through the lens will be displayed on the LCD monitor screen, together with the Live View Information Display and the AF point, which will vary in appearance according to the option selected for Live View AF-Area mode. Press the ▣ button to scroll through the Live View Display Options as described in the previous section.

Next, choose the focus mode by rotating the Focus Mode switch to AF, and then press the center button of the Focus Mode switch and rotate the Main Command dial until the required AF mode is displayed on the screen. The following options are available:

○ AF-S (Single-Servo AF): Ideal for stationary subjects, the focus will be adjusted and locked when the shutter release button is pressed down halfway. The shutter can only be released if focus is acquired.

○ AF-F (Full-Time servo AF): This is intended for moving subjects, because the camera focuses continuously during Live and D-Movie mode until the shutter release button is pressed. Focus locks when the shutter release button is pressed down halfway. The shutter can only be released if focus is acquired.

NOTE: To use Manual focus, rotate the Focus Mode switch to **M.**

Assuming that either AF-S or AF-F mode is selected, it is also necessary to set the AF-Area mode. AF-Area mode can be selected in all exposure modes. Press the center button of the Focus Mode switch and rotate the Sub-Command dial until the required AF-Area mode is displayed on the screen. The following options are available:

🖭 Face-Priority AF: The D7000 detects faces and focuses on them automatically. The subject's face usually needs to be square to the camera lens for positive detection. A double yellow border displays when the camera detects a persons face (if there are multiple faces the camera, which can detect a maximum of 35 faces, will focus on the one it considers to be closest; to focus on an alternative face, shift the AF point using the Multi Selector). Press the shutter release down halfway and the AF point will turn green if the D7000 can acquire focus on the subject, or it will blink red if it cannot. If the subject looks away from the lens so their face is no longer visible to the camera, the AF point borders will no longer be displayed.

⌷ᵂᴵᴰᴱ **Wide-Area AF:** Ideal for hand-held picture taking of large subjects or scenes, as the AF point covers a large area of the frame. Use the Multi Selector to shift the AF point to the required spot in the frame area. Initially, the AF point will be displayed as a red square. Use the Multi Selector button to shift the AF point to the required spot in the frame area, or press the ⊛ button to position the AF point at the center of the frame. Press the shutter release down halfway to focus and the AF point will turn green if the D7000 can acquire focus on the subject, or it will blink red if it cannot acquire focus.

⌷ᴺᴼᴿᴹ **Normal-Area AF:** Use this option for precision focus on a very specific area in the frame. It is best suited to shooting from a tripod and is particularly useful in close-up photography. Use the Multi Selector to shift the AF point to the required spot in the frame area. The AF point in Normal-Area AF behaves exactly as it does in Wide-Area AF.

⊕ **Subject-Tracking AF:** In this mode, the D7000 will attempt to track a selected subject as it moves within the frame area; it is most effective and reliable when the camera-to-subject distance remains constant (i.e., the subject moves laterally across the frame). Initially, the AF point will be displayed as a white square with four additional corner markings. Position the AF point over the subject and press the ⊛ button. The focus point will turn yellow and track the subject as it changes position within the frame area. Press the shutter release down halfway to focus and the AF point will turn green if the D7000 can acquire focus on the subject, or it will blink red if it cannot acquire focus, Once focus is acquired, the AF point will continue to track the subject. To end AF tracking, press the ⊛ button.

NOTE: The Live View AF and AF-Area modes can also be selected using CS-a8 [**Live view/movie**].

NOTE: Subject Tracking is unlikely to track subjects that are small, moving quickly (especially toward or away from the camera), of very similar color to the background, if the subject and background are particularly bright or dark, or if the subject leaves the frame area or changes size significantly.

NOTE: The exposure level can be locked by pressing the ᴬᴱᴸ/ᴬᶠᴸ button, and focus can be locked by pressing the shutter release button down halfway.

To take a picture from Live View, press the shutter release down all the way. The LCD monitor will turn off. If the [Image review] item in the ▶ Playback menu is set to [On], the picture will be displayed on the screen (a light touch on the shutter release button will return the camera to its Live View mode). If the [Image review] item is set to [Off], the screen will remain blank and the camera will then return to its Live View mode. Finally, to exit Live View, rotate the Ⓛⓥ switch clockwise again. There are a few general points to consider when shooting in Live View:

○ Since the sensor is exposed continuously during Live View, never point the camera directly at the sun or any other high-intensity light source, otherwise the sensor may be damaged.

○ The monitor display will adjust its brightness automatically, so the final exposure may differ from the image seen on the screen.

○ Exposure can be adjusted in P, S, A and M modes by ±5 EV in steps of 0.3 EV, although the effects of values above +3 EV and -3 EV will not be shown on the screen.

○ It is possible to magnify the image in Live View to assist in precise focusing. Press the ⊕ button to magnify the image by a maximum of approximately 6.7x, and press the ⊖ button to reduce magnification. In Wide-Area and Normal-Area AF, you can use the Multi Selector to scroll to other areas of the image. However, since the camera only uses a small proportion of its pixels in Live View, the resolution of an image enlarged in this way is very low, so it rather defeats the purpose of the function!

○ It is important to block light from entering the viewfinder eyepiece when shooting in Live View, as it may influence the TTL metering and therefore the exposure level, so be sure to use the supplied DK-5 cover.

○ A countdown of 30 seconds will be displayed before Live View ends automatically; the timer display will turn red when 5 seconds remain before the time selected at CS-c4 [Monitor off delay] > [Live View] runs out.

○ Live View may end automatically in advance of the normal countdown timer in conditions of high ambient temperature, if the camera has already been used for protracted periods in Live View or its D-Movie mode, or if you have been shooting in a Continuous release mode for extended periods; this feature is designed to prevent the sensor from overheating and to protect the other electrical circuitry of the camera from thermal damage.

- You may observe banding or flickering in the Live View image displayed on the screen under certain types of artificial lighting, such as fluorescent lighting. Use the **[Flicker reduction]** item in the ﾞ Setup menu to help reduce this effect by selecting the option that matches the frequency of the local AC supply.

D-MOVIE MODE

The D7000 is the second Nikon DSLR to offer a full HD 1080p resolution (previous models such as the D90 and D300s have a maximum resolution of HD 720p), plus it is also has a full-time AF capability during video recording, although this employs a contrast-detect method, as described in the Live View section, so it is inherently slower than the phase-detection AF used for normal autofocus shooting. The D7000 also uses a different compression regime for video, in place of the Motion JPEG used by previous models. The camera records a variety of different resolutions and frame rates, using the H.264 / MPEG-4 AVC compression and stores video in a .MOV container file (the H.264 / MPEG-4 AVC

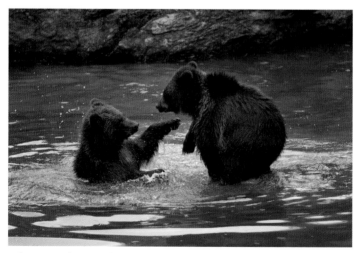

^ The contrast-detect autofocus system used during Live View and D-Movie modes is effective when the camera-to-subject distance is near constant; however, it is unlikely to keep up in a situation where the camera-to-subject distance changes rapidly.

compression is far more efficient in terms of file size compared with Motion JPEG). At all resolutions a frame rate of 24 frames per second (fps) is available, while at the lower resolution of 1280 x 720 pixels there are frame rates for 30 and 25 fps to match to the video standard (NTSC or PAL), as selected under the [Video mode] item in the ⚙ Setup menu. The built-in monaural microphone records in 16-bit PCM audio with an apparent sampling rate of 24 kHz (Nikon has not disclosed the precise figure), regardless of the video resolution and frame rate, and there is an option to use an external stereo microphone connected to the camera via the mini-pin 3.5 mm jack terminal under the smaller of the two rubber covers on the left side of the camera.

USING D-MOVIE MODE

To use the D-Movie mode, the first step is to set the options under the [Movie settings] item in the ◙ Shooting menu. Highlight [Movie settings] and press ▶.

Movie Quality: Select [Quality] and press ▶ to choose a frame size from the chart below, and then press ⊛. The frame rate will depend on the look you want to achieve and the type of device the video clip will be displayed on, as follows: 30 fps – NTSC devices, 25 fps – PAL devices, and 24 fps to emulate the frame rate of motion pictures (as described below).

Frame size (pixels)	NSTC		PAL	
	Frame rate	Maximum length	Frame rate	Maximum length
1920 x 1080	24 fps		24 fps	
1280 x 720	Choose 24 or 30 fps	20 minutes	Choose 24 or 25 fps	20 minutes
640 x 424	30 fps		25 fps	

NOTE: The actual frame rate when 24 fps is set is 23.976 fps, and it is 29.97 fps when 30 fps is selected.

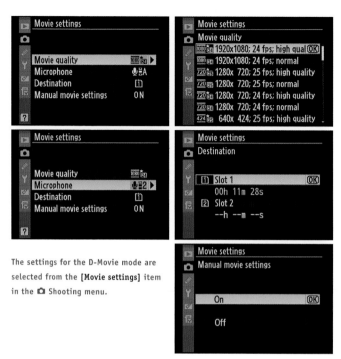

The settings for the D-Movie mode are selected from the [Movie settings] item in the ◘ Shooting menu.

Microphone: To set the options for the built-in or optional external microphone, highlight **[Microphone]** and press ▶. It is best to avoid the Auto setting, because Auto Gain will often produce variable recording levels that make achieving consistent sound impossible. For example, if you attempt to record a person talking against some low-level background noise, as soon as the person stops talking, the Auto Gain will boost the background noise and then suppress it as soon as the person begins speaking again. You should exercise as much manual control over the camera as possible when recording video. Therefore, use of the three other options is recommend as follows:

○ In a noisy environment, set microphone sensitivity to **[Low]**.

○ In a normal environment, like a conversation between two people with no strong background noise, microphone sensitivity can be set to **[Medium]**.

○ In very quiet environments, it can be set to **[High]**.

Highlight the required option and press ⊛.

> The built-in microphone, which is located on the front of the camera just below the camera badge, picks up the noise of camera operation distressingly well; for best audio results, use an external microphone.

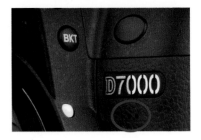

Destination: To record video to the card in Slot 1, select **[Slot 1]**. Select **[Slot 2]** to record video to the card in Slot 2. The menu indicates the recording time available on each card.

Manual Movie Settings: Choose **[On]** to allow manual adjustment of the shutter speed and ISO when the D7000 is set to **M** exposure mode. Shutter speeds can be selected between 1/8000 second and 1/30 second; ISO sensitivity can be set between ISO 100 and Hi 2 (the ISO value is fixed at the selected value and is not adjusted automatically by the **[Auto ISO sensitivity control]** option in the ⬛ Shooting menu).

RECORDING MOVIES

To record movies, perform the following steps:

1. Select the required lens aperture value in **A** or **M** mode, and set ᴬᴱ⁻ᴸ/ᴬᶠ⁻ᴸ button to the **[AE Lock (hold)]** option using CS-f5 in the ⬦ Custom Settings menu.

2. Rotate the ⃞ᴸᵛ switch to activate Live View and select the required AF mode and AF-Area mode as described in the Live View section.

3. Compose the opening frame of your video and acquire focus as described in the Live View section.

4. To start recording, press the record button at the center of the ⃞ᴸᵛ switch; a recording indicator and the time remaining for recording will be displayed on the monitor screen.

5. If you use the built-in microphone, which is located on the front of the camera just above the D7000 badge, take care not to obstruct it; also remember, the built-in microphone is prone to record the operation of camera controls.

6. To end the recording, press the record button again. Recording will stop automatically after 20 minutes, or when the memory card is full. A countdown display for 30 seconds will be shown in red before recording in the D-Movie mode ends automatically; this may appear considerably sooner than the full 20 minute duration if the camera's electronics have become warm. If this occurs, allow the camera to cool before resuming D-Movie mode recording.

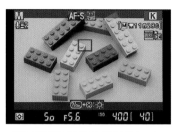

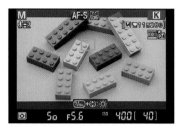

∧ The AF point can be positioned anywhere in the frame area; note the top and bottom edges of the frame are masked to show the 16:9 format of the video frame.

∧ The AF point turns green when focus has been achieved.

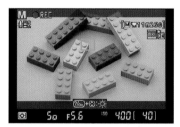

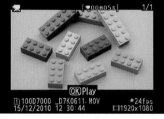

∧ The camera displays a recording indicator when the D-Movie mode is active; it can be seen in the top left corner of the LCD screen in the Show Movie Indicator display option (one of five information page options in D-Movie mode).

∧ The saved video file shown in Playback; note the icon in the top left of the screen to indicate it is a video file.

However, once you begin to peel away at what exactly the D7000 can deliver in its Movie mode, it soon becomes apparent that there are a number of restrictions imposed by the system. The D7000 is without doubt an extremely fine, state-of-the-art, mid-range DSLR camera, but it is not a full-fledged video camera by any stretch of the imagination!

Once the camera is in its Live View mode, which is a precursor to entering the D-Movie mode, you relinquish any control over the lens aperture; however, in D-Movie mode, it is possible to control the shutter speed and ISO level by setting the camera to its **M** exposure mode and selecting **[On]** for the **[Manual movie settings]** option under the **[Movie settings]** item in the ⚫ Shooting menu. Otherwise, if **[Off]** is selected for **[Manual movie settings]**, the camera shifts into a fully automated point-and-shoot mode. The reason behind this is the way that Nikon has implemented the recording of video in the D7000; in essence, the camera takes the video feed that provides the real-time image displayed on the monitor in Live View and uses this for its D-Movie mode. In this configuration, the settings for shutter speed and ISO sensitivity used for still picture shooting are totally irrelevant, since you cannot change them. As soon as the camera is in D-Movie mode, the only parameters you can control during video recording are: Manual focus, manual lens zooming, Exposure Compensation, autoexposure lock.

The lens aperture, which can be set to any value between the maximum aperture and f/16 when using a Nikkor lens with an electronic aperture control, should be selected prior to entering the Live View mode, as it is not possible to adjust the aperture value once in Live View or D-Movie mode. Likewise, any of the parameters that can be set within the Picture Control system must be set before entering Live View and D-Movie mode. It is important to avoid setting the level of contrast and sharpening too high when recording video, as the former will cause a reduction in the dynamic range the camera can record, and the latter can result in a "ghost" image, in which a black edge appears to follow any moving elements in the image. Similarly, the White Balance setting should also be selected prior to entering Live View.

Matrix metering is used exclusively during video recording, regardless of the metering pattern selected on the camera. This raises a series of issues: First, if the level of illumination in the scene being recorded changes—for example, the camera is panned from an area that is lit brightly to an area of deep shadow, or the lens is zoomed so the ratio of tones within the frame changes significantly, the camera will adjust shutter speed and ISO accordingly in order to maintain what the camera thinks is an appropriate level of exposure. As a consequence, the noise level in the image can increase perceptibly as the ISO level is increased. Furthermore, as with any automated exposure system, it is highly likely that if the scene is filled or nearly filled with particularly dark tones, it will be overexposed—or underexposed if the tones in the scene are primarily light. Allied to this problem is the way the camera adjusts

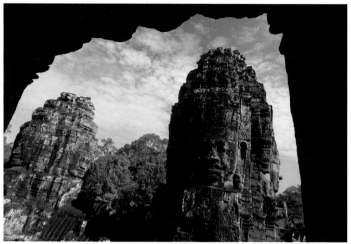

^ Locking the exposure level during video recording will help to produce a more consistent appearance in video clips, especially if the camera is panned from light to dark areas of a scene.

exposure changes in a distinctly stepped manner that is manifest in a noticeable shift in the level of illumination in the recorded image.

Unless you intervene, the D7000 will exercise fully automatic control of the exposure. So, if you choose not to use the [Manual movie settings] option how can you tame the automated exposure control of the D7000 in its D-Movie mode and exercise some degree of control to obtain both greater consistency and accuracy? Well, there are two options: It is possible to use the ⭤ Exposure Compensation feature; and second, you can set the [AE Lock (hold)] option for the ᴬᴱ⁻ᴸ button available under CS-f5 [Assign AE-L/AF-L button] item, so that you can lock exposure without having to press the shutter button. Both of these controls must be used after the camera has entered its Live View mode if they are to be effective during video recording, so the following is my suggested sequence for setting up the D7000 to achieve a consistent exposure level in its D-Movie mode, when [Manual movie settings] is not set:

1. Before activating Live View, set the camera to either A or M exposure mode and select the required lens aperture value in the camera's normal still-picture shooting mode (remember that the minimum aperture value available in Movie mode using a Nikkor lens with electronic aperture control is f/16). Also confirm that the [AE Lock (hold)] option is selected for operation of the ᴬᴱ⁻ᴸ button.

2. Activate Live View by rotating the ⓛⓥ switch. Next, set the AF mode and AF-Area mode as described previously in the Live View section.

3. Point the camera at the subject and focus using Live View autofocus; if the subject comprises tones that are significantly lighter or darker than middle-value tones, use the Exposure Compensation to set a positive or negative value, respectively, and then press the AE-L/AF-L button.

4. As an alternative to Step 3, use a middle-tone reference, such as a photographic 18% gray card. Ensure it is placed in the same light as the light falling on the subject, and then point the camera at the reference and press the AE-L/AF-L button. This approach ensures that the camera will record average tones accurately, while lighter and darker tones will also be rendered accurately, provided they are within the dynamic range of the sensor, plus the lens can be zoomed without risk that the camera will shift the exposure level if the tonal range in the scene changes significantly.

5. By pressing the AE-L/AF-L button as described in either Step 3 or Step 4, the exposure level calculated by the camera will be locked until the AE-L/AF-L button is pressed again (the **[AE Lock (hold)]** feature can be switched on and off as required during a video recording by pressing the AE-L/AF-L button); when it is active, "AE-L" is displayed in the lower left corner of the monitor screen next to the ⚫⚫ Matrix-metering icon.

NOTE: It appears that the application of an Exposure Compensation value also influences the shutter speed that the D7000 will use during video recording. Although no definitive values are available, setting any negative Exposure Compensation seems to result in the use of a faster shutter speed, while positive Exposure Compensation values cause a slower shutter speed to be set.

ACHIEVING THE CINEMATIC LOOK

Several aspects of the way the D7000 records video are different from those of a conventional video camera and it is important to appreciate this, because it is what sets the two devices apart in terms of the look they produce.

Shooting moving pictures requires different techniques compared with shooting still pictures. In still photography, it is common practice to set the ISO sensitivity according to the prevailing light conditions and leave it fixed at that value, before controlling the exposure through adjustment of the shutter speed and lens aperture. In shooting motion picture film or video, it is the shutter speed that is usually set and locked, with the aperture value then being selected to achieve the required depth of field, while exposure is controlled by adjusting the ISO sensitivity, often in combination with the use of neutral density filtration on the lens.

The design decision for the D7000 to record moving images at 24 frames per second (fps) was not arbitrary; 24 fps is the standard frame rate of cameras used by cinematic photographers when shooting motion picture films. By comparison, typical television broadcast video is recorded at 30 fps in NSTC standard, and 25 fps in PAL standard; for some applications, such as recording sports and other high-speed action, a frame rate of 60 fps is used by a process known as "over cranking" before it is slowed down to 30 fps in post production.

To emulate the appearance of a cinematic film, there should be a direct correlation between the frame rate of the D7000 and the shutter speed selected in its D-Movie mode. The shutter mechanism in a motion picture camera uses a rotating disc to alternately expose the film to light and then block the light, as the film is transported through the film gate; this type of shutter is often known as a "180-degree shutter," because it is open during 180 degrees of the disc rotation and then closed for the other 180 degrees. At a frame rate of 1 fps, the shutter would be open for 1/2 second, so extrapolating from this to a frame rate of 24 fps, the shutter is open for 1/48 second. The closest available shutter speed on the D7000 is 1/50 second, so this is the shutter speed that should be set to match its frame rate in D-Movie mode to simulate the motion blur perceived with a cinematic film camera shooting at 24 fps.

Another key difference between the D7000 and video camera is the size of the sensor (chip). At 15.6 x 23.6 mm, the camera's Nikon DX-format sensor is significantly larger than the sensor used in a typical consumer video camera and even those of many professional video camera models. As the size of a sensor in a camera increases, so the depth of field for any given lens aperture value decreases. On a typical video consumer camera, or point-and-shoot digital camera with video capability, the smaller size of the sensor means that virtually everything is in focus, because even at large lens aperture values (low f/numbers), the depth of field is so extensive. By comparison, the D7000 can achieve a far more limited (shallower) depth of field at equivalent lens aperture values, which allows you to isolate a subject by differential focus far more effectively, thereby directing the viewer's attention to a precise point in the scene.

The following is my suggested method on how to set up the D7000 to achieve a classic cinematic motion-picture effect, while maintaining full control over the camera to achieve a consistent exposure level, exploit the depth-of-field characteristics of the DX-format sensor in combination with the lens aperture, and produce smooth focus transitions, while recording in its D-Movie mode:

1. Before activating Live View, select **M** exposure mode and set the required lens aperture (this cannot be adjusted in Live View / D-Movie mode). Also, adjust settings for sharpening and contrast as required (I recommend exercising restraint with both for the reasons stated on pages 179-180) via the Picture Control system.

2. Set the camera to Manual focus mode. If you use an AF Nikkor lens, set any focus mode switch on it to M (manual). For most shooting in D-Movie mode, I prefer to use manual focus Nikkor lenses, as the action of their brass metal helicoid focusing mechanism is far smoother and has a much longer throw compared with modern AF Nikkor lenses, giving you far more control over focusing for smooth transitions; make sure the relevant non-CPU data is entered via the **[Non-CPU lens data]** item in the **Y** Setup menu.

3. Select **[On]** for the **[Manual movie settings]** option under the **[Movie settings]** item in the **📷** Shooting menu. Also, under the **[Movie settings]** item, select the required settings for **[Movie quality]** (which should be set to either 1920 x 1080, or 1280 x 720 to allow selection of a frame rate of 24 fps), **[Microphone],** and **[Destination]**.

4. Activate Live View by rotating the **🔲** switch, and then press the **📷** button to scroll to the required information page; you will probably find either the **[Show movie indicators]**, **[Hide all indicators]**, or **[Framing grid]** displays.

5. Point the camera at the subject and focus manually.

6. Adjust the shutter speed to 1/50 second by rotating the Main Command dial. Finally, adjust the ISO sensitivity by pressing the **ISO** button and rotating the Main Command dial to achieve a proper exposure, changing the exposure level as required for recording a subject / scene with significantly light or dark tones; if necessary, use a neutral density filter to reduce light transmission through the lens (a variable neutral density filter can be very useful for this purpose).

7. As an alternative to step 6, use a middle tone reference, such as a photographic 18% gray card. Ensure it is placed in the same light as the light falling of the subject before pointing the camera at the reference and adjusting the ISO sensitivity and neutral density lens filtration if applied, to achieve a proper exposure. This approach ensures that the

camera will record average tones accurately, while lighter and darker tones will also be rendered accurately, provided they are within the dynamic range of the sensor.

8. Press ⊡ switch center button to start recording; press it again to stop recording.

MOVIE MODE CONSIDERATIONS

Shooting moving images is quite different from shooting still pictures, and shooting in D-Movie mode is different again from shooting with a video camera. Your approach to planning, preparing, and shooting needs to considered accordingly:

○ Plan your movie. It's a story, so give it a beginning, middle, and end; consider writing out a storyboard to detail each clip you will want to shoot (this will help at the editing stage as well).

○ Prepare the camera as described above. Think about how you can use depth of field to direct the viewer's attention by emphasizing a subject or section of a scene. Use Manual focus control to adjust the focus point during recording.

○ Use a solid, heavy tripod for maximum stability and mount the camera on a fluid or friction type tripod head for smooth pan and tilt movements.

○ If the camera lens has the Nikon Vibration Reduction (VR) system, switch it off; when recording in D-Movie mode, even when the camera is mounted on a tripod head that has been left loose to facilitate pan or tilt movement, the VR action can cause the image of a stationary subject to appear to drift slightly due to the movement of the VR lens group.

○ Shoot short clips, typically 15 to 45 seconds in duration; short clips makes editing them to produce the finished movie much easier.

○ Think about audio. If you want to record sounds associated with the subject and its surroundings, consider using an external microphone or separate recording device. Avoid using any Auto Gain setting to control recording level automatically, as this can lead to variability in sound levels.

○ Remember, the D-Movie mode is just an extension of the Live View function, so while active, the sensor is exposed continuously to light passing through the lens. Therefore, it is absolutely essential that the camera is never pointed directly at the sun or any other very strong light source, as doing so risks damage to the sensor and / or associated electrical circuitry.

ROLLING-SHUTTER EFFECT

There is one other surprise that awaits the uninitiated user of the D7000 in Movie mode. It concerns the way the readout from the sensor is handled. The CMOS sensor does not capture each frame of video simultaneously, but records it in a scanning process of horizontal lines that starts from the top edge of the sensor and works toward the bottom. The consequence of this shows up when the camera and / or the subject moves rapidly during recording, as the subject can appear at different parts of the frame leading to vertical lines in static subjects that are skewed in a diagonal direction, or moving subjects that appear to have a cartoon-like, exaggerated lean.

A more pernicious version of this skewing effect occurs with a handheld camera that, due to a lack of stability, moves laterally left and right during recording with the result that vertical static lines in the frame, such as the edge of a building, take on a wavy appearance and look as though they are wobbling. If the lens in use offers Nikon's Vibration Reduction (VR) feature, I recommend very strongly that you switch it on for hand-held video recording.

In my opinion, the results produced by the D7000 in terms of the rolling-shutter effect are as well suppressed as in other recent Nikon DSLR cameras, such as the D3s, but the effect is still perceptible; therefore, it is a matter of anticipating them in certain situations and attempting to mitigate the worst effects by shooting appropriately— for example, panning the camera slowly or following a moving subject accurately and accepting the inevitable distortion in the foreground and background. The single most effective step you can take is to use a tripod to support the D7000 when recording in D-Movie mode.

BUILT-IN LIMITATIONS

There are several limitations you may confront when using the D7000's D-Movie mode:

- O Due to the high data rates at Full HD resolution, Nikon recommends the use of at least a Class 6 SD memory card for recording video clips.
- O The maximum duration for a single video clip recording is twenty minutes.
- O It is important to keep the autofocus capabilities during video recording in perspective. The contrast-detect system used for Live View and D-Movie mode is slower than the phase-detection system used in

normal shooting. Do not expect too much of the system and you will not be disappointed. For example, it may not keep pace with a subject involved in fast-paced action or sport, but may do better with more modest levels of subject movement, especially if the subject is not too close to the camera.

o The camera controls the maximum duration for the use of the Live View and the D-Movie mode automatically to prevent overheating, which can damage the camera's circuitry. In high ambient temperatures or after protracted use of Live View and / or D-Movie mode, the camera may end Live View unexpectedly.

o The audio recording of the D7000, achieved using its built-in 16-bit mono channel microphone, which has a relatively low sampling rate of just 11 kHz (most dedicated video cameras provide stereo channel sound recording with a sampling rate of 48 kHz), leaves something to be desired—the sounds generated by camera operation, such as rotating the Command dials, adjusting the zoom position of a lens, or the AF and Manual focus actions, are recorded with distressing clarity! The built-in microphone may be acceptable for casual recording but if you want to include ambient sounds with video clips, I would recommend either the use of a good quality external stereo microphone in combination with one of the fixed audio sensitivity levels (i.e., do not use the Auto Gain option), or the use of a separate audio recorder with stereo microphones, so that the video and audio tracks can be edited together in appropriate video editing software.

o In addition to continuous data-writing to the memory card and Live View running, it is likely the VR function of appropriate Nikkor lenses will also be active; these two latter actions are the most power-demanding functions of the D7000, so pack plenty of spare batteries if you anticipate making protracted use of the Live View and / or D-Movie mode.

VIEWING MOVIES

A video file is indicated by a 🎥 icon in full-frame Playback; press the ⊛ button to begin viewing it. The following operations can be performed:

o To pause, press ▼

o To resume Playback, press the ⊛ button.

o To rewind / advance press ◀ or ▶, respectively; speed doubles with each press, from 2x to 4x to 8x to 16x.

o To increase the volume, press ⌕; to decrease the volume, press ⌕⊟.

o To edit the video clip, press the ?/⊶ button.

○ To resume shooting, press the shutter release down halfway.

○ To display menus, press the MENU button.

○ To exit to full-frame Playback, press ▲ or ►.

EDITING MOVIES

To edit a movie clip directly from the full frame Playback:

1. Display the movie clip full-frame on the monitor by pressing the ► button and selecting it by pressing ◄ or ►.

2. Play the movie clip back by pressing ⊛. Use the ⊛ button to start and resume Playback, and press ▼ to pause the Playback. To trim the opening section of the movie clip, pause on the first frame you wish to retain. Alternatively, to trim the end of the movie clip, pause on the last frame you wish to retain.

3. Press the ?/oₙ button to display the [Edit movie] item from the ⊠ Retouch menu.

4. To create a copy that includes the current frame and all subsequent frames, highlight [Choose start point] and press ⊛. Alternatively, select [Choose end point] to create a copy that includes the current frame and all preceding frames and press ⊛. Next, press ▲ to delete all frames before the current frame when [Choose start point] is selected, or after the current frame when [Choose end point] is selected.

5. Highlight [Yes] and press the ⊛ button to save the edited copy. The saved copy can be trimmed further by repeating the process just described. A movie clip must be at least 2 seconds long to be edited.

NOTE: To edit D-Movie clips in the D7000 or capture a single frame from a video clip within the ⊠ Retouch menu use the [Edit movie] item.

TWO-BUTTON RESET: RESTORE DEFAULT SETTINGS

If you ever want to restore the camera's settings to their default values, press and hold the QUAL and 🖾 buttons at the same time for more than 2 seconds (they have green dots beside them). The following settings will change back to their default options, which are listed in the right-hand column:

OPTION	DEFAULT
Image Quality	JPEG Normal
Image Size	Large
White Balance	Auto > Normal
Fine-Tuning	Zero
ISO (Sensitivity)	
ᴬᵁᵀᴼ🖻 and SCENE modes	Auto
P, S, A, and M	100
Autofocus (viewfinder)	
Autofocus mode	AF-A
AF-Area mode	
🌷 ♟ 🍴 🏔 🖼 🖼	Single-Point
🏃 🐾	39-Point Dynamic-Area
Other shooting modes	Auto-Area AF
Autofocus in Live View / D-Movie mode	
🏃 🖼 🐾 🏔 🖼 🖼	Wide-Area AF
🌷 🍴	Normal-Area AF
Other shooting modes	Face-Priority AF
Focus point [1]	Center
Metering	Matrix
AE/AF Lock (hold)	Off
Active D-Lighting	Off
Bracketing	Off
Picture Control Settings [2]	Unmodified
Flash Compensation	Off
Exposure Compensation	Off
Flash mode	
ᴬᵁᵀᴼ🖻 🌸 🍴 🌷 🐾	Auto Front-Curtain sync
👤	Auto + Red-Eye Reduction
🖼	Auto Slow sync
🍴 P, S, A, M	Front Curtain sync
FV Lock	Off
Multiple Exposure	Off
Flexible Program	Off

1. Focus point is not displayed if Auto-area AF is slected for AF-area mode.
2. Current Picture Control only

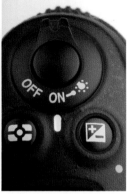

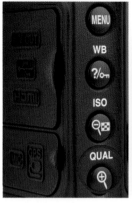

> The QUAL and ⊞ buttons together are used to restore a range of default settings on the D7000.

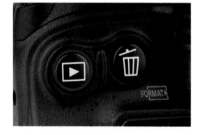

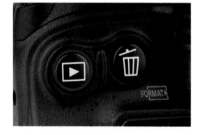

> The ▶ Playback button located on the back of the camera, to the left of the viewfinder.

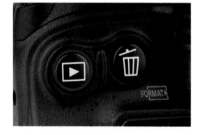

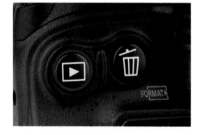

SHOOT AND REVIEW

NOTE: If the current Picture Control has been modified, the existing, saved settings for the Picture Control will also be restored.

IMAGE REVIEW OPTIONS

One of the most useful features of a digital camera is the ability to get near-instant feedback on photographs as you shoot. Using the Playback functions on the D7000 will allow you to see not only the images you have taken, but also a range of useful information.

The 3-inch, 921,000-dot, color TFT LCD monitor of the D7000 offers a viewing angle of 170° and displays 100% of the image when it is reviewed. Pictures can be displayed either as a single image or in multiples. When used to display a single still image, the review function has a zoom facility that enables you to enlarge the image by up to 31x for large size images (4928 x 3264 pixels) by pressing the ⊕ button.

Lower magnifications are available for medium (23x) and small (15x) size images, to produce a greater than 400% view. To get a 100% view (i.e., an actual pixel view), back up from the 400% view two presses on the ⊖ button. At this magnification, it is possible to make a sound assessment of the sharpness and noise level in the image.

Any critical analysis regarding color and contrast should be left until the image is displayed on a computer screen; but that said, the screen of the D7000 is certainly capable of providing a good representation of the image. However, do remember that the preview image, including those for NEF files, is always derived from a JPEG file to which the camera settings (White Balance, contrast, saturation, etc.) have been applied. An NEF file will actually contain more data and have a wider range of tonal values than this preview image; therefore, an overexposed highlight in the JPEG preview may not really be an overexposed highlight when the NEF file is examined in a RAW file converter such as Nikon Capture NX2.

> **HINT:** At its default setting, the LCD monitor of the D7000 is overly bright in my opinion, so I usually select -1 for the **[LCD brightness]** item in the ¥ Setup menu.

Immediately after making an exposure on the D7000, the Image Review function will provide a brief display of the photograph on the LCD monitor (assuming **[On]** is selected for **[Image review]** in the ▶ Playback menu). In Single Frame release mode, the image is displayed almost immediately after the exposure is made. In either of the Continuous shooting modes, the camera must write the image data from the buffer memory to the memory card for each image recorded, so a short delay is induced; the camera displays each image chronologically as soon as it has been saved.

> **NOTE:** Select **[Off]** for the **[Image review]** option in the ▶ Playback menu if you do not want the camera to display the image automatically after shooting to help to conserve battery power.

SINGLE-IMAGE PLAYBACK

To view the last image recorded by the camera, press the ▶ button. If you wish to view other images saved on the memory card, press ◀ or ▶ to scroll through them. To return to the Shooting mode, press the ▶ button again, although the quicker method if you are in the midst of shooting is to press the shutter release button down halfway.

PLAYBACK INFORMATION PAGES

A very useful feature of the image Playback function on the D7000 is the host of information that can be accessed while viewing the image on the monitor. This information can help you ensure that you have achieved a good exposure, as well as give you detailed information about how, when, and where the exposure was made. Depending on the selections made using the [Display mode] item in the ▶ Playback menu, and whether an image file contains data recorded from a GPS, there are up to nine different pages of information that can be displayed for each image file.

To access the information pages, press ▼ to scroll through each page in the following order: File Information, Highlights Warning, RGB and Composite Histograms, Shooting Data (1), Shooting Data (2), Shooting Data (3), Shooting Data (4), GPS Data (only displayed if file contains GPS data), and Overview data. Press ▲ up to scroll through in the reverse order.

The File information and Overview data pages are always displayed. The additional pages can be selected / deselected using the options of the [Display Mode] item of the ▶ Playback menu: [Highlights], [RGB Histogram], and [Data]. Focus point information can also be selected using the [Basic photo info] > [Focus point] option of the [Display Mode] item; it will then be displayed on the File Information page.

File Information: This page displays an unobstructed view of the image while providing additional information:

- O Protect status (if any)
- O Retouch indicator (if any has been applied)
- O Focus point (set from **[Display Mode]**)
- O AF area brackets (set via **[Display Mode] > [Basic photo info] > [Focus point]**)
- O Frame number / total number of frames
- O File name
- O Image Quality
- O Image Size
- O Image Authentication
- O Time of recording
- O Date of recording
- O Current card slot
- O Folder name

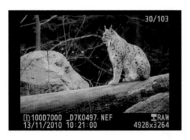

Highlights: Displayed only if **[Highlights]** is selected for **[Display mode]**, this screen shows an unobstructed view of the image; and any areas that may be overexposed will flash black and white. It also shows:

- Protect status (if any)
- Retouch indicator (if any has been applied)
- Folder number / frame number
- Current channel
- Highlight display indicator

NOTE: Press ◀ or ▶ while pressing ⚏ to scroll through RGB channels for the Highlights Warning.

> The Highlights Warning is based on the data of an an 8-bit JPEG file, so it should be treated with some caution when recording 12-bit or 14-bit NEF (RAW) files, as these will frequently hold more detail in highlight areas than JPEGs.

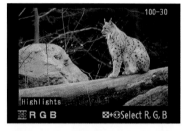

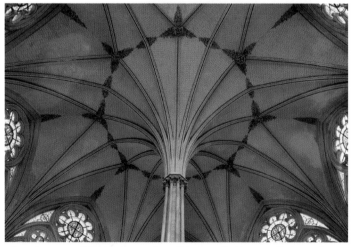

∧ In an image containing large areas of very light tone, the histogram display can be extremely helpful for assessing the exposure level and ensuring important detail is not compromised due to overexposure.

RGB Histogram: Displayed only if **[RGB histogram]** is selected for **[Display mode]**, it provides an individual histogram for each of the red, green, and blue channels, together with an RGB composite histogram and a thumbnail of the image file. (See pages 139-142 for more information about the histogram.)

- O Image highlights
- O Folder number / frame number
- O Protect status (if any)
- O Retouch indicator (if any has been applied)
- O White Balance (color temperature / setting, Fine-Tuning, Preset Manual)
- O Current channel
- O Histogram, RGB composite
- O Histogram, red channel
- O Histogram, green channel
- O Histogram, blue channel

NOTE: To show a Highlight Warning display, which indicates areas of the image that may be overexposed press ◀ or ▶ while holding the ◗▨ button down to scroll through a Highlight Warning for each channel; a yellow frame will surround the histogram of the selected channel.

NOTE: To enlarge the image, press ⊕ while the histogram is displayed. Use ⊕ and ◗▨ buttons to zoom in and out of the image, and the Multi Selector to scroll through images; the histogram is updated to reflect only the area of the image displayed in the monitor.

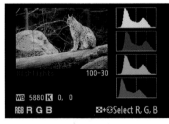

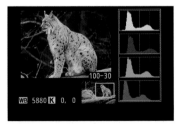

∧ The histogram display provides the most useful assessment of the range of tones recorded by the camera.

∧ If a section of the image is enlarged on the monitor, the histogram will reflect only the tones recorded in the area of the image bounded by the yellow frame.

Shooting Data, page 1: Displayed only if **[Data]** is selected for **[Display mode]**; a block of information will be superimposed over the center portion of the screen, obstructing the view of the image.

- O Protect status (if any)
- O Retouch indicator (if any has been applied)
- O Metering method
- O Shutter speed
- O Aperture
- O Exposure mode
- O ISO sensitivity (displayed in red if ISO auto control was on)
- O Exposure Compensation
- O Optimal exposure tuning
- O Focal length
- O Lens data
- O Focus mode
- O VR lens (only displayed if VR lens attached)
- O Flash type / Commander mode
- O Flash mode
- O Flash Control
- O Flash Compensation
- O Camera name
- O Folder number / frame number

NOTE: This screen can be particularly useful if you are trying to reproduce similar results in a similar environment, learn about your shooting style, or learn what settings produce particular results.

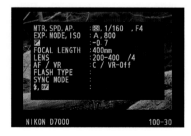

Shooting Data, page 2: Displayed only if **[Data]** is selected for **[Display mode]**; a block of information will be displayed superimposed over the center portion of the screen, obstructing the view of the image.

O Protect status (if any)

O Retouch indicator (if any has been applied)

O White Balance (color temperature / setting, Fine-Tuning, Preset Manual)

O Color space

O Picture Control

O Quick Adjust or original Picture Control (whichever is applicable)

O Sharpening

O Contrast

O Brightness

O Saturation

O Filter effects

O Hue

O Toning

O Camera name

O Folder number / frame number

NOTE: This screen can help you understand the effects of image settings and adjustments on the appearance of your picture.

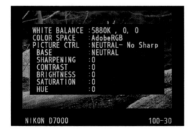

Shooting Data, page 3: Displayed only if **[Data]** is selected for **[Display mode]**; a block of information will be displayed superimposed over the center portion of the screen, obstructing the view of the image.

- Protect status (if any)
- Retouch indicator (if any has been applied)
- High ISO Noise Reduction / Long Exposure Noise Reduction
- Active D-Lighting
- Retouch history
- Image comment
- Camera name
- Folder name / frame number

Shooting Data, page 4: Displayed only if **[Data]** is selected for **[Display mode]**; a block of information will be displayed superimposed over the center portion of the screen, obstructing the view of the image.

- Protect status (if any)
- Retouch indicator (if any has been applied)
- Name of photographer
- Copyright holder
- Camera name
- Folder name / frame number

GPS Data: This screen will only be displayed if the camera was connected to the Nikon GP-1 GPS unit and it was active at the time the exposure was recorded; a block of information will be displayed superimposed over the center portion of the screen, obstructing the view of the image.

- Protect status (if any)
- Retouch indicator (if any has been applied)
- Latitude
- Longitude
- Altitude
- Coordinated Universal Time (UTC)
- Camera name
- Folder number / frame number

Overview Data: This screen is always available and offers a swift way to review camera settings plus a composite (luminance) histogram; a thumbnail image is displayed.

- O Frame number / total number of frames
- O Protect status (if any)
- O Camera name
- O Retouch indicator (if any has been applied)
- O Histogram (composite only)
- O Metering method
- O Exposure mode
- O Shutter speed
- O Aperture
- O ISO sensitivity (shown in red if picture taken when **[ISO Auto]** was **[On]**)
- O Focal length
- O Exposure Compensation
- O Flash Compensation
- O Flash mode (if any)
- O Image Comment indicator
- O GPS data indicator (only appears if applicable)
- O White Balance (color temperature / setting, Fine-Tuning, Preset Manual)
- O Color space
- O Picture Control
- O Active D-Lighting
- O Current card slot
- O Folder number
- O File name
- O Image Quality
- O Date of recording
- O Time of recording
- O Image Authentication indicator
- O Image Size

VIEWING MULTIPLE IMAGES: THUMBNAIL PLAYBACK

If you wish to view multiple images on the monitor, press the ⊖▦ button; from single-image Playback, you can choose to view either four (press once), nine (press twice), or seventy-two images (press a third time); to return to a single-image view, press ⊕ or ▶.

A yellow border surrounds the highlighted image; to scroll through the images, use the Multi Selector. Once the image is highlighted, you can use the ⊛ button to view the image full frame. To protect a highlighted image, press the ?/o‑ button; to delete it, press ⛊.

CALENDAR PLAYBACK

To view images taken on a specific date, press the ⊖▦ button while in the 72-image display. Once the Calendar Playback display is shown any date on which one or more images was recorded will be indicated by a thumbnail image on that date, use the ⊖▦ button to switch back and forth between the calendar of dates [Date list] and the list of thumbnails [Thumbnail list] displayed to the right of the calendar. To highlight a specific date or image in the thumbnail image list use the Multi Selector.

In the [Date list], use ⊕ to exit to the 72-thumbnail display, ⊛ to view the first picture taken on the selected date, ⊕ to highlight a date, or ⛊ to delete all the pictures taken on the selected date. In the [Thumbnail list] press and hold ⊕ to enlarge the highlighted picture, ⊛ to view highlighted picture, ⊕ to highlight picture, or ⛊ to delete highlighted picture; to return to the Shooting mode press the ▶ button, or press the shutter release button down halfway.

PLAYBACK ZOOM

The image displayed on the monitor is usually too small to check with any certainty that it is sharp, but the Playback zoom will allow you to enlarge the image by up to 31x for a large size image (which is equivalent to a 400% view on a computer screen), 23x for a medium size image, and 15x for a small size image.

To zoom into the image displayed on the monitor, press the ⊕ button. The image will appear slightly enlarged. To decrease the degree of magnification, press the ⊖▦ button. A navigation window is displayed when the zoom ratio is changed; the area currently visible in the monitor is shown with a yellow border. To scroll around the enlarged image, use

Multi Selector, and to view the same area at the current zoom ratio in other images, rotate the Main Command dial. This is a useful feature if there are a number of similar images of the same subject and you want to check a specific detail, such as a certain person's eyes in a group portrait. To return to the shooting mode, press the ► button or the shutter release button.

PROTECTING IMAGES

To protect an image against inadvertent deletion, display the image on the monitor in full-frame single-image Playback and press the ?/o☞ button. A small key icon will appear in the upper left corner, superimposed over the image. To remove the protection, open the image and press the ?/o☞ button again, and check that the key icon is no longer displayed.

> **NOTE:** Any protected image will be deleted if the memory card is formatted. However, the protect status is preserved when any image file is transferred to another storage device or a computer.

DELETING IMAGES

Images can be deleted using one of two methods. The quickest and easiest is to press the 🗑 button when the image to be deleted is displayed on the monitor. The first press of the button opens a warning dialog box that asks for confirmation of the delete command. To complete the process, press the 🗑 button again. To cancel the delete process, press the ► button to return to viewing the image. Images can also be deleted via the [Delete] item in the ► Playback menu.

ASSESSING THE HISTOGRAM DISPLAY

The histogram is a graphical display of the tonal values recorded by the camera. The shape and position of the histogram curve indicate the range of tones that have been captured in the picture. The horizontal axis represents 256 different tonal values from pure black at the extreme left end to pure white at the extreme right end; so darker tones will be distributed to the left of the histogram graph and lighter tones to the right. The vertical axis represents the number of pixels that have that specific tonal value.

In a well exposed picture of a scene containing an average distribution of tones that includes a few dark shadows, a sizable number of midtones, and a few bright highlights, where no clipping of shadow or highlights has occurred, the curve will extend across much of the horizontal axis; in this case, all tones in the scene will have been recorded.

Naturally, not all scenes contain an even spread of tones; many have a natural predominance of light or dark areas. In these cases, the histogram curve will be biased to the right with scenes containing mainly light tones, or the to left when the scene contains mainly dark tones; this is not an indication of over- or underexposure respectively, but an indication of the limited range of tones in the scene. Hence, there is no single perfect or ideal histogram curve for all scenes and subjects; the shape of the histogram curve will vary widely depending on the nature of the scene recorded.

Provided the histogram curve stops on the bottom axis before it reaches either end of the graph, the image will contain the fullest range of tones from the darkest to the lightest in the scene being photographed. However, if the curve begins at a point partway up the left or right vertical axis of the histogram display (i.e., it does not end on the horizontal axis but the histogram curve looks as though it has been cut off abruptly), the camera will not have recorded some tones. This is often referred to as "clipping." If the curve is stacked up against the left axis, or there is a peak in the histogram against the left axis, some of the darker tones (i.e., shadow areas in the image) will likely be compromised due to underexposure, whereas if the curve is stacked up against the right axis, or there is a peak in the histogram against the right axis, some of the lighter tones (i.e., highlight areas) will likely be compromised due to overexposure. The exception would be in a scene were there were very bright specular highlights, such as the sun reflecting off water, or streetlights in a nighttime cityscape—these small areas will almost invariably be much brighter than most of the other light tones in the scene and, therefore, it is of little consequence if they are overexposed.

Significant under- or overexposure is to be avoided if possible but especially the latter, as it is unlikely that highlight areas that have been overexposed will be able to render any detail and nothing can be done to rectify this in post processing. It is often possible to recover shadow detail lost due to underexposure; however, there is likely to be a penalty of reduced image quality in these areas due to the effects of an increased level in noise.

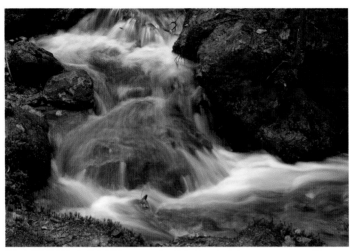

∧ The histogram was extremely helpful for this shot, which has a fairly wide tonal range. Using the histogram curve as a guide, I adjusted the exposure to the maximum level at which highlight detail was retained, thus exposing fully for the shadows as well.

Many photographers use a technique known as "expose to the right," in which they adjust the exposure to the point that the histogram curve is as far to the right as it can be without clipping in order to ensure they capture as wide a tonal range as possible and with as many levels to describe those tones. While this is a valid technique, for best results, do not base your exposure on just the composite RGB histogram; rather, look carefully at the histograms for each of the three individual channels, as it is often possible for one of the color channel histograms to show clipping not apparent in the composite RGB histogram. A common example of this is a sunrise or sunset, when it is likely the red channel will begin to clip first due to the higher level of red / orange light in the scene.

As mentioned, the clipping of the histogram curve is usually an indication of under- or overexposure, but do remember that the preview image, including those for NEF files, is always derived from an 8-bit JPEG file to which the camera settings (White Balance, contrast, saturation, etc.) have been applied, and it is the tonal distribution of this JPEG file that the histogram describes. An NEF file will contain more data and have a wider range of tonal values; therefore, an overexposed highlight in the JPEG preview may not be an overexposed highlight when the NEF file is examined in a RAW file converter such as Nikon Capture NX 2.

Even if an NEF file has been incorrectly exposed, it is possible to apply retroactive Exposure Compensation using software such as Nikon View NX2 or Nikon Capture NX2, between about -1.0 and +1.5 EV; no such flexibility is possible with a JPEG file.

Scenes that are low in contrast will have a rather narrow curve that ends before reaching either the left or right-hand extremities of the bottom axis. You have two choices about how to deal with this situation: (1) Use the Picture Control System to increase the contrast level, or (2) adjust the contrast level at a later stage using an image-processing software application. I would recommend the latter approach, as it offers a far greater degree of control.

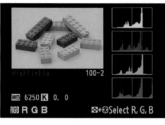

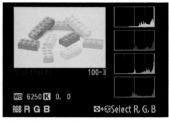

∧ This histogram indicates that a full range of tones has been recorded.

∧ This histogram indicates overexposure; note how the histogram curve is stacked to the right side.

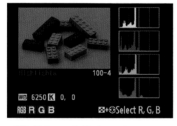

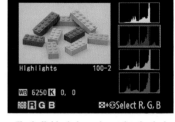

∧ This histogram indicates underexposure; note how the histogram curve has moved to the left.

∧ The individual channels can be checked for the warning by holding the ⌗ button and pressing ◀ or ▶; here the red channel has been selected.

HINT: It is always preferable to err on the side of lower image contrast because it is easier to boost contrast than it is to try and reduce it at any stage subsequent to the original exposure.

SD (Secure Digital) memory cards are small, solid-state cards that measure 1.3 x 0.9 x 0.08 inches (34 x 22 x 2 mm), have a capacity of up to 2GB, and are structured rather like the hard drive disk of your computer in that they have a file directory, a file allocation table, folders, and individual files. They are capable of retaining data even when they are not powered, and since they have no moving parts they are reasonably robust, so a minor impact from the card being dropped 8 to 10 feet (2.7 – 3 m) or exposure to the natural elements should not cause any problems. But total immersion in water should be avoided! Obviously, you should treat any memory card with the same care you would all your camera equipment, and it is advisable to keep them in the small plastic case supplied with each card.

Typically, SD cards have a temperature-operating range of -4°F to 167°F (-20°C to 75°C), and no altitude limit. They also have a small, sliding write-protect switch on one edge that, when set to the locked position, prevents any data being written or deleted (if you insert a locked SD card into the D7000, the camera will emit a beep sound as a warning if you try to release the shutter). Finally, unlike photographic film, they are not affected by ionizing radiation from X-ray security equipment that is used widely these days.

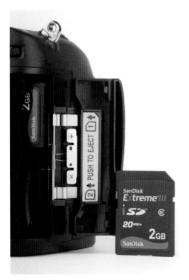

‹ The D7000 is compatible with SD, SDHC, and SDXC memory cards and has two memory card slots

SDHC & SDXC CARDS

As camera development led to larger file sizes there was soon a requirement for SD cards with a capacity greater than 2GB. Secure Digital High Capacity (SDHC) cards, were introduced as a new standard to meet this demand. They have the same physical dimensions and write-protect feature of SD cards, and comply with the SD specification version 2.0 (which supports a card capacity of 4GB and over), and come in a variety of speed classes with different performance capabilities and minimum requirements. Full details on the SD 2.0 specification can be viewed at: www.sdcard.org.

The D7000 is fully compatible with memory cards that comply with the SDHC standard, and at the time of writing most manufacturers already offer card capacities up to 16GB, with some producing 32GB cards. While such capacious storage may sound tempting, I believe it is important to consider the potential risks of placing all your proverbial "eggs in one basket," and suggest it would be prudent to disperse the risk of loss or corruption of image data by using a number of cards with smaller capacities.

More recently, SDXC memory cards, which represent the next generation of flash memory card, based on the latest SD 3.0 specification, have been introduced and in time will be the natural successor to the popular SDHC card format. Capacities of the new SDXC cards are planned to range between 32GB and 2TB (terabytes), and already SanDisk has released a 64GB SDXC card. The file structure of the SDXC format cards enables long duration HD video recording at a high data transfer rate, so widespread adoption of the new format is expected as many cameras, such as the D7000, incorporate an HD video capability.

APPROVED MEMORY CARDS

There is a plethora of memory cards on the market, but Nikon has only tested and approved those listed in the table found at the top of the next page for use with the D7000; all cards of the make and capacity listed there can be used regardless of their read / write speed. SD, SDHC and SDXC card technology is well established, so although Nikon will not guarantee operation with other makes of cards, you should not experience any problems or have any concerns if you use an alternative brand. If you have any doubt, test your memory card before using it to record any important pictures.

BRAND NAME	SD MEMORY CARDS	SDHC MEMORY CARDS	SDXC MEMORY CARDS
SanDisk		4, 8, 16, 32 GB	64 GB
Toshiba		4, 8, 16, 32 GB	
Panasonic	1 GB, 2GB	4, 6, 8, 12, 16, 32 GB	48 GB, 64 GB
Lexar Media		4, 8 GB	
Lexar Platinum II		4, 8, 16, 32 GB	N/A
Lexar Professional		4, 8, 16, 32 GB	

Nikon states that other brands and capacities of cards have not been tested with the D7000; therefore, operation cannot be guaranteed. If you intend to use a memory card not listed in the table above, it is advisable to check with the manufacturer in relation to its compatibility with the D7000. If you purchase a new memory card, always test it a few times before using it for any important photography. Should you experience any problems related to the memory card, use one of the approved cards for the purposes of troubleshooting. It is essential to also check that any card reader or other device is compliant with the respective SD memory card standard (SD, SDHC, and SDXC). For example, an SDHC-compliant card reader supports both SD and SDHC cards but will not support the SDXC format.

MEMORY CARD CAPACITY

When considering the capacity of the memory cards you will use, bear in mind that the 16.2MP resolution of the D7000 will result in larger file sizes compared with the 12.3MP D300S camera model, or earlier 6MP Nikon camera models such as the D100. So if you have been in the habit of using 1GB or 2GB memory cards regularly with your 6MP to 8MP DSLR, you may want to think about stepping up to 8GB. On average, I find that when shooting NEF (RAW) files, I can expect to record about 450 images on a 8GB card. This provides plenty of scope, especially if you shoot for techniques such as high dynamic range (HDR) or panoramic, requiring multiple shots per final image. I find a 8GB card offers a good compromise between storage capacity and the risks (card failure or loss) inherent with saving all your shots to a single, high-capacity 16GB or 32GB card; however, if you expect to use the HD video capability of the D7000 such high capacity cards will be more convenient.

The table below provides information on the approximate number of images that can be stored on an 8GB SanDisk Extreme SDHC memory card at the various image quality, and size settings available on the D7000. All memory cards use a small proportion of their memory capacity to store data required for the card to operate. Therefore, the amount of memory available for storing image files will be slightly less than the quoted maximum capacity of the card. Likewise, capacities may vary slightly if a different brand of memory card is used.

IMAGE CAPACITY	IMAGE SIZE	FILE SIZE (MB)[1]	NO OF IMAGES[1]	BUFFER CAPACITY[2]
NEF (RAW) Lossless compressed, 12-bit	-	15.5	291	11
NEF (RAW) Lossless compressed, 14-bit	-	19.4	223	10
NEF (RAW) Compressed, 12-bit	-	13.6	398	15
NEF (RAW) Compressed, 14-bit	-	16.7	330	12
JPEG Fine [3]	L	7.8	813	32
	M	4.4	1400	100
	S	2.0	3100	100
JPEG Normal [3]	L	3.0	1600	100
	M	2.2	2800	100
	S	1.0	6000	100
JPEG Basic [3]	L	2.0	3100	100
	M	1.1	5500	100
	S	0.5	11000	100

1 All figures are approximate. File size varies with scene recorded.
2 Maximum number of exposures that can be stored in memory buffer drops if [Optimal quality] is selected for JPEG compression, or if High ISO NR is on.
3 Figures assume JPEG compression is set to [Size priority]. Selecting [Optimal quality] increases the file size of JPEG images; number of images and buffer capacity drop accordingly.

FORMATTING A MEMORY CARD

The memory of an SD card has a similar structure to that of a hard disk drive, with a file directory, file allocation table, folders, and files. As data is written to and deleted from the card, small areas of its memory can become corrupted and fragmented, particularly if you delete individual image files (pictures). When you format the card in the camera, the worst effects of fragmentation are, for the most part, cleaned up.

Nikon states in the D7000 instruction book that formatting a memory card "permanently deletes all pictures and other data on the card." While this is a salutary warning, it is somewhat misleading, because the process of formatting actually causes the existing file directory information to be overwritten, so that the pointers that direct any reading device, including the camera itself, to the image data held on the card are removed; the process of formatting does not delete all the data as Nikon states it does. That said, once the card is formatted, it is difficult—although far from impossible—to recover previously written data from the card. If you should format a card inadvertently, it is often possible to recover the image files using appropriate recovery software, provided no further data is written to the card. Since prevention is always better than a cure, save your images to a computer or other storage device (and make a backup copy) before formatting a card.

To format a card using the D7000, insert the card in a card slot, making sure the main (top) label of the card faces the back of the camera, and then switch the camera on. Press and hold the ⚏ and 🗑 buttons for approximately two seconds, until For appears flashing in the control panel, together with a flashing frame-count display, and flashing card-slot identifier. If two memory cards are installed in the camera, the card Slot 1 (top) will be formatted; Slot 2 can be selected by rotating the Main Command dial. To proceed with the formatting process, you must release the ⚏ and 🗑 buttons momentarily and then press them again, while For appears flashing. During formatting, For appears continuously within the frame-count brackets of the control panel. Once formatting is complete, the frame-count display shows the approximate number of photographs that can be recorded at the current size and quality settings.

Alternatively, you can use the [Format] item in the ⚙ Setup menu, but this method is slower to perform and involves using the LCD monitor, which increases power consumption. If you press any other button after For begins to flash, the format function is cancelled, and the camera returns to its previous state. Never switch the camera off or otherwise interrupt the power supply to the camera during the formatting process, as this may corrupt the memory card.

IMAGE QUALITY (FILE FORMAT)

The D7000 saves images to the memory card in two file formats, Joint Photographic Experts Group (JPEG), and Nikon Electronic File (NEF) RAW format.

Using Nikon's Expeed2 processing regime, the D7000 records images in the JPEG file format via the integrated analogue-to-digital converter (ADC) on the sensor. The ADC converts the electrical signals generated by the photodiodes at a 12-bit depth to produce 12-bit raw data before the value for each pixel is rendered via a demosaicing process at a 12-bit depth. Thereafter, all in-camera processing, such as color manipulation, contrast control, and sharpening is performed in a 16-bit depth space. Additionally, there is an automated reduction of the effects of lateral chromatic aberration to reduce color fringing at distinct edges in image detail. Finally, the image data is only reduced to 8 bits once the encoding for the JPEG file is actually performed, after all the other processing stages have been completed.

When the D7000 is set to record an image in the Nikon Electronic File (NEF) format, the data that is saved is essentially the "raw" data generated via the ADC with no interpolation or other adjustment of the information from the sensor; hence, this is often referred to as the RAW format file. Recording NEF files, you can select the bit depth used to hold the image data: either 12 bits or 14 bits. The data is maintained in the selected bit depth both while it is built and subsequently output. This means that at a 12-bit depth, each pixel can have one of 4096 distinct values for its color (red, green, or blue), while at a 14-bit depth, the same pixel can have one of 16,384 values, which means potentially that color and tone graduation in the 14-bit file will be improved; however, this is not necessarily the case (see NEF file attributes, pages 151-152). Furthermore, shooting in NEF format allows you to select whether this data is retained in a lossless compressed or compressed state.

If the camera is set to record lossless compressed NEF files, the original data values calculated for each pixel are preserved (i.e., no data is discarded). Lossless compression uses a reversible algorithm to retain all of the image information. For this reason, this type of compression may also be referred to as "data lossless." However, if the camera is set to record normally compressed NEF files, some of the information from the sensor is discarded in a process that Nikon describes as being "visually lossless" (see pages 152-153 for the explanation of what actually occurs).

Regardless of whether the camera saves lossless compressed, or compressed NEF files, the files are constructed in the same way. Essentially, an NEF file uses the same structure as a TIFF file; it starts with tags that point to the EXIF and White Balance value information (this describes the camera settings in use at the time the image was recorded). Then a small JPEG "thumbnail" image is produced, followed by the raw pixel data.

To summarize, the principal difference between the JPEG format compared with the NEF format concerns how the camera deals with the data from the sensor. Using the JPEG format, the camera produces a finished image from the sensor data with the settings at the time of the exposure embedded in the file. The file is finished in the sense that it is possible to use a JPEG file direct from the camera to produce a print or post to a website. These files can, however, still be subjected to post processing if required or desired, although they are nowhere near as flexible in post processing as NEF files. Using the NEF format, on the other hand, absolutely requires post processing to produce a finished image, using a computer with an appropriate RAW file converter and usually some additional image-editing software. If you are relying on post processing to get a final result that is significantly different from the image at the time of capture, NEF will make those results much easier to achieve.

If you are beginning to form the impression that to eek out every last ounce of quality the D7000 has to offer, you should shoot in the NEF (RAW) format, you are not too far off the mark! However, that last sentence requires justification because, while many photographers refer to the RAW format as being better than JPEG, I prefer to consider the issue in terms of the flexibility the formats offer (see the section entitled "File Format Attributes" on the following page), and recommend that you use the one that is best suited to your specific requirements.

FILE FORMAT ATTRIBUTES

It is worth taking a look at the attributes of each format so you can make an informed decision:

JPEG Format: Probably the greatest benefit of the JPEG format is that it can be read by most software and is supported by HTML, the computer language used to build web pages. Such ubiquitous acceptance of the JPEG format enables these files to be shared widely, regardless of the type of computer or software that may be used.

NOTE: Strictly speaking, JPEG is a data compression regime and not a file format, but since a file saved using this regime is usually assigned an extension of .jpg or .jpeg, it has become common convention to refer to it as a file format.

The process of saving a file in the JPEG format involves taking blocks of 8 x 8 pixels from the image and subjecting each block to a series of calculations, the results of which are then compressed. Essentially, the numerical value of the each block of pixels is converted into an equation that represents an average value of the pixels in that block. While this compression process is variable in its level, depending on the range of pixel values in each block, it still results in the permanent loss of some data. The compressed result for each block is then brought together as a single sequence of binary values, which is encoded using a further lossless form of compression. As a rule of thumb, using a JPEG compression ratio of 1:4 or less will produce an image in which the effects of the compression process are, for all intents, imperceptible. However, the JPEG format has three attributes that can potentially influence image quality in adverse ways:

O The in-camera processing reduces the 12-bit data from the sensor to 8-bit values when it creates a JPEG file. The D7000 does have the advantage that it makes all in-camera adjustments to image attributes such as sharpening, contrast, and saturation at a 12-bit level before the data is reduced to 8 bits, so if you do not intend post processing work on your images, the reduction to 8-bits is of no real consequence. However, if you make significant changes to an image using software in post processing, the 8-bit data of a JPEG file can impose limits on the degree of manipulation that can be applied, particularly in respect of the level of color and contrast adjustments that can be made.

O When the camera saves an image using the JPEG format, it encodes most of the camera settings for attributes such as White Balance, sharpening, contrast, saturation, and hue into the image data. If you make an error and inadvertently select the wrong setting, it may be challenging and time consuming to rectify the mistake in post processing.

O The technology of digital imaging is fast paced, and the electronics used in any particular camera are only as good as they were the day the manufacturer decided on their specification and finalized the design of the camera. Granted, most modern cameras can have their firmware (installed software) upgraded, and to some extent, this helps to off set obsolescence, but it is only effective for so long. By processing images in software on a computer, you can often take advantage of the very latest advances in image processing, which may be unavailable in the camera.

NEF (RAW): Using the NEF format has only limited disadvantages in my opinion: It does require some extra time for post processing each image to produce a finished picture; the larger file size of the NEF format can be an issue in terms of the amount of available storage, both in terms memory-card capacity and external storage for archiving your pictures, but these days, data storage devices are relatively cheap; and finally, there can be limitations and variability with some third party software when it comes to their ability to read and interpret Nikon NEF files. The benefits of NEF format, on the other hand, include:

O More consistent and smoother tonal gradations

O Color that is more subtle and accurate to the original subject or scene

O A slight increase in the level of detail that is resolved

O The ability (within fairly limited parameters) to adjust exposure in post processing to correct for slight exposure errors

O The ability, in post processing, to correct and / or change image color by resetting attributes such as the White Balance value, saturation, and hue; plus, effect control over image contrast and brightness

NOTE: Most modern software is capable of reading NEF files generated by the D7000. For compatibility between NEF files from the D7000 and Nikon software, you will require: Nikon View NX2 2.0.3 or Nikon Capture NX2 2.2.6 or later. There are a wide variety of third-party RAW file converters that enable NEF files to be opened in most popular digital imaging software, such as Adobe Camera Raw 6 (for Adobe Photoshop CS5, Photoshop Elements 9) and Adobe Lightroom 3. Most manufacturers offer their software for a free trial period, so I recommend you try a few to see which meets your requirements before you commit to a license purchase.

I have already discussed briefly that the D7000 can be configured to save NEF files at either a 12-bit or a 14-bit depth and with two options for file compression. So which of these options should you choose, and why?

As far as selecting the bit depth is concerned, the most likely benefit this will bring is to the appearance of the deepest shadow values in the image, which can be rendered with richer, smoother-looking tones, particularly at higher ISO settings. I say "can be," as this will in part be dependent on properties of the RAW file converter that you decide to use; hence, my recommendation is that you experiment with a few. Even then, the improvement is modest at best. If you are intent on extracting the very best an NEF has to offer, and assuming your camera technique and workflow thereafter are impeccable, you will want to shoot using the 14-bit option.

Allied to the choice of bit depth will be the level of compression; again, to maximize potential quality and flexibility in post processing, you will want to avoid conventionally compressed RAW files. So, I recommend choosing lossless compressed. I would suggest that, for most users, 12-bit depth and lossless compression offers the best combination for most shooting situations.

Conventionally Compressed NEF File: If the camera is set to record lossless compressed NEF files, the data value for each pixel is preserved; however, if the camera records compressed NEF files, some of the image data is discarded. Nikon has described the compression applied to NEF files as being "visually lossless," by which they mean it is impossible to differentiate visually between an image produced from an uncompressed file and one produced from a compressed file. The compression process used by Nikon is selective; that is to say, it only works on certain image data, while leaving other data unaffected. Nikon's use of the word "compression" in this context is rather misleading, as the process involves two distinct phases. The first phase sees certain tonal values grouped and then rounded, and the second phase is the point at which compression is actually applied. It works as follows: Once the analog signal from the sensor has been converted to digital data, the first phase of the compression process separates the values that represent the very darkest tones from the rest of the data. Then, the data with values that represent the remaining lighter tones is divided into groups, but this process is not linear; as the tones become lighter, the size of the groups increases, so the group with the lightest tones is larger than a group containing midtone values. A lossless compression is then applied to each individual dark tone value and the rounded value of each group in the mid and light tones.

When an application such as Nikon View NX2 or Nikon Capture NX2 opens an NEF file, it reverses the lossless compression process, or at least part of it. The individual dark tone values are unaffected (remember the compression applied to these is lossless) but, and here is the twist, each of the grouped values for the mid and light tones must be expanded to fit its original range. However, since the rounding error in each group becomes progressively larger as the tonal values it represents become lighter and lighter, the "gaps" in the data caused by the rounding process also become progressively larger at lighter tonal values.

It is important to put these data "gaps" into perspective. A single compression / decompression cycle performed on an NEF file produces an image that is visually indistinguishable that of an uncompressed NEF file, because the human eye does not respond in a linear way to increased levels of brightness; therefore, it is incapable of resolving the very minor changes that take place, even in the lightest tones where the rounding error is greatest and therefore the data gap is largest (remember Nikon's phrase—visually lossless).

Furthermore, our eyes are generally only capable of detecting tonal variations equivalent to those produced by 8-bit data, and since even a compressed NEF file has the equivalent of more than 8-bit data, the data gaps caused by Nikon's compression process are of no consequence. Similarly, many photographers will ultimately reduce their 12-bit NEF files to 8-bit JPEG files prior to printing or web publishing, which can mask any loss of tonal gradation caused by compressing NEF files.

In spite of this, it is important to understand that the data loss caused by compression of NEF files can affect final image quality, with the appearance of posterization that creates course shifts in color and tone where there should be gentle, smooth transitions. This is most likely to manifest in any highlight area of an image that is subjected to a significant level of adjustment during post processing, such as a considerable shift of color or contrast, or where excessive sharpening is applied.

WHICH FORMAT?

In considering the attributes of the JPEG and NEF formats, many photographers make an analogy with film photography; they think of the NEF file like an original film negative, and the JPEG file as being akin to a print. I do not disagree, but this is where my point about the flexibility of the two formats comes back to be relevant; not every photographer has the desire, ability, or time to spend post processing NEF files. The good news is that we have a choice, so consider the points made in this section and choose the format that is most suited to your purposes. If you have sufficient storage capacity on your memory card(s), you could always select one of the NEF + JPEG combinations from the Image Quality options (either directly using the **QUAL** button and Main Command dial, or via the [Image quality] option in the ◘ Shooting menu), as the D7000 can save a copy of a single image in both formats.

IMAGE QUALITY & SIZE

JPEG Format Files: The D7000 saves JPEG files at three different levels of quality:

- O FINE – uses a low compression ratio of approximately 1:4
- O NORMAL – uses a moderate compression ratio of approximately 1:8
- O BASIC – uses a high compression ratio of approximately 1:16

Each JPEG file can also be saved at one of three different sizes:

- O L – Large (4928 x 3264 pixels)
- O M – Medium (3696 x 2448 pixels)
- O S – Small (2464 x 1632 pixels)

As the processing involved in the creation of JPEG files uses compression that discards data, you should select the lowest level of compression if you want to maintain the highest image quality; a file saved at the FINE setting will be visually superior to a file saved at the BASIC setting. JPEG compression can generate visual artifacts, and the higher the compression ratio, the more apparent these become. If you are shooting for web publication, this is unlikely to be an issue, but if you intend to make prints from your JPEG file pictures, you will probably want to use the Large and FINE settings.

NEF (Raw) Format Files: There are two decisions to be made when setting the camera controls to record NEF files. The bit depth used to record the file, and what type of compression should be applied. As stated earlier, the D7000 offers either a 12-bit or 14-bit-depth NEF file, either of which can be saved in either a lossless compressed, or compressed form. A compressed NEF file is approximately 40-50% smaller than an uncompressed NEF file would be, while a lossless compressed NEF file is approximately 20-40% smaller.

NOTE: Compressed black-and-white NEF files are slightly smaller than color NEF files due to the thumbnail image embedded in the NEF file being grayscale, with no color information.

NOTE: NEF files taken with the D7000 using the Monochrome Picture Control are only slightly smaller than color files, because the NEF file retains all the original raw data, including the color information. Consequently, using the appropriate options in a raw file converter, an NEF file saved as a black-and-white image can be converted to produce a color image.

Setting Image Quality and Size: To set image quality (i.e., file format or combination of formats) on the D7000, open the ◘ Shooting menu and highlight the [Image quality] item; press ▶ to open the list of quality options and use ▲ or ▼ to highlight the required setting, then press the ⑧ button to confirm the selection. Alternatively, and in my opinion, the more convenient and quicker way to select image quality is to use the button-and-dial method. Press and hold the QUAL button, then rotate the Main Command dial; the selected value is displayed in the control panel. There are seven options available: NEF (RAW), JPEG Fine, JPEG Normal, JPEG Basic, NEF (RAW) + JPEG Fine, NEF (RAW) + JPEG Normal, and NEF (RAW) + JPEG Basic.

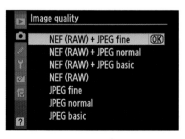

To set image size for the JPEG format on the D7000, open the ▲ Shooting menu and highlight the [Image size] item (note if you only have NEF selected for Image Quality, this option is grayed out); press ▶ to open the list of options and use ▲ or ▼ to highlight the required setting. Again, in my opinion, it's easier to use the button-and-dial method. Press and hold the QUAL button, and then rotate the Sub-Command dial; the selected value is displayed in the control panel, as L (large), M (medium), or S (small).

FILE COMPRESSION OPTIONS

JPEG: In addition to the Image Quality settings that apply a varying degree of compression to the image data when saving JPEG format files, the D7000 has two further options in respect to JPEG compression. Open the ▲ Shooting menu and highlight the [JPEG compression] item. Press ▶ and use ▲ or ▼ to select one of the two options:

○ [Size Priority] (default) – Image files are compressed to a near-uniform size, which results in a variation of quality dependent on the level of fine detail in the subject or scene. The more detail the subject or scene contains the more likely that image quality will be reduced.

○ [Optimal Quality] – Image files are compressed to varying sizes to allow for different levels of detail in the subject or scenes being photographed, maintaining a uniform level of quality. Unless you really need files of a consistent size, and as long as image storage capacity is not an issue, I recommend you use this option in preference to Size Priority.

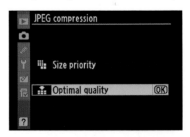

Once your required option is highlighted, press ⊛ to confirm the selection.

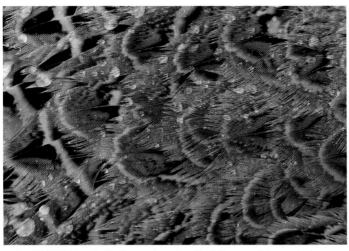

∧ The NEF (RAW) format will allow you to capture the full nuances of tone and color gradations in a subject, as well as provide a more flexible image file for post-processing.

NEF (RAW): To choose compression for NEF files, open the ▢ Shooting menu and highlight the **[NEF (RAW) recording]** item. Press ▶ and use ▲ or ▼ to select one of the two items displayed:

○ **[Type]** offers two options: **[Lossless compressed]** (default) and **[Uncompressed]**. Select the required option and press ⓞ to confirm the selection.

○ **[NEF (RAW) Bit Depth]** offers two options: **[12-bit]** (default), and **[14-bit]**. Select the required option and press ⓞ to confirm the selection.

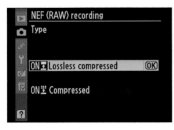

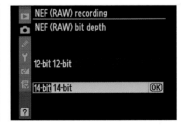

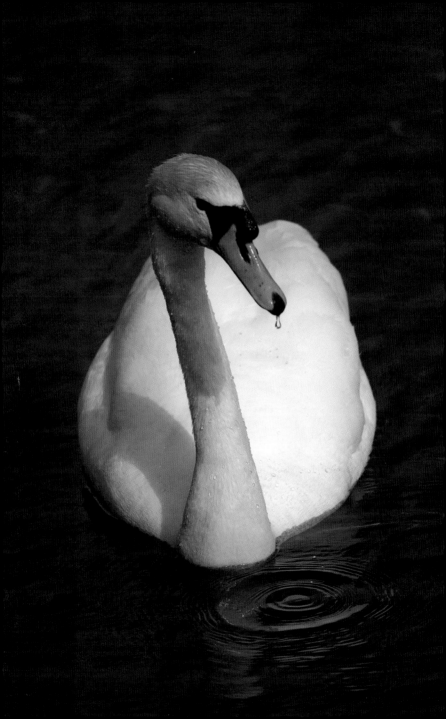

In-Camera Processing

WHITE BALANCE

We are all familiar with the way the color of sunlight changes during the course of a day from the warm orange and yellow colors immediately after sunrise, to the cooler, blue color of light around midday, returning to the oranges and yellows that appear as the sun sets. These changes are significant, and our eyes can see them quite clearly. However, the color of light (not to be confused with the color of the objects from which it is reflected) changes in subtle ways at other times of the day and in different climatic conditions. Furthermore, artificial light sources, such as a household light bulb or camera flash unit, emit light with a wide range of different colors. In many instances, our eyes and brain are remarkably good at adapting to these changes in the color of the light, so they are not visibly apparent to us. Think about what you see when you stand outside a building in which the interior lamps are switched on in daylight—the light the lamps emit often appears very yellow. But, if you look into the same building after dark, the light from the lamps now appears to be white. This is an example of the adaptive process that our eyes and brain apply to light, one which cameras, regardless of whether they use film or a digital sensor, cannot perform!

Cameras have a fixed response to the color of the light they record. Film has a response limited to a specific color (for daylight-balanced film, this is equivalent to direct sunlight at midday under a clear sky). Digital cameras, such as the D7000, are far more flexible; they can process the picture data to equate to a variety of specific light colors, either automatically or by selecting settings manually. This function is known as the White Balance control.

The color of light is often referred to as its color temperature, which is expressed in units called degrees Kelvin (K). It sounds counterintuitive, but warm light (red / orange colors) has a low color temperature and cool light (blue tones) has a high color temperature.

Why is this? Well, the color temperature of a light source equates to the color of something called a black body radiator—a concept used by scientists that involves a theoretical object that can re-emit 100% of the energy it absorbs. As heat is applied to this "black body radiator," it becomes hotter and its color changes from black to red, orange, yellow, through to blue. The color temperature of a particular light source is said to approximate the color of a black body radiator at the same temperature. Thus, at a low temperature, the color of the light emitted would contain a high proportion of red wavelengths; and at a high temperature, the light would contain a high proportion of blue wavelengths.

Generally, film is balanced to either direct sunlight under a clear sky at midday (a color temperature around 5500K) or the light emitted by a tungsten photoflood lamp (a color temperature around 3400K). If the temperature of the ambient light you are shooting under differs from these values, your photographs will take on a color cast, and you will need to use color correction filters to counter the effects.

NOTE: The color temperature of daylight will vary according to a number of factors including time of day, time of year, latitude, altitude, and the prevailing atmospheric and climatic conditions. The color temperature of 5500K, to which daylight film is balanced, is a somewhat arbitrary value and should only be used as a rough guide.

Digital cameras are far more versatile and can either automatically adjust their response to light within a range of different color temperatures or allow the user to set a specific color temperature. This feature is known as the White Balance control. Assuming the color temperature value of the chosen White Balance corresponds to the color temperature of the prevailing light in the scene, it will be rendered without any noticeable color cast (unnatural tint). You can also use the White Balance feature creatively by setting an alternative value that does not correspond to the prevailing light, thereby inducing a deliberate color shift.

The White Balance options of the D7000 camera can be selected in one of two ways:

○ Open the ⬛ Shooting menu and navigate to the **[White balance]** option, press ▶ on the Multi Selector, and highlight the required option from the displayed list by pressing either ▲ or ▼ (you must take this route if you want to alter the color temperature value for the Fluorescent option; see page 163). Then press ▶ to open the Fine-Tuning control and set any desired adjustment (see pages 169-171). Finally, press ⓞⓚ to confirm the selection.

○ Alternatively, and in my opinion the quicker way, is to use the button-and-dial method. Press the **WB** button and then rotate the Main Command dial until the required White Balance option is displayed in the control panel. To scroll and select a value for ⬛ **[Choose color temp]** (see pages 164-165); hold down the **WB** button while rotating the Sub-Command dial. The color temperature value, which is shown in degrees Kelvin (K), is displayed in the control panel.

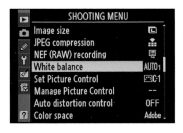
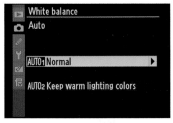

WHITE BALANCE OPTIONS

The White Balance control of the D7000 offers nine principal options: Auto, Incandescent, Fluorescent (with seven sub-options), Direct Sunlight, Flash, Cloudy, Shade, Choose Color Temperature, and Preset Manual. In addition to these options, the White Balance control has a Fine-Tuning feature. The approximate color temperature for each option (except the Preset Manual) is given in parentheses in the following list of descriptions for the various White Balance options:

A **Automatic (3500 – 8000K):** The D7000 benefits from the Nikon Scene Recognition System (SRS), which enhances the abilities of the newly developed 2016-pixel RGB-metering sensor. For example, the system helps enable the D7000 to distinguish between the greens of foliage and the green wavelengths produced by a flourescent light bulb. Nikon states that the effective color temperature range of the Automatic White Balance option on the D7000 is 3500K to 8000K. In practice, while I have found this option to be very effective and more reliable than on previous Nikon DSLR cameras when shooting in the middle of that range (i.e., typical daylight conditions), I would suggest that in practice, the color temperature range is closer to 4000K to 7000K. For example, in lighting conditions with low color-temperature values, typically incandescent lighting, I find the **[Auto1 - Normal]** option consistently sets a color temperature that is a little too high, resulting in a perceptibly warm (too much yellow) cast, which curiously is the very purpose of the **[Keep warm lighting colors]**. As with all automatic features, you will need to be aware of the limitations of the Auto White Balance option, especially in situations such as the following: under normal household lighting when the color temperature of light sources is likely to be lower than 4000K, outdoors in bright overcast conditions, or at high altitude where the color temperature of daylight is likely to exceed 6500K.

As I've said, Auto White Balance allows selection of two options **[Auto1 - Normal]** and **[Auto2 - Keep warm lighting colors]**; the difference between the results produced by these options is subtle, but **[Auto2 - Keep warm lighting colors]** produces a perceptibly warmer color rendition. To access these two options, open the ◘ Shooting menu and navigate to the **[White balance]** item, then press ▶ to display the White Balance settings. Highlight the **[Auto]** item and press ▶ to display the two options. Press either ▲ or ▼ to highlight the required setting, and press ▶ to open the Fine-Tuning option, adjust if required, and then press ⊗ to save the setting. The two options available under the **[Auto]** item can only be selected from within the ◘ Shooting menu; it is not possible to access them via the **WB** button route.

☀ **Incandescent (3000K):** Use this option when shooting under typical household incandescent lighting, as its color temperature is a better match; however, you may find that results still have a color cast and look too warm (i.e., the red content is too high), in which case, you should use either the Fine-Tuning feature or a Preset Manual measurement.

☼ **Fluorescent (2700K – 7200K):** The light emitted from fluorescent tubes is notorious for causing unwanted color casts. This is due to the way these tubes work and the variability in the color temperature of the light they produce. In an effort to increase the accuracy of color rendition under the wide variety of fluorescent bulbs, the D7000 has seven sub-options available under the **[Fluorescent]** White Balance option in the ◘ Shooting menu. To access these options, open the ◘ Shooting menu and navigate to the **[White balance]** option, press ▶ on the Multi Selector and highlight **[Fluorescent]**, and then press ▶ again to display the seven bulb types. Highlight the required bulb type and press ▶ to open the Fine-Tuning control if you wish to make any Fine-Tuning adjustments (see pages 169-171 for more on Fine-Tuning). Make any required adjustment before pressing ⊛ to set the bulb type and Fine-Tuning factor (if selected). The bulb type will be displayed in the ◘ Shooting menu, as ☼ next to a number from 1 to 7 (see table below). Selecting **[Fluorescent]** from the Information Display will select the bulb type set via the **[White balance]** option in the ◘ Shooting menu, but only ☼ is displayed; it is not possible to select the bulb type when setting the White Balance via the Information Display. The details of the seven bulb types found in the **[Fluorescent]** option are as follows:

BULB TYPE	COLOR TEMPERATURE	SHOOTING MENU DISPLAY
Sodium-vapor lamps	2700	☼ 1
Warm-white fluorescent	3000	☼ 2
White fluorescent	3700	☼ 3
Cool-white fluorescent	4200	☼ 4
Day white fluorescent	5000	☼ 5
Daylight fluorescent	6500	☼ 6
High temp. mercury vapor	7200	☼ 7

☀ **Direct sunlight (5200K):** This option is intended for subjects or scenes photographed in direct sunlight during the middle part of the day (i.e., from around two hours after sunrise to two hours before sunset). At other times, when the sun is low in the sky, the light tends to be warmer; using this setting at those times will produce pictures with a higher red content.

HINT: White balance is a very subjective issue, but to my eye, Nikon's color temperature for the Direct Sunlight option is too low. When shooting in these conditions I often prefer to use either the [Flash] or [Cloudy] option. I recommend you experiment to find a setting that meets your requirements.

HINT: Similar to the [Direct Sunlight] option, I consider the color temperature of the Flash option to be slightly too low. The color temperature of light emitted by Nikon Speedlights is generally in the range of 5500 – 6000K, so I often select the [Cloudy] option when working with Nikon flash units as the main lighting source.

☘ Flash (5400K): As its name implies, this option is intended for use whenever a flash (Nikon refers to their own flash units as Speedlights) is the main lighting source.

☁ Cloudy (6000K): This White Balance option is intended for shooting under overcast skies, when daylight has a high color temperature. It ensures the camera renders colors properly without the typical cool, blue tone, which can impart a cold appearance to a photograph, particularly in pale skin tones.

🏠 Shade (8000K): This option applies a greater degree of correction than the Cloudy option and is intended for those situations when your subject or scene is in open shade beneath a clear blue sky. Under these conditions the light will have a very high blue content, as it is principally comprised of light reflected from the blue sky above.

K Choose Color Temp. (2500 – 10,000K): If you know the specific color temperature of the light source(s) illuminating the subject and / or scene, the camera can be set to match it. The [Choose color temp] option under the [White balance] item in the ◙ Shooting menu allows selection from 31 different predetermined color temperature values that range from 2500K to 10,000K in increments of approximately 10 MIRED.

Open the ◙ Shooting menu and navigate to the [White balance] item, then press ▶ to display the options. Highlight the [Choose color temp] option and press ▶ to display the color temperature values. Press either ▲ or ▼ to highlight the required value and press ▶ to open the Fine-Tuning option, and then press ⓞⓚ to save the setting.

Alternatively, press and hold the **WB** button and rotate the Main Command dial to select the [Choose color temp] option in the control panel display. To select the required color temperature, press and hold the **WB** button and rotate the Sub-Command dial; the color temperature value is displayed in the control panel while the **WB** button is pressed.

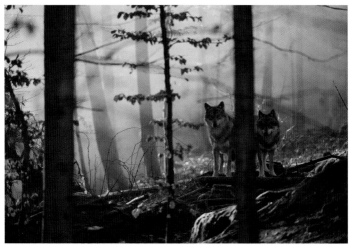

∧ Reproducing the natural color of light is important if the picture is to retain the atmosphere of the original scene. Here, I used a White Balance Choose Color Temperature setting of 5560K to capture the warmth of the early morning light.

PRE Preset Manual: This option allows you to obtain a measurement of the exact color temperature of the light illuminating the subject or scene by making a test exposure of a white or neutral gray test target, or by using the value from an existing image stored on the memory card. I understand from engineers at the Nikon Corporation that the Preset Manual White Balance option of the D7000 sets an infinitely variable color temperature value within the range available on the camera (which is 2500K to 10,000K), not one of the 31 fixed color temperature values available under the Choose Color Temp option. (See pages 164-165 for more on how to use this function.) However, there is no software (proprietary or otherwise) that will reveal the actual numerical Kelvin value of the color temperature used by the Preset Manual option; it will only show that the Preset option was used.

NOTE: As is the case with other image attributes, such as contrast level and sharpening, the White Balance settings used at the time of capture are embedded in JPEG files. NEF (RAW) files, on the other hand, simply have those attributes attached as a separate set of instructions that can be changed easily after the event in post processing. In terms of achieving the "as shot" White Balance, the highest level of compatibility comes with Nikon software, whereas most third-party software only calculates an approximation for the color temperature value of any White Balance set on Nikon DSLR cameras, including the D7000.

ALL ABOUT PRESET MANUAL WHITE BALANCE

The Preset manual option allows you to manually set a White Balance value from the scene, and as such, provides probably the most accurate way of setting a White Balance value in conditions of mixed light sources or any type of lighting that has a strong color bias. The D7000 provides two methods of selecting a Preset Manual White Balance setting: either by using the camera to measure light reflected from a white or neutral gray card test target, or by using the White Balance value from a picture recorded previously by the camera (see page 168). Furthermore, the camera can store up to five different values for a Preset White Balance.

HINT: In place of a test target such as a piece of gray card, there are a number of products that can be attached directly to the lens and allow the camera to not only obtain a White Balance measurement, but also take an incident reading for the ambient light using its TTL metering system. Probably the best device I have used for this purpose is the ExpoDisc (www.expodisc.com).

HINT: In the Nikon instruction manual, it is suggested that you can use either a white or neutral gray card as a reference target for the [Preset manual] White Balance option. I strongly recommend that you use only a neutral gray card for two reasons: First, white cards often contain pigments used to whiten them, which can cause the camera to render colors inaccurately. And second, it is more difficult to expose correctly for a pure white subject, despite the fact that the D7000 will automatically increase exposure by 1 EV when measuring for the Preset Manual White Balance; errors in exposure can affect the White Balance reading you obtain from the test target.

To measure a Preset Manual White Balance value, start by placing your test target in the same light that is illuminating subject to be photographed, and then press the **WB** button and rotate the Main Command dial until **PRE** is displayed in the control panel. Release the **WB** button briefly, and then press and hold it until **PRE** begins to flash in the control panel, and *PrE* flashes in the viewfinder display. Point the camera at the reference target (make sure you do not cast a shadow over the test target card) and make sure that it fills the viewfinder frame (there is no need to focus on the test target card). Exposure is automatically increased by 1 EV when measuring White Balance in the Preset Manual option; in Manual exposure mode, ensure the exposure scale is set to ±0. Now, press the shutter release. If the camera is able to obtain a measurement and set a White Balance value, *Good* will be displayed in the control panel and *Ud* will appear in the viewfinder, both icons blinking. The camera's White Balance is now set for the prevailing light falling on your subject, and this value will be stored and retained automatically in d-0, replacing any previous value stored there, until you make another Preset option measurement. To use the new White Balance value immediately, ensure that d-0 is selected for the White Balance file by pressing the **WB** button and rotating the Sub-Command dial until you see d-0 displayed in the control panel.

If the camera is unable to set a White Balance value, typically because the light level is either too low or too high, *no Ud* will appear blinking in the viewfinder and the control panel. In this case, repeat the process until a measurement is achieved.

To retain the value at d-0 and store it before taking a new White Balance measurement, open the [White balance] item in the ◙ Shooting menu and select the [Preset manual] option, and then press ▶. Highlight the destination Preset (d-1 to d-4) and press the ⊕⊟ button. Finally, highlight [Copy d-0] and press ⊛. If a comment has been attached to the Preset Manual value stored at d-0, it will be transferred to the new preset value. (See page 168 for more on comments.)

NOTE: If no White Balance value is measured for d-0 the color temperature will be set to 5200K (the same as the [Direct sunlight] option).

Copying a White Balance Value: If you want to use the White Balance value of an existing photograph recorded by the D7000, open the [White balance] item in the ◘ Shooting menu, highlight the [Preset manual] option and press ▶. Highlight the destination preset (d-1 to d-4) and press the ⊞ button. Highlight [Select image] and press ▶ to display a thumbnail view of images stored on the installed memory card; press and hold ⊕ if you wish to display the image full-frame on the screen. Highlight the photograph to be the source of the White Balance value; a narrow yellow border will surround it. Finally, press the ⊛ button to copy the White Balance value and any stored comment (see below) to the selected preset (d-1 to d-4).

Selecting a White Balance Preset Value: One way to select a stored Preset Manual White Balance value is via the [White balance] item in the ◘ Shooting menu: Highlight the [Preset manual] option, and then press ▶. Highlight the required preset (d-0 to d-4) value and press the ⊞ button. Next, highlight [Set] and press ▶ to display the Fine-Tuning options. Adjust if required, and finally, press ⊛ to save the settings.

Alternatively, press the **WB** button and rotate the Main Command dial until **PRE** is displayed in the control panel. Then press the **WB** button and rotate the Sub-Command dial to display the Preset value (d-0 to d-4) in the control panel.

Attaching a Comment to Preset Value: To help identify a Preset value (d-0 to d-4), a comment of up to 36 characters can be attached to it. Open the [White balance] item in the ◘ Shooting menu and highlight the [Preset manual] option, then press ▶. Highlight the required Preset (d-0 to d-4) value and press the ⊞ button. Highlight [Edit comment] and press ▶. Use the characters and controls displayed at the bottom of the screen to create a comment. Press ⊛ to save it.

HINT: The ability of the D7000 to store Preset White Balance values is very useful. If the camera is to be used at a variety of different locations with different lighting conditions during the course of an event, a White Balance value can be measured and stored (and named) for each location in advance. You can then recall the appropriate Preset value for each location as the event progresses. Alternatively, if you frequently return to a particular location, the White Balance value for the lighting can be stored and recalled on each visit.

This feature enables the White Balance settings to be fine-tuned to compensate for variations in the color temperature of a particular light source or to create a deliberate color cast in a picture. The system effects change in equally spaced MIRED values (see the "What is MIRED" panel, page 171) and offers considerably more precise and consistent results when compared with the somewhat arbitrary and counterintuitive Kelvin scale. If you have become familiar with the Kelvin system, where positive and negative values create cooler and warmer results, respectively, you will need to invest some time to learn MIRED; the results may not be what you expect.

The fine-tuning of White Balance can be achieved via two different routes: the [White balance] item in the ◘ Shooting menu or the **WB** button and Sub-Command dial. Using the [White balance] item in the ◘ Shooting menu provides the greatest level of fine-tuning over both color temperature and color. Open the ◘ Shooting menu and navigate to the [White balance] item; press ▶ to display the list of White Balance options. Highlight the required one, and then, other than for the four options listed below, press ▶ to display a color graph; its horizontal axis is used to fine-tune for the level of amber (A) to blue (B), while the vertical axis is used to adjust the level of magenta (M) to green (G).

If you select either [Auto], [Fluorescent], [Choose color temp], or [Preset manual], one additional step has to be performed before the color graph is displayed, as follows:

- ○ If you select the [Auto] option, select either [Auto1 - Normal] or [Auto2 - Keep warm lighting colors] and press ▶.
- ○ If you select the [Fluorescent] option, select a bulb type and press ▶.
- ○ If you select the [Choose color temp] option, highlight a color temperature value and press ▶.
- ○ If you select the [Preset manual] option, select a Preset value (see page 168) and press ▶.

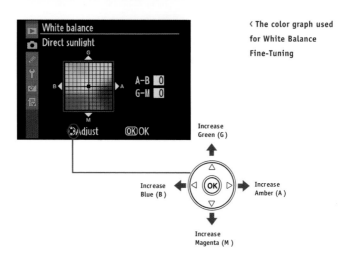

< The color graph used for White Balance Fine-Tuning

Increase Green (G)

Increase Blue (B)

Increase Amber (A)

Increase Magenta (M)

Using the Multi Selector, select an adjustment value between one and six along each axis of the color graph, working from the central point (see graphic above). Color temperature is fine-tuned by shifting along the amber (A) / blue (B) axis, while color balance is shifted along the green (G) / magenta (M) axis. On the A-B axis, each step is equivalent to about 5 MIRED; the higher the number, the greater the color shift, making the picture appear warmer as the level of amber is increased or cooler as the level of blue is increased. Adjusting the color balance through this Fine-Tuning option is similar to using color-compensating (CC) filters. A combined color temperature and color balance shift is possible by moving the cursor of the graph display into one of the four quadrants of the graph. Once you have set the Fine-Tuning adjustment, press ⊛ button to save the setting and return to the ◘ Shooting menu.

> A shift to an amber (warmer) tint has been set.

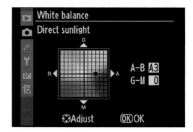

IN-CAMERA PROCESSING

It is important to appreciate that the colors on the axes of the color graph are relative and not absolute. This means, for example, shifting the cursor toward A (amber) when a White Balance option with a high color temperature value, such as ☁ Cloudy, is selected will make the picture slightly warmer still.

WHAT IS MIRED?

MIRED (Micro Reciprocity Degree) is a method of defining a shift in color in such a way that each shift in MIRED value is equivalent to the difference in color we perceive. The disadvantage of degrees Kelvin (K) is that a relatively small shift in Kelvin value at low color temperatures (below 4000K) creates a much larger perceived shift in visible color than the same small shift in Kelvin value at high color temperatures (above 6000K). The MIRED value is calculated by multiplying the reciprocal of the color temperature by ten to the power six (10^6). For example, the difference of 1000K between a color temperature of 3000K and 4000K is equal to 83 MIRED, whereas the difference between 6000K and 7000K is only 24 MIRED.

WHITE BALANCE BRACKETING

The White Balance Bracketing feature creates multiple copies of a single image recorded by the camera, but each one has a different White Balance value as determined by the selected settings.

NOTE: White Balance Bracketing is not available with the following Image Quality settings: NEF (RAW) or NEF (RAW) + JPEG (Fine, Normal, Basic). Selection of any of these options will cancel White Balance Bracketing.

NOTE: White Balance Bracketing only affects color temperature on the amber – blue axis; it does not affect the color balance on the green – magenta axis.

Select the [WB bracketing] option at CS-e5 [Auto bracketing set]. Press the **BKT** button and rotate the Main Command dial to select the number of different White Balance values to be created by the bracketing process; a scale is displayed in the control panel to indicate the number of images that will be created (only one exposure is made; the camera applies the different White Balance values to copies of the original as it processes the image data).

To select the adjustment to be applied to the White Balance value, press the **BKT** button and rotate the Sub-Command dial. Each increment is approximately equal to 5 MIRED. Choose from increments of 1 (5 MIRED), 2 (10 MIRED), or 3 (15 MIRED); higher A values correspond to an increased shift in color temperature toward an amber (warmer) tint, while higher B values shift color temperature toward a bluer (cooler) tint.

CONTROL PANEL		BRACKETING PROGRESS INDICATOR	NO. OF SHOTS	INCREMENT	BRACKETING ORDER
b2F	1	÷◀▮	2	1B	0 / 1 B
A2F	1	▮▶÷	2	1A	0 / 1 A
3F	1	÷◀▮▶÷	3	1A, 1B	0 / 1 A / 1 B

NOTE: The effect of applying a White Balance Fine-Tuning factor and White Balance Bracketing are cumulative (i.e., the bracketed values will be added to the Fine-Tuning factor for each file the camera creates).

NOTE: If the number of shots in the bracketing sequence is greater than the remaining capacity of images on the installed memory card, the remaining-exposures counter will blink *FuLL* in the control panel and *Ful* in the viewfinder, while the shutter release will be disabled. If this occurs, simply insert a new memory card, format it, and you can resume shooting the White Balance Bracket sequence.

CREATIVE USE OF WHITE BALANCE

Feel like getting creative? It is easy with the White Balance control on the D7000. You do not have to set the White Balance to match the color temperature of the prevailing light. Try mismatching it instead! For example, rather than shoot a subject or scene lit by daylight using one of the Daylight White Balance values, set it to [Incandescent]—now your picture will have a strong blue color cast. The great appeal of digital photography is the ability to experiment!

Remember, if the color temperature of the prevailing light is lower than the color temperature of the White Balance value set on the camera, the subject or scene will be rendered with a warmer appearance. Conversely, if the color temperature of the prevailing light is higher than the color temperature of the White Balance value set on the camera, the subject or scene will be rendered with a cooler appearance.

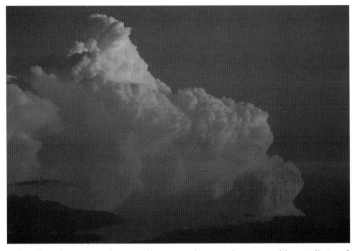

∧ The Nikon Picture Control system allows extensive control over several key attributes of an image, including its color saturation and level of contrast.

THE PICTURE CONTROL SYSTEM

The Picture Control System (PCS) replaces the color mode options and optimizes image features that were used in previous Nikon DSLR cameras, such as the D200 and D80 models, to influence the appearance of pictures in terms of sharpening, contrast, brightness (gamma), color saturation, and hue.

The purpose of the PCS is to provide a single, all-encompassing solution for obtaining consistent results with different Nikon cameras, while also integrating Nikon software, particularly Nikon View NX2 and Capture NX2. Once you have adjusted settings to achieve your desired result on one camera, it can be replicated using the same settings on another D7000 camera to produce pictures with identical attributes. Furthermore, within Nikon Capture NX2 software, it is possible to apply the same settings to an NEF (RAW) file recorded by a Nikon DSLR camera that has the PCS.

It is important to mention that full integration of the PCS with Capture NX2 means that the settings made within the PCS on the D7000 are only really relevant if you shoot in the JPEG format. The values for the various parameters are embedded in those file types and cannot be altered at a later stage, at least not without a lot of trial-and-error testing, and even then, there is no guarantee the process will be successful! Since the full range of the PCS settings is replicated in Nikon View NX2 and Nikon Capture NX2 (both are RAW-compatible), it is possible to adjust all PCS settings at will subsequently, if pictures are recorded in the NEF format.

The Picture Control System of the D7000 offers six preset Picture Controls: Standard, Neutral, Vivid, Monochrome, Portrait, and Landscape. Depending on which item is selected, a range of attributes can be adjusted, including sharpening, contrast, brightness, saturation, and hue. The Monochrome item offers controls to simulate traditional contrast-control filters used for black-and-white photography, as well as toning effects. The [Standard], [Vivid], [Portrait], and [Landscape] items also have a Quick Adjust feature that allows sharpening, contrast, and saturation to be adjusted simultaneously. Plus, there is also an automated option to adjust sharpening, contrast, and saturation. Finally, a graphical display available on the camera's monitor maps contrast against saturation to help you understand how one group of settings relates to another.

The full flexibility of the PCS comes with the ability to either modify the Nikon Preset Picture Controls or create your own Custom Picture Controls within the D7000. A maximum of nine Custom Picture Controls can be saved in the camera; they can also be copied to a memory card and transferred to other compatible cameras or to a computer for use with Nikon View NX2 and / or Nikon Capture NX2. Likewise, Custom Picture Controls can be created using the Picture Control Utility within Nikon View NX2 or Nikon Capture NX2 software and uploaded to the camera.

SELECTING A NIKON PICTURE CONTROL

In the **P**, **S**, **A**, and **M** exposure modes, select one of the Preset Nikon Picture Controls to suit the type of subject or scene being photographed. To do this, press the [Info] button to open the Information Display, and then press the [Info] button again and use the Multi Selector button to highlight the [Set Picture Control] item and press ⓞ. Highlight the required option from the list of Preset Picture Controls using the Multi Selector button, pressing it up or down as required, and then press ⓞ.

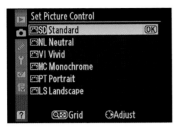

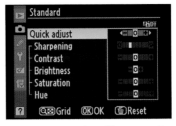

∧ Opening the [Set Picture Control] item will display a list of the available Picture Controls. Use the Multi Selector to highlight the required option (here, [Standard] is selected). Press ⊛ to display the attribute options for the selected Picture Control.

∧ The Picture Control provides a range of options for adjusting its characteristics, including a [Quick adjust] option that produces a global adjustment. Alternatively, each parameter can be adjusted individually.

Another method of accessing the Picture Controls is via the ⏢ Shooting menu: Navigate to the [Set Picture Control] item, then press ▶ to display the six preset Nikon Picture Control options. Highlight the required option and press ⊛.

PRESET NIKON PICTURE CONTROLS

Whichever method you use to access the Picture Controls, the following are your choices:

o ⏢SD Standard: Probably the most useful option for most shooting situations. Modest levels applied to image attributes such as color saturation and contrast. Sharpening is set to 3.

o ⏢NL Neutral: Provides a good starting point for any image that will be subjected to extensive post-processing, as processing applied in camera is very restrained. Sharpening is set to 2.

o ⏢VI Vivid: Useful for images that will be printed directly from the camera. Saturation, contrast, and sharpening are relatively high.

o ⏢MC Monochrome: Use for producing black-and-white images direct from the camera. Sharpening is set to 3.

o ⏢PT Portrait: Color rendition is optimized for skin tones, while sharpening is reduced to 2.

o ⏢LS Landscape: Saturation of blues and greens tends to be boosted, plus sharpening level is raised. Sharpening is 4, same as Vivid.

HINT: There is no indication in the viewfinder as to which Picture Control is selected, but if you press the ⊞PT button, the information will be shown in the Information Display.

MODIFYING A PICTURE CONTROL

The PCS enables you to modify any one of the six preset Nikon Picture Controls so that settings match a particular shooting situation more appropriately, or so you can use the settings for a specific creative purpose. However, it is not possible to create an entirely new Picture Control, but only modify an existing set of parameters provided by the Nikon Picture Control settings to make modified Picture Controls.

Start by navigating to the [Set Picture Control] item in the ◻ Shooting menu, and then press ▶ to display the six preset Picture Control items, along with any previously saved Custom Picture Controls (see next section, Creating a Custom Picture Control). Highlight the required Picture Control and press ▶ to display the settings for the various attributes; use ▲ or ▼ to select the required attribute and use ◀ or ▶ to adjust its value. Alternatively, where available, you can use the Quick Adjust to select a preset combination of adjustments (rather than adjusting each attribute individually), which will be displayed against each attribute as you change the levels. If at any time you want to restore a Picture Control to its original settings, press the 🗑 button, highlight [Yes], and press ⊛. Press the ⊛ button to save the settings you have selected. When you adjust the level of a Picture Control setting, a yellow line is displayed beneath the previous level for your reference. If a Picture Control is modified from its default settings (or original settings in the case of a Custom Picture Control) it will be marked with an asterisk.

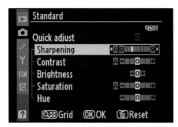

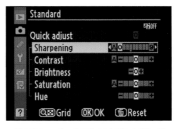

∧ The default setting for [Sharpening] in the [Standard] Picture Control is 3, as indicated by the yellow cursor.

∧ The sharpening level, as indicated by the yellow cursor, has been adjusted to 0 by pressing the Multi Selector to the left.

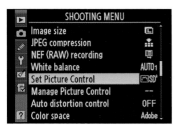

< Once Nikon Picture Control has been adjusted from its default settings, such as changing the sharpening level from 3 to 0, and the new settings has been saved, the Picture Control will be marked with an asterisk (*) to indicate it has been modified.

NOTE: To access the graphical display of contrast and saturation, in order to compare the selected option with the others, press and hold the ⊕▦ button. (If the Monochrome option is selected, only the value for contrast is shown.) Release the ⊕▦ button to return to the menu for the selected Picture Control.

NOTE: I would not recommend relying on the LCD screen of the D7000 to make any critical assessment of the sharpness, color, or contrast in an image, as it simply does not have a sufficiently high resolution, or the ability to display the full gamut of colors defined by the Adobe RGBcolor space, with greens being restricted in particular; its capabilities are closer to approaching the narrower gamut of sRGB.

The settings available for each of the Picture Control options is outlined in the following table:

OPTION	SETTINGS
Quick Adjust	Choose values between ±2 to reduce (negative value) or enhance (positive value) the effect of the selected Picture Control. This option resets any manually adjusted settings; it is not available with the Neutral, Monochrome, or any Custom Picture Control.
All Picture Controls	
Sharpening	Auto (A), or a manually set value between 0 (no sharpening) and 9; the higher the value, the greater the degree of sharpening.
Contrast	Auto (A), or a manually set value between ±3; negative values reduce contrast, while positive values increase contrast.
Brightness	Choose values between ±1 to reduce (negative value) or enhance (positive value) brightness (luminance) of an image.
Picture Controls (except Monochrome)	
Saturation	Auto (A), or a manually set value between ±3; negative values reduce saturation, while positive values increase saturation.
Hue	Manually set value between ±3; see description of the effect below.
Monochrome Picture Controls only	
Filter Effects	Use to emulate the effect of contrast control filters used with traditional black-and-white photography.
Toning	Use to emulate the effect of chemical toners used in traditional black-and-white photography.

HINT: Unless you need to produce images direct from the camera, I personally believe it is better to leave adjustment of contrast, saturation, brightness, and hue until post-processing. Appropriate software offers a far greater degree of control over these adjustments.

Sharpening: Sharpening is a process applied to digital data that can increase the apparent sharpness (acuity) of a picture. It is applied to correct the side effects of converting light into digital data, which often causes distinct edges between colors, tones, and objects in a digital picture to look ill-defined (fuzzy). The process identifies an edge by analyzing the differences between neighboring pixel values. It then lightens the pixels immediately adjacent to the brighter side of the edge and darkens the pixels adjacent to the dark side of the edge. This causes a local increase of contrast around the edge, making it appear sharper; the higher the level of sharpening applied, the greater the contrast at the edge. Sharpening is not a method for rescuing an out-of-focus picture—remember, once out of focus, always out of focus!

If you select the automatic setting for this option, you surrender all control to the camera and have no way of ensuring consistency in the degree of sharpening it applies; the camera will vary the amount of sharpening according to the nature of the scene being photographed. A scene with a lot of fine detail will receive a greater degree of sharpening compared with a scene that contains large area(s) of continuous tone.

HINT: There is no single level of sharpening that is appropriate for all shooting conditions. With JPEG files, it is fixed by in-camera processing and any sharpening applied in post-processing will be cumulative. With an NEF RAW file, the original in-camera sharpening can be removed, but only by selecting a different picture control option within Nikon View NX2 or Capture NX 2 and then adjusting the settings. The level of sharpening should be based on your ultimate intentions for the image (i.e., display on a web page, publication in a book or magazine, or producing a print for framing). Therefore, it is often preferable to only apply sharpening during the final stages of post-processing, particularly if you want to work on images for a range of different output purposes.

I would make the following suggestions with regard to in-camera sharpening when shooting with the D7000:

○ For general photography, using JPEG files: If you intend to work on these images in post-processing, set sharpening to zero or a low value.

○ For general photography, using JPEG files: If you intend to print pictures directly from the camera without any further processing, set sharpening to a mid-range value.

○ On occasions when you need to expedite the output of pictures for publishing on a website or in newsprint, use the JPEG format and set the sharpening level in the mid to higher range. In this specific case, a slightly stronger degree of sharpening is probably more appropriate, as images will be viewed on computer screens or at low reproduction resolutions. It is probably also more prudent because it will save valuable time in post-processing.

○ If you shoot in the NEF file format, I recommend setting sharpening to zero. Otherwise, there is a risk that any in-camera sharpening, when applied by a RAW file converter, will create a cumulative effect with any sharpening that is subsequently applied.

Contrast: The contrast control allows you to adjust the distribution of tones in an image and works by applying a curve control similar to those used in post-processing software. I feel the D7000 tends to err toward too much contrast when left to set it automatically; and with the exception of the Neutral option, the default level of contrast in the other Nikon Picture Controls is also slightly too high; therefore, I recommend that this control be used judiciously. It is important to remember that it is far easier to increase contrast than reduce it. This is especially important if you intend to subject the image to further contrast adjustments in post-processing.

Brightness: While the contrast control is used to increase or reduce the difference between lighter and darker tones in an image, the brightness (luminance) control is used to make an overall image lighter or darker. Adjusting the brightness affects all three of the color channels (red, green, and blue); a positive value increases brightness, and a negative value decreases it. Adjusting the brightness level of an image does not affect the exposure.

Saturation: Adjusting the saturation of an image changes the overall vividness (chroma) of color without affecting the brightness (luminance). A positive value increases saturation, and a negative value decreases it. As with contrast, I have found the D7000 sets saturation a little too strongly for my liking in both the automatic option and at the default settings in the Standard, Vivid, and Landscape Picture Controls. I suggest you exercise restraint with the saturation control—overdoing it will make returning an image to a more natural-looking appearance a difficult task.

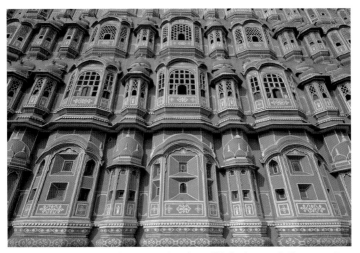

∧ The settings applied in a Picture Control can be modified subsequently if you record an NEF (RAW) file; however, it is still advisable to use low values for color saturation and contrast. Otherwise, these may affect the histogram display, which is derived from a preview JPEG.

There will always be a degree of subjective opinion when assessing color, but I find the D7000 tends to produce a slightly oversaturated color. A combination of the Neutral Picture Control and Adobe RGB color space renders the most natural and neutral colors with the right amount of saturation, so this probably represents a good reference point when adjusting other Picture Controls.

> **NOTE:** If achieving consistent results is important to you, I recommend that you avoid using the A (Auto) options for contrast and saturation, since the level applied by the D7000 with this setting will vary depending on the exposure level and is influenced by the position of the subject in the frame area.

Hue: The RGB color model (sRGB or Adobe RGB) used by the D7000 to produce images is based on combinations of red, green, and blue light. By mixing two of these colors, a variety of different colors can be produced. If the third color is introduced, the hue of the final color is altered. For example, applying a positive adjustment will make reds look more orange, greens more blue, and blues more purple. If you apply a negative adjustment, the hue shifts so that red is more purple, blue is more green, and green is more yellow.

Monochrome Filter Effects: In the Monochrome Picture Control, there are options to select filter effects that emulate the results of using contrast-control filters with traditional black-and-white film. These filters modified the tonal response of the film to certain wavelengths (colors) of light. The options available in the D7000 are [Off] (default), [Yellow], [Orange], [Red], and [Green]. Just like their optical filter counterparts, these filter effects reduce the amount of their complimentary color in the image. For example, the yellow, orange, and red options reduce the level of blue, making a blue sky appear darker; the yellow filter has the least effect and the red the greatest. One result of this effect is an increase in the level of contrast between the blue sky and any white clouds, making the clouds more prominent. The green option reduces the amount of red, making red and orange colors appear darker. This option can be useful for enhancing the range of skin tones in a portrait picture and making them appear more natural or separating the tones of the various shades of green in landscape photography. My advice is to experiment with these options to determine if, how, and when they will best suit your needs.

Monochrome Toning: In addition to the filter effects described above, the Monochrome Picture Control also offers a range of options that emulate the effects of traditional chemical toning of black-and-white prints. The options include [B&W] (black-and-white, the default setting), [Sepia] (yellow/brown), [Cyanotype] (blue tint), [Red], [Yellow], [Green], [Blue-green], [Blue], [Purple-blue], and [Red-purple] (similar to selenium toning). Once you have selected the [Toning] option and the desired tone, press ▼ to display a saturation control and use ◄ or ► to adjust the saturation of the toning effect (this is not available with the [Black-and-white] option).

NOTE: Regardless of the black-and-white option selected under the [Monochrome] Picture Control option, the D7000 always saves black-and-white pictures recorded in the NEF RAW format as an RGB file. Therefore, it can always be converted back to a full color image using the Picture Control utility in Nikon View NX2 or Nikon Capture NX2.

NOTE: The Picture Control system provides a tremendous level of control. I recommend you spend some time experimenting with the settings for the various attributes in the Picture Control system, based on the file type you intend to record and the way in which you will use your pictures, particularly if you shoot using the JPEG format.

CREATING A CUSTOM PICTURE CONTROL

The PCS enables you to modify any one of the six preset Nikon Picture Controls and save the new settings to create a Custom Picture Control; furthermore, once a Custom Picture Control has been saved, it can be modified at any time subsequently. However, it is not possible to create an entirely new Picture Control, but only modify an existing set of parameters provided by the Nikon Picture Control settings and then save those settings.

Start by opening the ▢ Shooting menu and navigating to the [Manage Picture Control] item, and then press ▶ to display the next menu page. Highlight the [Save/edit] option and press ▶ to display the six preset Nikon Picture Control options (remember, if a preset Picture Control option has been modified, it will be marked with an asterisk). Highlight the required option and press ▶ to display the current Picture Control settings, and then use ▲ or ▼ to select the required attribute and use ◀ or ▶ to adjust its value. Once all the required adjustments have been made, press the ⊛ button. Highlight a destination (C-1 to C-9) for the new Custom Picture Control and press ▶. This opens a text-entry field with a selection of characters displayed above it. By default, the new Custom Picture Control is given a two-digit suffix assigned automatically to the name of the existing preset or modified Picture Control. If you wish, you can use the controls displayed below the text-entry field to create a different name for the new Custom Picture Control comprising up to nineteen characters. To rename or delete a Custom Picture Control, see the "Managing Custom Picture Controls" section below.

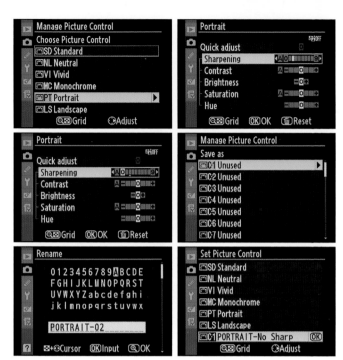

This sequence of screen shots shows the steps involved in selecting, adjusting, saving, and naming a Custom Picture Control. Starting from the [Manage Picture Control] item, the [Portrait] Picture Control has been adjusted, and its level of sharpening is zero. It has been named [Portrait-No Sharp] and saved as a Custom Picture Control at the [C-1] position.

SHARING CUSTOM PICTURE CONTROLS

Custom Picture Controls can be created in Nikon View NX2 or Nikon Capture NX2 software using the Picture Control Utility, or they can be created in another compatible camera, saved to a memory card, and then loaded into the D7000. To copy a Custom Picture Control to the D7000, highlight the [Manage Picture Control] item in the ○ Shooting menu and press ▶ to display the options. Highlight [Load/Save] and press ▶, then highlight [Copy to camera] and press ▶. Highlight the required Custom Picture Control and either press ▶ to display the current Picture Control settings, or press ○K. Select the destination for the Custom Picture Control and press ▶ to display the text-entry dialog box. Name the Custom Picture Control, as described previously under Creating Custom Picture Controls. Finally, press ○K to save the name and return to the Picture Control list.

To copy a Custom Picture Control to a memory card, display the [Load/Save] menu as described above, highlight [Copy to card], and press ▶. Highlight the required Custom Picture Control and press ▶ to display the [Choose destination] list. Select the destination for the Custom Picture Control from one of the 99 locations listed, and press ⓞⓚ to save the Custom Picture Control to the memory card. If you select a destination that already has a Custom Picture Control saved to it, it will be overwritten by the new save command. A maximum of 99 Custom Picture Controls can be stored on a memory card.

To delete a Custom Picture Control from a memory card, highlight the [Load/Save] item in the [Manage Picture Control] option of the ◘ Shooting menu and press ▶. Highlight the [Delete from card] option and press ▶ to display the list of Custom Picture Controls stored on the card. Highlight the desired Custom Picture Control and either press ▶ to display its settings or press ⓞⓚ to display the [Yes] / [No] options in the [Delete from card] dialog box. Highlight the required option and press ⓞⓚ to confirm the action.

MANAGING CUSTOM PICTURE CONTROLS

To rename a Custom Picture Control, highlight the [Rename] item in the [Manage Picture Control] option of the ◘ Shooting menu and press ▶. Highlight the required Picture Control and press ▶ to display the text-entry dialog box. Create the new name for the Custom Picture Control. Finally, press ⓞⓚ to save the name and return to the Picture Control list.

To delete a Custom Picture Control from the camera, highlight the [Delete] item in the [Manage Picture Control] option of the ◘ Shooting menu and press ▶. Highlight the required Custom Picture Control and press ▶ to display the [Yes] / [No] options. Highlight one and press ⓞⓚ to confirm the action.

NOTE: The options available under sharing and managing Custom Picture Controls do not apply to the six Preset Nikon Picture Controls; these cannot be copied, renamed, or deleted.

COLOR SPACE

A color space (sometimes called color gamut) defines the range of colors that are available for reproduction and what particular RGB values should represent those colors in the digital image file. Unless you know your pictures will only ever be displayed on a computer monitor (i.e., as part of a website) or you will be using a direct printing method with no intention of carrying out any post-processing, I would recommend using the Adobe RGB color space option on the D7000—it provides the widest range of colors, permitting more subtle rendition and well-graduated tonal transitions. This increases the flexibility of an image file that will be subjected to post-processing, as well as the quality of any print made from that image file using an appropriate printing process. The sRGB color space is more suited to an image that will be used directly from the camera with no post-processing.

HINT: It is essential that any software used for post-processing be set to the same color space as the image file recorded by the camera. Otherwise, it is more than likely the application will assign its own default color space and you will lose control over the rendition of colors during the course of your workflow from initial capture to final output of the picture.

To choose a color space, highlight the [Color space] item in the ◘ Shooting menu and press ▶ to display the two choices: sRGB (default) and Adobe RGB. Highlight the required option and press ⓦ to confirm the selection, returning to the ◘ Shooting menu.

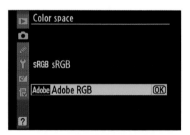

NOTE: While it comes very close, the Adobe RGB color space option on the D7000 does not appear to be capable of reproducing the complete gamut of the full Adobe RGB color space, as the camera does not replicate some of the green values; however, the camera's Adobe RGB color space option is still significantly broader than its sRGB color space.

NOTE: The monitor screen on the D7000 falls a little short of being able to display the sRGB color space, so it certainly doesn't show anything like the full gamut of the Adobe RGB space, so do not attempt to make a critical assessment of color from the camera's display.

ACTIVE D-LIGHTING

Active D-Lighting (not to be confused with the D-Lighting option available in the ☑ Retouch menu) applies a localized adjustment to contrast to improve the rendition of areas of deep shadow and bright highlights. It can be thought of as an automated dodge-and-burn effect, as opposed to a global adjustment to brightness (gamma) and contrast. It is designed for use with Matrix metering, which assesses scene contrast, and is intended for situations where the scene has a naturally high level of contrast. If necessary, it will modify exposure by reducing it accordingly—the adjustment is quite modest, typically 0.3 or 0.7 EV—to preserve highlight detail, then after the exposure has been made and the image data is being processed, the shadow and middle tones are adjusted to optimize the dynamic range by adjusting the tone curve applied to the image data.

I recommend exercising restraint if using Active D-Lighting feature, by choosing either the Low or Normal settings if recording JPEG files, since this function modifies the exposure settings before recording an original file, unlike the normal D-Lighting feature in the ☑ Retouch menu where a copy file is created from the original to which the adjustments are then applied. Any Active D-Lighting setting applied to an NEF file can always be modified later, using Nikon Capture NX2 software. If the effect of the Active D-Lighting setting is too strong, it may compromise the tonal range of the entire image, especially if the contrast in the scene is very high. To maintain image quality, I suggest you avoid using Active D-Lighting at ISO settings of 800 or above.

To select the Active D-Lighting from the Information Display, press the 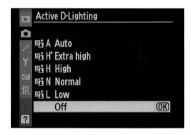 button and then press the ⓘⓝⓕⓞ button again. Now, move the highlight cursor to the Active D-Lighting item in the Information Display and press ⓞⓚ. Highlight the required option from the list of settings using the Multi Selector button, pressing it up or down as required, and then press ⓞⓚ.

Alternatively, it can be selected via the menu system. Highlight the [Active D-Lighting] item in the ⚪ Shooting menu and press ▶ to display the options: OFF [Off], 畦 L [Low], 畦 N [Normal], 畦 H [High], 畦 H⁺ [Extra high], and 畦 A [Auto]. Highlight the required option, and press ⓞⓚ to confirm the selection and return to the ⚪ Shooting menu.

Active D-Lighting

畦 A Auto
畦 H⁺ Extra high
畦 H High
畦 N Normal
畦 L Low
Off   (OK)

NOTE: While in M exposure mode, an Active D-Lighting setting of 畦 A [Auto] is equivalent to 畦 N [Normal].

NOTE: Using Active D-Lighting increases recording time and reduces buffer memory capacity.

BRACKETING ACTIVE D-LIGHTING

Using the [ADL bracketing] option under CS-e5 [Auto bracketing set], it is possible to bracket exposures with and without the Active D-Lighting being applied. Select CS-e5 [Auto bracketing set], press ▶, and then highlight [ADL bracketing] and press ⓞⓚ. To select the number of pictures in the bracketing sequence, press the BKT button and rotate the Main Command dial; choose to take either two or three pictures. If you select two, the D7000 will make two exposures: one with ADL off, and another at the Active D-Lighting value currently selected in the ⚪ Shooting menu. If that value is [Off], the second picture will be taken with ActiveD-

Lighting set to **[Auto]**. If you choose three pictures, the camera will make a series of exposures in the following sequence: OFF, 🎚N (normal), and 🎚H (high).

The Active D-Lighting Bracketing ends after the selected number of exposures has been made, even if the camera is set to a Continuous release mode. To cancel the bracketing sequence, press the **BKT** button and rotate the Main Command dial until the number of pictures in the bracketing sequence is set to zero.

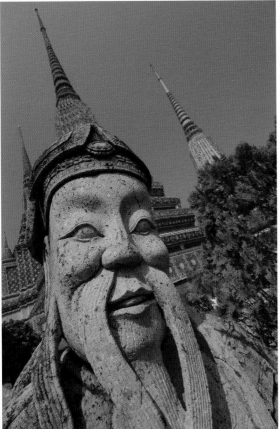

> The Active D-Lighting feature will help to retain detail in bright highlight areas of an image. For best results, use moderate levels of adjustment and low ISO values.

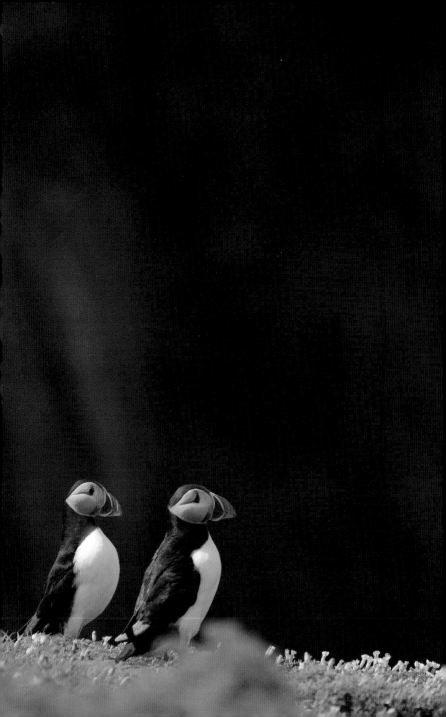

The Menu System

INTRODUCTION

The control of many features and functions on the D7000 relies on an extensive and comprehensive menu system that is displayed on the LCD monitor. It is divided into six main sections:

- O The Playback menu is used to review, edit, and manage the pictures stored on the memory card.

- O The Shooting menu is used to select more sophisticated camera controls that have a direct influence on the quality and appearance of the pictures recorded by the camera. The menu also contains several special features, such as Picture Controls, Active D-Lighting, Multiple Exposures, and a time-lapse (Interval Timer) setting.

- O The Custom Settings menu, as its name suggests, allows you to select and set a wide range of controls to fine-tune camera operation to meet your specific requirements. The menu is subdivided in to six groups that each deal with a specific area of camera operation: autofocus, metering / exposure, timers / AE lock, shooting / display, bracketing / flash, and controls.

- O The Setup menu is used to establish the basic configuration of the camera; once the settings for the items in this menu are made, they are generally not changed very frequently.

- O The Retouch menu is only available when a memory card containing picture files is inserted in the camera. It offers a range of items that enable you to crop, enhance, and add effects to a picture, and save it as a separate copy without affecting the integrity of the original file.

- O The My Menu allows you to create your own fully customized menu from any of the items contained in the Setup, Shooting, Custom Settings, Playback, or Retouch menus. This menu improves the efficiency of camera operation, since it saves you from having to scroll through the full menus to access frequently used items. The menu can be edited and reordered at will.

The 🔳 My Menu item on the D7000 is not only helpful, but is also a recognition that the menu system has become even more complex compared with previous Nikon DSLR cameras, due to the incorporation of more features and functions. There is a total of 123 main menu items, many of which have numerous sub-options. Since each page in the menu system can only display eight main items, you can spend a lot of time scrolling through subsequent pages with the Multi Selector.

Unfortunately, with the exception of My Menu, it is not possible to rearrange the order of items in the menus, which can be inconvenient because, in many cases, the item you are most likely to want to access is located behind the first page of the menu display. That said, it is only possible to add up to five items to the My Menu display before it becomes necessary to start scrolling to a subsequent page!

In short, the menu system has become cumbersome and overly extended. Many of the options within the menu system can be set using buttons and dials located on the camera body; where such an alternative route is available, I would recommend using it, as this will improve the efficiency of camera handling, with the added benefit of reduced battery consumption due to less use of the LCD monitor.

ACCESSING MENUS

To access any menu, push the MENU button and press ◀ to highlight one of the five tabs used to identify each menu (top to bottom): ▶ Playback menu, ◻ Shooting menu, ✐ Custom Settings menu, ⵎ Setup menu, ⅗ Retouch menu, and 🔳 My Menu.

> The Multi Selector button is used to navigate the menu system.

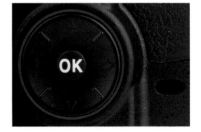

Highlight the required menu tab by using ▲ or ▼ and the menu will open. Press ▶ to highlight an option. Navigate to a specific menu item by pressing ▲ or ▼; each menu has multiple pages, so keep scrolling up and down using ▲ and ▼ to access options not shown on the current page of the menu. To display the sub-options available for each menu item, press ▶. Again, use ▲ or ▼ to highlight the required option and press the ⊛ button to confirm the selection. Pressing ▶ generally has the same effect as pressing the ⊛ button; however, there are some menu options that will only be selected or set by pressing ⊛. To exit the menu system, press the shutter release button down halfway.

> **NOTE:** If a menu option is displayed in gray, it is not available; this can be for one of a number of reasons including the following: the current camera settings, state of the memory card, or condition of the battery.

▶ PLAYBACK MENU

The Playback menu will only be displayed if a memory card is currently installed in the camera.

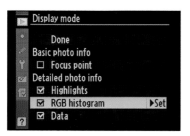

> **NOTE:** A number of items in the Playback menu involve selecting images saved to the memory card(s) installed in the camera. To view images stored at another location to the current one, hold down the **BKT** button and press ▲ to display Slot 1 and Slot 2; highlight the required item and press ▶ to display a list of folders stored on that memory card. Highlight the required folder and press ⊛.

DELETE

Using the [Delete] item in the Playback menu, you can choose to erase individual images, a group of images, all images taken on a specific date, or all of the images on the card (note that this last action does not have the same effect as formatting the memory card). To delete a group of images:

1. Highlight the [Delete] item in the Playback menu and press ▶.
2. Highlight [Selected] and press ▶.
3. Thumbnails of all of the images stored on the card will be displayed on the monitor. Scroll through the images using the Multi Selector button; a yellow frame will be displayed around the selected image. To see an enlarged view of the selected image, press and hold the ⊕ button. To view images stored in an alternative location, hold down the BKT button, press ▲, and select the required card / folder.
4. To select the highlighted image for deletion, press the ⊟ button; 🗑 will appear in the upper right corner of the thumbnail image. Repeat steps 3 and 4 to select additional pictures. To deselect a picture for deletion, highlight it and press ⊟ again.
5. Once all the files to be deleted have been selected, press the ⊗ button.
6. The total number of images to be deleted will be displayed, along with two options: [No] and [Yes]. Highlight [No] to cancel and [Yes] to confirm; press ⊗ to complete the process.

To delete images taken on a selected date:

1. Highlight the [Delete] item in the Playback menu and press ▶.
2. Highlight [Select date] and press ▶.
3. Highlight the required date. To view the pictures taken on that date press ⊟. Scroll through the images using the Multi Selector button; a yellow frame will be displayed around the selected image. To see an enlarged view of the selected image, press and hold the ⊕ button. To return to the date list, press the ⊟ button.
4. To select all pictures taken on the highlighted date press the ▶ button; a check mark icon will appear in the upper right corner of the thumbnail image. Repeat steps 3 and 4 to select additional pictures. To deselect a date, press the ▶ button again.
5. A confirmation message will be displayed with two options: [No] and [Yes]. Highlight [No] to cancel and [Yes] to confirm; press ⊗ to complete the process.

To delete all images:

1. Highlight the **[Delete]** item in the Playback menu and press ▶.
2. Highlight **[All]** and press ▶.
3. Highlight either **[No]** or **[Yes]** as required.
4. Press the ⊛ button to complete the process.

NOTE: It is not possible to delete pictures that have been protected. Images that have been hidden will not be displayed; therefore, they cannot be selected for deletion.

PLAYBACK FOLDER

The **[Playback folder]** option in the Playback menu allows you to determine which images on the installed memory card will be displayed during playback. There are three options available:

O **[D7000]** (default): Images in all folders recorded by the D7000 are capable of being displayed.

O **[All]**: All of the images stored on the memory card(s) can be displayed, regardless of the camera used to record them, provided it conforms to the Design Rule for Camera File System (DCF). All Nikon digital cameras and most other current digital cameras are DCF compatible.

O **[Current]**: Only the images in the folder currently set for image storage via the **[Storage Folder]** item in the Shooting menu will be displayed.

To select the Playback Folder:

1. Highlight the **[Playback folder]** item in the Playback menu and press ▶.
2. Highlight the desired option.
3. Press ⊛ to confirm the selection.

HIDE IMAGE

The **[Hide image]** option of the Playback menu enables you to hide or reveal selected images. Images that are hidden cannot be viewed during normal image Playback. Hidden images can only be viewed using the **[Hide image]** item, and they are also protected against deletion; they can only be deleted from the memory card by formatting it. To use Hide Image to hide or reveal selected pictures:

1. Highlight the [Hide image] item in the Playback menu; press ▶.
2. Highlight [Select/set] and press ▶.
3. Thumbnails of all of the images stored on the card will be displayed on the monitor. Scroll through the images using the Multi Selector button; a yellow frame will be displayed around the selected image. To see an enlarged view of the selected image, press and hold the ⊕ button. To view images stored in an alternative location, hold down the BKT button, press ▲ and select the required card / folder.
4. To select the highlighted image to be hidden, press the ⊞ button. An ⊠ icon will appear in the upper right corner of the thumbnail image. To deselect a picture for deletion, highlight it and press ⊞ again.
5. Once you have selected all images to be hidden, press the ⊗ button to hide all selected images.

To hide, or reveal pictures taken on a specific date:

1. Highlight the [Hide image] item in the Playback menu and press ▶.
2. Highlight [Select date] and press ▶.
3. A list of dates is displayed. Highlight the required date and press ▶. Selected dates are indicated with a check mark; to reveal all pictures taken on a selected date, highlight it and press ▶.
4. Once you have selected the required dates, press the ⊗ button to complete the process.

To reveal all hidden images:

1. Highlight the [Hide image] item in the Playback menu and press ▶.
2. Highlight [Deselect All?] and press ▶.
3. A message is displayed on the monitor, "Reveal all hidden images?" Highlight either [Yes] or [No] as required.
4. Press the ⊗ button to confirm the action.

NOTE: Images can be protected by selecting them using the Image Review function and pressing the ?/○ᵣ button.

DISPLAY MODE

The [Display mode] option determines which pages of image information are displayed during single-image Playback, in addition to the File Information and Overview Data pages. The [Basic photo info] item is used to select display of the [Focus point], while the [Detailed photo info] item is used to select display of [Highlights], [Display mode] and [Data], which comprises up to four pages of detailed shooting information (see pages 130-137 for full details). To select an option(s) for Display mode:

1. Highlight the [Display mode] item in the Playback menu and press ▶.
2. Highlight the desired option using ▲ or ▼, and then press ▶; a check mark will appear in the box to the right of the option title.
3. Repeat Step 2 for any other required option(s).
4. Finally, highlight [Done] and press ▶ to confirm the selection and return to the Playback menu.

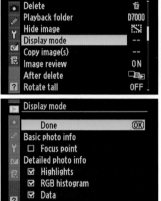
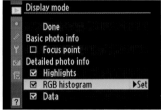

In the [Display mode] menu item, an option is only activated if a check mark appears next to it in the menu page; this sequence of screen shots shows selection of the [Display mode] option.

COPY IMAGE(S)

The [Copy image(s)] enables you to copy images from one memory card to another; obviously, there must be two memory cards installed in the camera for this feature to be available. To copy images:

1. Highlight [Copy image(s)] in the Playback menu and press ▶.
2. Highlight [Select source] and press ▶; highlight the memory card from which the image(s) will be copied, and press ⊛.

3. Highlight [Select image(s)] and press ▶ to display a list of folders stored on the memory card; highlight the source folder and press ▶.

4. All images or all protected images can be selected by highlighting the relevant options, [Select all images] or [Select protected images], and pressing ▶. To select individual images for copying, highlight [Deselect all] and press ▶.

5. Scroll through the individual images using the Multi Selector; a yellow frame will be displayed around the selected image. To select or deselect a highlighted picture, press the ▣ button. To see an enlarged view of the selected image, press and hold the ⊕ button. Selected images are marked with a check mark; press ⊛ once all desired images have been selected.

6. Highlight [Destination folder] and press ▶; to use a folder number, choose [Select folder by number] and enter the folder number before pressing ⊛; to choose from a list of existing folders, highlight [Select folder from list] and press ⊛. Select the desired folder from the list and press ⊛.

7. Next, highlight [Copy image(s)?] and press ▶; a confirmation dialog is displayed, highlight [Yes] and press ⊛. Press ⊛ again when copying is complete.

NOTE: If the destination folder does not have sufficient space for the images to be copied, the copying process will not be performed.

NOTE: If the destination folder contains an image with the same file name as one of the images being copied, a dialog box will be displayed: select [Replace existing image] to overwrite the image with the image to be copied; or select [Replace all] to overwrite all existing images with duplicate file names with the files to be copied. To continue the copying process without overwriting the image, select [Skip], and to stop the copying process without copying any further images, select [Cancel]. The Protect status of any images copied will be maintained but printing instructions will not be copied.

IMAGE REVIEW

The [Image review] option in the Playback menu determines if an image will be displayed on the monitor immediately after it is recorded. There are situations when reviewing every image recorded by the camera is undesirable—for example, when shooting in low-light conditions where the light from the screen is a distraction. You should also consider the necessity of displaying every exposure, as the monitor consumes a relatively large amount of power, which will increase the drain on the battery considerably. My recommendation is to switch this option off and use the ▶ button whenever you wish to review an image. To select an Image Review option:

1. Highlight [Image review] in the Playback menu and press ▶.
2. Highlight [On] or [Off] (default), as desired.
3. Press ⊗ to confirm the selection.

AFTER DELETE

The [After delete] option in the Playback menu enables you to select whether the following or the previous image (based on the order in which they were recorded) is displayed after an image is deleted. To set After Delete:

1. Highlight the [After delete] item in the Playback menu and press ▶.
2. Highlight the desired option from the following:
   - ○ [Show next] (default): The next image to be displayed will be the image recorded after the one deleted. If the deleted picture was the last to be recorded, the previous picture will be displayed.
   - ○ [Show previous]: The next image to be displayed will be the image recorded before the one deleted. If the deleted picture was the first to be recorded, the following picture will be displayed.
   - ○ [Continue as before]: The next image to be displayed after an image is deleted will be the image recorded either after or before the one deleted, depending on the direction in which you were scrolling through the recorded images.

HINT: In my opinion the [After delete] option is a prime example of the unnecessary complexity of the menu system. Not only does it take up valuable space in the menu, it burdens the user with yet more decisions. Personally, I leave this option at its default setting and forget it is there.

ROTATE TALL

The [Rotate tall] item determines whether pictures shot in the vertical (portrait) format are displayed automatically in that orientation, or displayed in the horizontal (landscape) format. Displaying an image in the vertical orientation will decrease the overall size of the image to about 2/3 the size of an image displayed horizontally, as the horizontal orientation uses the full viewing area of the screen. Pictures taken with **[Off]** selected for **[Auto image rotation]** in the Setup menu will be displayed in the horizontal orientation, regardless. To select **[Rotate Tall]**:

1. Highlight the **[Rotate Tall]** item in the Playback menu and press ▶.
2. Highlight **[On]** or **[Off]**.
3. Press ⊗ to confirm the selection.

The **[Slide show]** option in the Playback menu allows you to view all of the images stored on the current playback folder in sequential order. This can be a useful and enjoyable feature, especially if the camera is connected to a television or monitor for viewing. To view a slide show:

1. Highlight the **[Slide show]** item in the Playback menu and press ▶.
2. **[Start]** will be highlighted; to commence the slide show immediately, press ⊗.
3. To select the display duration for each image, highlight **[Frame interval]** and press ▶ to display the four options: 2, 3, 5, or 10 seconds. Highlight the desired interval duration, and press ⊗ to confirm the selection and return to the **[Slide show]** page.
4. Repeat Step 2 above to start the slide show.

There are a variety of control options when the Slide show function is active:

O To return to previous image, press ◀.

O To skip to the next image, press ▶.

O To display and scroll the photo information pages, press ▲ or ▼.

O To pause the display, press the ⊗ button. A submenu with three options is displayed: **[Restart]**, **[Frame interval]**, or **[Exit]**. Highlight as required and press ⊗ to select the option.

O To stop the display and return to the Playback menu, press the MENU button.

O To stop the display and return to the Playback mode (full-frame or thumbnail view), press ▶.

O To stop the display and return to the Shooting mode, press the shutter release button down halfway.

At the end of the display, the same menu displayed when the slide show is paused will be displayed with the following options: [Restart], [Frame interval], or [Exit]. Highlight the desired option and press ®.

NOTE: Hidden images do not appear during the slide show display.

HINT: The [Slide show] function consumes a lot of power, especially if a large number of images are stored on the memory card, due to the protracted use of the LCD screen. Ensure you use a fully charged battery, or use the EH-5a AC adapter with EP-5B connector.

PRINT SET (DPOF)

The [Print Set (DPOF)] item in the Playback menu enables you to create and save an instruction set for a group of images to be printed automatically by a compatible printing device. This "print order set" will communicate which images should be printed, how many prints of each image, and the information that is to be included on each print. The information is saved on the installed memory card in the Digital Print Order Format (DPOF) and can be read subsequently by any DPOF-compatible printing device (see pages 347-348 for full details).

◘ SHOOTING MENU

The Shooting menu offers options that will dictate how the camera will operate when you are actually taking pictures. Many of the options available in the Shooting menu can also be accessed more quickly using various buttons on the camera and / or the Information Display (see page 33).

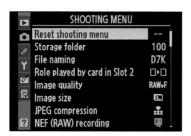

RESET SHOOTING MENU

The [Reset shooting menu] item allows you to restore all settings in the Shooting menu back to their default values. To reset the Shooting menu:

1. Highlight [Reset shooting menu] in the Shooting menu and press ▶.
2. Highlight [No] (default) or [Yes] as required.
3. Press the ⊛ button to confirm the selection and return to the Shooting menu.

> The Shooting menu contains most of the key items that determine the appearance of a picture, such as White Balance and Picture Controls.

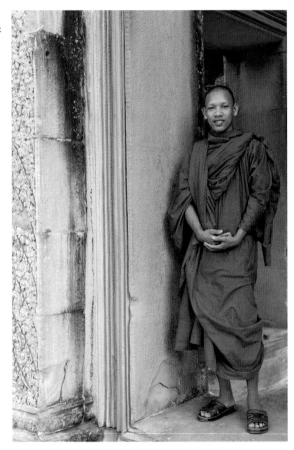

A list of the affected functions and their default settings is shown in the following chart:

OPTION	DEFAULT
File Naming	DSC
Role Played by Card in Slot 2	Overflow
Image Quality	JPEG Normal
Image Size	Large
JPEG Compression	Size Priority
NEF (RAW) Recording > Type	Lossless Compressed
NEF (RAW) Recording > Bit Depth	14-Bit
White Balance	Auto > Normal
White Balance > Fine-Tuning	Off
White Balance > Choose Color Temp	5000K
Set Picture Control	Standard
Auto Distortion Control	Off
Color Space	sRGB
Active D-Lighting	Off
Long Exp. Noise Reduction	Off
High ISO Noise Reduction	Normal
ISO Sensitivity in P, S, A, and M	100
ISO Sensitivity in other modes	Auto
ISO Sensitivity Auto Control	Off
Multiple Exposure	Reset
Movie Settings > Quality	1920 x 1080 / 24 fps
Movie Settings > Microphone	Auto Sensitivity
Movie Settings > Destination	Card Slot 1
Movie Settings > Manual Settings	Off
Interval Timer shooting	Reset
Remote Control mode	Delayed Remote

NOTE: The default settings for Image Quality, Image Size, White Balance, and ISO sensitivity can also be reset using the Two-Button Reset option as described on pages 126-128.

The D7000 uses a folder system to organize images stored on the memory card installed in the camera. The [Storage folder] item in the Shooting menu allows you to select the folder that the images that are currently recording will be saved to, and enables creation of new folders.

If you do not use any of the options pertaining to folders, the camera creates a folder named 100D7000 automatically, in which the first 999 pictures recorded by the camera will be stored on the memory card. If you were to exceed 999 pictures, the camera would create a new folder named 101D7000, and so on, for each set of 999 pictures. You can create your own folder(s); a three-digit number between 100 and 999 that you assign always prefixes the folder title. The suffix—D7000—remains the same.

If you use multiple folders, you must select one as the active folder to which all images will be stored until an alternative folder is chosen or the maximum capacity of 999 pictures in the active folder is exceeded. At this point, the D7000 will create a new folder using the same five-character suffix and assign a three-digit prefix with an incremental increase of one (e.g., if folder 100D7000 became full, the D7000 creates folder 101D7000 and pictures will now be stored in this new folder). To select the folder in which subsequent images will be stored:

1. Highlight [Storage folder] in the Shooting menu and press ▶.
2. Highlight the [Select folder by number] option and press ▶.
3. Press ◀ or ▶ to select a digit, and then press ▲ or ▼ to select the desired number.
4. If a folder with the selected number already exists, a small icon will be displayed to the left of the folder number to indicate: Folder is empty ▢, folder is partially full ▤, or folder is full / contains a file numbered 9999 ▤. The card slot icon in the top right corner of the menu page indicates which card the folder is stored on. The card used for the new folders depends on the option currently selected for [Role played by card in slot 2].
5. Press ⊛ to confirm the action and return to the Shooting menu.

To select an existing folder:

1. Highlight the [Storage folder] in the Shooting menu and press ▶.
2. Highlight the [Select folder from list] option and press ▶.
3. A list of the currently stored folders is displayed; highlight the folder you wish to use by pressing ▲ or ▼.
4. Press ⊛ to confirm the action and return to the Shooting menu.

HINT: Personally, I find using multiple folders to be time consuming and potentially confusing. I would rather use a browser application such as Nikon View NX2 to organize my image / video files.

FILE NAMING

The file names of all images you take with the D7000 contain three letters, a four-digit number, and the three-letter file extension (JPG, NEF, MOV, or NDF). The default for the three letters in the name is DSC, and depending on the selected color mode, they will have an underscore mark either as a prefix to denote Adobe RGB or as a suffix to denote sRGB (e.g., DSC_0001.JPG would be a JPEG file, number 0001, saved in the sRGB color space). The [File Naming] item in the Shooting menu is used to select three letters to replace the default DSC (this section of the file name must contain three letters—no more or less). To rename files:

1. Highlight the [File Naming] item in the Shooting menu and press ▶.
2. [File Naming] is highlighted on the next page, and two examples of file names are displayed to indicate the position of the underscore in relation to the color space used. Press ▶ to open the keyboard display (note that only upper-case letters and numbers 0 – 9 are available).
3. To enter a new file name, highlight the character you wish to input using the Multi Selector and press its center button to select the character. If you accidentally enter the wrong character, use the ⊕⊞ button in combination with the Multi Selector to move the cursor over the unwanted character and press the 🗑 button to erase it.
4. Press the ⊕ button to save the name and return to the Shooting menu.

ROLE PLAYED BY CARD IN SLOT 2

When two memory cards are inserted in the camera, this item can be used to determine the role of the card in Slot 2. The options are as follows:

O **[Overflow]**: The card in slot 2 is only used when the card in Slot 1 becomes full.

O **[Backup]**: Each file is recorded twice; once to the card in slot 1 and again to the card in slot 2.

O **[RAW Slot1 - JPEG Slot 2]**: When the camera is set to record NEF (RAW) + JPEG, the NEF (RAW) files are saved to the card in Slot 1, while the JPEG files are saved to the card in Slot 2.

IMAGE QUALITY

The Image Quality item in the Shooting menu allows you to select the file format for images recorded by the camera; the D7000 can record images in JPEG or NEF format (see pages 148-157 for full details).

IMAGE SIZE

Image Size determines the file size (resolution) of an image, and is expressed as a number of pixels (see pages 154-156 for full details).

NOTE: Image size adjustments will only apply to images saved using the JPEG or TIFF Format. NEF (RAW) files are always saved at the camera's highest resolution.

JPEG COMPRESSION

The complexity of a scene being recorded will affect the size of an image file recorded in the JPEG format. Usually, a more intricate scene will require more information to be recorded, which increases the file size. However, the [JPEG compression] option in the Shooting menu enables you to determine whether the camera places a priority on recording JPEG files at a fixed size, or varies the file size according to the scene in order to optimize image quality (see page 156 for full details).

NEF (RAW) RECORDING

The D7000 provides the option of saving NEF files in either a lossless compressed or compressed form. Losslessly compressed NEF files are approximately 20 – 40% smaller than uncompressed files, while compressed NEF files are approximately 40 – 55% smaller than uncompressed files. This increases the number of pictures that can be stored in any given storage capacity (see pages 151-157 for full details).

WHITE BALANCE

The [White balance] option in the Shooting menu allows you to select the color temperature or light type to which the images you are shooting will be balanced (see pages 159-173 for full details).

SET PICTURE CONTROL

The D7000 has six basic Nikon Picture Controls: Standard, Neutral, Vivid, Monochrome, Landscape, and Portrait (see 173-185 for full details).

MANAGE PICTURE CONTROL

You can create and save Custom Picture Controls, which can be copied to a memory card and applied to another D7000 camera or used in compatible Nikon software. Picture Controls created in compatible Nikon software can also be uploaded to another D7000 (see page 185 for full details).

AUTO DISTORTION CONTROL

The **[Auto distortion control]** feature offers correction to reduce the effects of linear distortion, an optical aberration that occurs in lenses. Wide-angle lenses produce "barrel distortion" that causes straight lines to bow outward, away from the center of the image; and long focal length lenses produce "pin cushion distortion," which causes straight lines to bend inward toward the center of the image. Select **[On]** for this feature to take advantage of it. It is possible that the extreme edges of an image may be cropped by this function and the recording time of the picture will be increased. Best results are achieved with D- or G-type Nikkor lenses (distortion is not corrected with PC-E, fisheye, or other certain types of lens).

> **HINT:** I recommend leaving this option set to **[Off]**, as more precise control in correcting optical distortion can be achieved using post-processing software.

COLOR SPACE

The range of colors capable of being displayed in an image recorded by the D7000 is determined by the Color Space setting. The D7000 provides two options for color space: Adobe RGB and sRGB (see pages 186-187 for full details).

ACTIVE D-LIGHTING

The Active D-Lighting feature (not to be confused with the D-Lighting item in the Retouch menu) can be used to optimize the exposure settings when using Matrix metering. Since the effects of Active D-Lighting are applied during the processing of an image file, it is not possible to reverse them when recording JPEG files. The effects of Active D-Lighting on an image recorded in the NEF format can be altered subsequently using appropriate Nikon software (see pages 187-189 for full details).

LONG EXPOSURE NOISE REDUCTION (NR)

Images taken at long shutter speeds will often exhibit a higher level of electronic noise. Noise is the result of the amplification process that is applied to the data captured by the sensor, which is compounded by a higher internal temperature of the camera due to extended shutter speeds. It manifests as irregularly placed, bright, colored pixels that disrupt the appearance of an image, particularly in areas of even tonality. The [Long Exp. NR] item will help reduce the appearance of noise when shooting with exposures times of 8 seconds or more. To set [Long Exp. NR]:

1. Highlight [Long Exp. NR] in the Shooting menu and press ▶.
2. Highlight [On] or [Off] (default) as required.
3. Press the ⊛ button to confirm the selection and return to the Shooting menu.

If [On] is selected for [Long Exp. NR], the processing time for each recorded image will increase by approximately 100%. While the image data is being processed, "job nr" will appear, blinking, in place of the shutter speed and aperture values in the control panel. No other picture can be recorded while this is displayed and image processing is in progress.

HINT: Nikon states that the Long Exposure Noise Reduction feature of the D7000, when switched on, will operate whenever the shutter speed exceeds 8 seconds approximately. Personally, I have found that the in-camera signal processing of the camera is so effective that there is often no necessity for this feature until a shutter speed of 30 seconds or longer is used.

NOTE: The process used by the D7000 to perform the [Long Exp NR] involves the camera making a second "exposure" known as a "dark frame exposure" during which the shutter remains closed but the camera maps the sensor and records the values of each photodiode (pixel). Sometimes a photodiode (pixel) can lock up and retain a value that is erroneous; this can often occur if the sensor gets hot due to use over a protracted period, as would occur in a long time exposure, or due to a high ambient temperature. After mapping the sensor for hot (overly bright) photodiodes (pixels), the camera subtracts the dark frame photodiode values from the photodiode values of the main exposure in an effort to reduce the effect of noise in the final image.

HIGH ISO NOISE REDUCTION (NR)

At high ISO settings, the presence of electronic noise in an image increases due to the greater degree of signal amplification that takes place during in-camera processing (it is analogous to the more visible grain structure of higher ISO film). The High ISO Noise Reduction feature, abbreviated to High ISO NR, will help to reduce the amount of noise in images taken at ISO sensitivities of 800 and higher. To set High ISO NR:

1. Highlight [High ISO NR] in the Shooting menu and press ▶.
2. Highlight the required option from [High], [Normal], [Low], or [Off] (see chart below).
3. Press the ⊛ button to confirm the selection and return to the Shooting menu.

OPTION	EFFECT
High	
Normal	Noise reduction is applied at ISO sensitivities of ISO 800 or higher. Select the level of Noise Reduction from one of the three options
Low	
Off	Noise reduction is only applied at ISO sensitivities of 1600 and higher. The level applied is lower than the amount applied when Low is selected for High ISO NR.

HINT: The Noise Reduction functions will affect the resolution of fine detail, and at high levels, the saturation of colors. The in-camera noise reduction for higher ISO sensitivities does not offer the same level of control as dedicated noise reduction software, so unless you really must use the camera options, I recommend applying noise reduction during post-processing.

ISO SENSITIVITY

ISO Sensitivity in the D7000 emulates the sensitivity of film to any given intensity of light bearing the same ISO number; the higher the ISO number, the greater the sensitivity to light (see pages 47-51 for full details).

MULTIPLE EXPOSURE

The Multiple Exposures item enables a number of different exposures to be made (up to ten) that the camera will combine into a single image; the individual files must be shot in consecutive order and are not saved as separate files (see pages 102-104 for full details).

MOVIE SETTINGS

The Movie Settings item encompass options for quality, microphone, the storage destination for video recordings made using the D7000, plus manual control of shutter speed and ISO when the camera is set to M exposure mode (see pages 114-116 for full details).

INTERVAL TIMER SHOOTING

The Interval-Timer shooting feature of the D7000 enables the camera to take a set number of pictures over a period of time, at predetermined intervals—a technique often called time-lapse photography (see pages 104-106 for full details).

REMOTE CONTROL MODE

This item determines the timing of the shutter release when using the optional ML-L3 infrared remote control with the D7000 (see pages 99-100 for full details).

The Custom Settings menu allows you to fine-tune the performance of the D7000 to satisfy your particular requirements, and adapt the camera to meet the demands of specific shooting situations. It comprises a comprehensive set of no less than 49 items, each with a range of options that covers virtually every aspect of camera operation. The items are grouped logically by the nature of their function, as set out in the table below:

GROUP		CUSTOM SETTINGS
a	Autofocus	a1 – a8
b	Metering / Exposure	b1 – b5
c	Timers / AE Lock	c1 – c5
d	Shooting / Display	d1 – d14
e	Bracketing / Flash	e1 – e6
f	Controls	f1 – f10

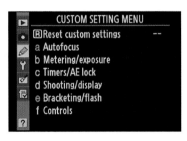

< The Custom Settings menu screen

SELECTING CUSTOM SETTING OPTIONS

The Multi Selector is used to navigate through the Custom Settings menu. Highlight ✐ (Custom Settings menu) to display the list of six Custom Setting groups, plus **[Reset custom settings]**. To use the ✐ menu:

○ Highlight the required group and press ▶ to display a full list of the items in the group.

○ Use ▲ or ▼ to highlight the required item, and press ▶ to display the options available for the item.

○ Use ▲ or ▼ to select the required option and use ⊗ to confirm the selection and return to the list of items in the group.

To reset the Custom Settings to the default settings, use the reset option. Select this item in the Custom Settings menu and highlight [Yes], then press ▶. Highlight either [No] or [Yes] as required and press ⊛. The default Custom Settings are set out in the table below:

	SETTING	DEFAULT
a1	AF-C Priority Selection	Release
a2	AF-S Priority Selection	Focus
a3	Focus Tracking with Lock-On	3 (Normal)
a4	AF Point Illumination	Auto
a5	Focus Point Wrap-Around	No wrap
a6	Number of Focus Points	39 points
a7	Built-In AF-Assist Illuminator	On
a8	**Live View / Movie AF**	
	Autofocus Mode	Single-Servo AF
	AF-Area Mode	
	In 🕺, 🖼, 🌾, ⛰, 📷, and 🌆	Wide-Area AF
	In 🌷 and 🍴	Normal-Area AF
	In other shooting modes	Face-Priority AF
b1	ISO Sensitivity Step Value	0.3 step
b2	EV Steps for Exposure Control	0.3 step
b3	Easy Exposure Compensation	Off
b4	Center-Weighted Area	ø 8 mm
b5	**Fine Tune Optimal Exposure**	
	Matrix metering	0
	Center-Weighted metering	0
	Spot metering	0
c1	Shutter-Release Button AE-L	Off
c2	Auto Meter-Off Delay	6 seconds
c3	**Self-Timer**	
	Self-Timer Delay	10 seconds
	Number of Shots	0
	Interval Between Shots	0.5 second

SETTING		DEFAULT
c4	**Monitor Off Delay**	
	Playback	10 seconds
	Menus	20 seconds
	Information Display	10 seconds
	Image Review	4 seconds
	Live View	10 minutes
c5	Remote On Duration	1 minute
d1	**Beep**	
	Volume	Off
	Pitch	High
d2	Viewfinder Grid Display	On
d3	ISO Display and Adjustment	Show frame count
d4	Viewfinder Warning Display	On
d5	Screen Tips	On
d6	CL Mode Shooting Speed	3 fps
d7	Maximum Continuous Release	100
d8	File Number Sequence	On
d9	Information Display	Auto
d10	LCD Illumination	Off
d11	Exposure Delay Mode	Off
d12	Flash Warning	On
d13	MB-D11 Battery Type	LR6 AA Alkaline
d14	Battery Order	Use MB-D11 batteries first
e1	Flash Sync Speed	1/250 second
e2	Flash Shutter Speed	1/60 second
e3	Flash Control for Built-In Flash (or accessory flash)	TTL
e4	Modeling Flash	On
e5	Auto Bracketing Set	AE and Flash
e6	Bracketing Order	MTR > under > over
f1	☼ Switch	LCD backlight
f2	⊛ Button (Shooting Mode)	Select center focus point
f3	Assign Fn Button	FV Lock
f4	Assign Preview Button	Preview

SETTING		DEFAULT
f5	Assign AE-L/AF-L Button	AE/AF Lock
f6	**Customize Command Dials**	
	Reverse Rotation	No
	Change Main / Sub	Off
	Aperture Setting	Sub-Command dial
	Menus and Playback	Off
f7	Release Button to Use Dial	No
f8	Slot Empty Release Lock	Enable Release
f9	Reverse Indicators	✚◀ıⅼıⅼıⅼ⁰ıⅼıⅼıⅼ▶➖
f10	Assign MB-D11 AE-L/AF-L button	AE/AF Lock

AUTOFOCUS (a)

a1: AF-C Priority Selection: Controls whether an exposure is made whenever the shutter release is pressed (release priority) or only when focus has been attained (focus priority), in Continuous-Servo AF mode. The options are as follows:

- ○ **[Release]** (default): Exposure can be made whenever the camera is in Continuous-Servo AF mode and the shutter release is pressed.
- ○ **[Focus]**: The shutter can only be released in Continuous-Servo AF mode once focus has been attained, although focus does not lock in this autofocus mode.

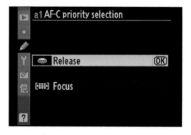

a2: AF-S Priority Selection: Controls whether an exposure can be made only when focus has been attained (focus priority), or whenever the shutter release is pressed (release priority) in Single-Servo AF mode. Regardless of the selected option, focus is always locked when the in-focus indicator ● is displayed in the viewfinder. The options are:

○ [Release]: Exposure can be made whenever the camera is in Single-Servo AF mode and the shutter release is pressed.

○ [Focus] (default): Exposure can be made in Single-Servo AF mode only when focus has been attained and the in-focus indicator ● is displayed in the viewfinder.

HINT: I recommend leaving CS-a1 and CS-a2 set to their default options, at least until you are familiar with the focusing system of the D7000.

a3: Focus Tracking with Lock-On: This item determines how the autofocus system adjusts to abrupt changes in the camera-to-subject distance. The options are:

○ [Normal] (default): The D7000 delays adjusting the focus point when the camera-to-subject distance changes suddenly; there are five options: 1 (Short), 2, 3 (Normal), 4, 5 (Long). The purpose is to keep the camera from refocusing inadvertently when an object passes briefly between the camera and the subject (Nikon provides no information on the duration of the three delay options).

○ [Off]: The camera readjusts focus immediately when the camera-to-subject distance changes suddenly.

a4: AF Point Illumination: To facilitate the identification of the active AF point, particularly in low-light situations, it can be set to be highlighted in red. The options are:

○ [Auto] (default): The selected AF point is highlighted in red if required, depending on the level of ambient illumination.

○ [On]: The selected AF point is always highlighted in red, regardless of the level of ambient illumination.

○ [Off]: The selected AF point is never highlighted.

a5: Focus Point Wrap-Around: This item controls how the selection of an autofocus sensing area is performed. The options are as follows:

O **[Wrap]:** This allows the selection of AF points to "wrap around" from top to bottom, bottom to top, left to right, and right to left. If the point reaches the left-hand edge of the AF area and you continue to press ◄, the point will jump to the right hand side and keep moving left from there.

O **[No Wrap]** (default): The AF point selection cannot "wrap" from one side of the AF area to the other, for example, pressing ► has no effect if the selected AF point is at the right-hand edge of the AF area marked on the viewfinder screen.

a6: Number of Focus Points: You can set the number of AF points the D7000 will use when selection of the AF point is performed manually. The options are:

O **[AF39]** (default): The camera uses all 39 AF points of its autofocus system.

O **[AF11]:** The camera uses just 11 AF points.

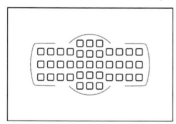

^ 39 AF points

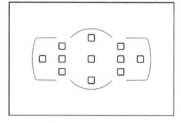

^ 11 AF points

a7: Built-In AF-Assist Illuminator: The D7000 has a built-in lamp that activates to assist autofocus operation in low-light shooting situations. This item determines whether the lamp operates or not. The options are as follows:

O **[On]** (default): The built-in lamp activates to assist autofocus operation in low-light shooting situations.

O **[Off]:** The lamp does not light, regardless of the level of ambient illumination.

a8: Live View / Movie AF: The D7000 offers a number of different focusing options when operated in its Live View and D-Movie modes (see pages 110-111 for full details).

- O To select the autofocus mode, choose from: **[Single-servo AF]** or **[Full-time-servo AF]**.
- O To select the AF-Area mode, choose from: **[Face-priority AF] [Wide-area AF] [Normal-area AF]** or **[Subject tracking AF]**.

METERING / EXPOSURE (b)

b1: ISO Sensitivity Step Value: Use this item to select the size of the step when adjusting ISO sensitivity. The options are as follows:

- O **[1/3 step]**: (default) 0.3 EV
- O **[1/2 step]**: 0.5 EV

b2: EV Steps for Exposure Control: Use this item to select the size of the step when adjusting shutter speed, lens aperture, and exposure bracketing. The options are:

- O **[1/3 step]** (default): Shutter speed and aperture change in steps of 0.3 EV.
- O **[1/2 step]**: Shutter speed and aperture change in steps of 1/2 EV.

HINT: I recommend using the 0.3-step option for CS-b1 and CS-b2 to provide the finest degree of exposure control.

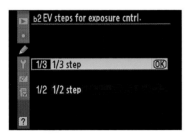

b3: Easy Exposure Compensation: This item controls whether or not the ⊠ button is required for setting an Exposure Compensation value. This item does not operate in Manual exposure mode. The options are:

- ○ **[On (Auto Reset)]**: Rotate the Main Command dial to set Exposure Compensation (see table below). Compensation set using the Command dial is reset when the camera or exposure meter is turned off (any compensation set via the ⊠ button is not reset).
- ○ **[On]**: Same as **[On (Auto Reset)]** (see above), except when the camera or the exposure meter is turned off, the Exposure Compensation is not reset.
- ○ **[Off]** (default): Set Exposure Compensation by pressing the ⊠ button and rotating the Main Command dial.

The choice of Command dial will depend on the exposure mode and which option is selected at CS-f6: **[Customize command dials]** > **[Change main/sub]**. The variations are as follows:

CS-F6 [Customize command dials] > [Change main/sub]		
Exposure Mode	**Off**	**On**
P	Sub-command dial	Sub-command dial
S	Sub-command dial	Main-command dial
A	Main-command dial	Sub-command dial
M	N/A	

b4: Center-Weighted Area: In Center-Weighted exposure metering, the D7000 assigns approximately 75% of the metering influence to a circular area in the center of the frame. This option allows you to select the diameter of the circular metering area, or have the camera average the exposure reading across the entire frame area. The options are:

- ○ **[6mm]**
- ○ **[8mm]** (default)
- ○ **[10mm]**
- ○ **[13mm]**
- ○ **[Average]**

b5: Fine-Tune Optimal Exposure: This option enables you to fine-tune exposure measurement; it can be set independently for each metering pattern over a range of +/-1 EV in steps of 0.15 (1/6) EV. Highlight **[CS-b5]** and press ▶ to display the options **[No]** and **[Yes]**.

- ○ **[No]**: Use this option to exit the item without adjusting exposure.
- ○ **[Yes]**: Highlight **[Yes]** and press ▶ to open a submenu that displays the three metering methods: Matrix, Center-Weighted, and Spot. Highlight the required metering pattern and press ▶ to open the next menu page that displays the exposure adjustment value. Use ▲ or ▼ to select an adjustment level and press ⑳ to save the setting.

HINT: I recommend you avoid this item if you use Matrix metering, as it will adjust exposure by unknown amounts based on each and every subject or scene that it meters from. However, if you use the Spot meter function to take a meter reading from a known test target, this item is useful to ensure the meter reading suggested by the camera matches the reflectivity of the test target. For example, if you use an 18% gray card as a test target, you will probably want to set a fine-tune value of +0.3 to +0.5 EV, due to the way the camera meter is calibrated. The key to using this option successfully is to test your own equipment with care and precision, and only make an adjustment when you are satisfied it is required.

TIMERS / AE LOCK (c)

c1: Shutter-Release Button AE-L: This option determines how the exposure value can be locked. Your options are:

- ○ **[Off]** (default): Exposure is only locked by pressing the ᴬᴱ⁻ᴸ/ᴬꜰ⁻ᴸ button.
- ○ **[On]**: Exposure can be locked by either pressing the ᴬᴱ⁻ᴸ/ᴬꜰ⁻ᴸ button or pressing the shutter release button down halfway.

c2: Auto Meter-Off Delay: This item determines how long the camera exposure meter remains active when no other camera operation is performed. The options are:

- ○ **[4s]**
- ○ **[6s]** (default)
- ○ **[8s]**

O [16s]

O [30s]

O [1 min]

O [5 min]

O [10 min]

O [30 min]

O [No Limit]

> The [Auto meter-off delay] item offers a wide range of display durations.

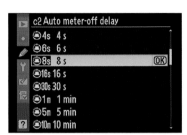

HINT: To prevent undue drain on the battery, I recommend using either the default setting or the 8 second option, as these provide a good compromise between having sufficient time to read and assess the meter reading, and conserving battery power.

c3: Self-Timer: This item controls the duration of the shutter release delay, the number of shots, and the interval between them in Self-Timer mode. The options are:

O **[Self-timer delay]:** Offers durations of 2s, 5s, 10s (default), or 20s.

O **[Number of shots]:** Use ▲ or ▼ to select a number between 1 and 9 (default is 0).

O **[Interval between shots]:** Offers durations of 0.5s (default), 1s, 2s, or 3s, when **[Number of shots]** is set to more than 1.

> The Self-Timer allows a number of pictures to be taken in a sequence with a variable delay.

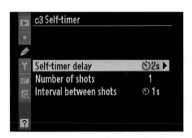

c4: **Monitor-Off Delay:** This option determines how long the LCD monitor on the back of the camera remains on if no other camera operation is performed in the following modes: [Playback], [Menus], [Information display], [Image review], or [Live View]. Select any of those five items, and you will see the following options:

- O [4s] (default for [Image review]): 4 seconds
- O [10s] (default for [Playback] and [Information display]): 10 seconds
- O [20s] (default for [Menus]): 20 seconds
- O [1 min]: 1 minute
- O [5 min]: 5 minutes
- O [10 min] (default for [Live View]): 10 minutes

HINT: Use the shortest convenient duration to prevent undue drain on the battery power.

---

c5: **Remote-On Duration:** This item determines how long the camera remains in standby in Remote release mode. If no camera operation is performed within the selected period, remote shooting will end, and the exposure meter turns off. To reactivate Remote mode, press the shutter-release down halfway. The options are: [1 min] (default), [5 min], [10 min], or [15 min].

SHOOTING / DISPLAY (d)

d1: **Beep:** Controls the pitch of the audible warning that sounds when the following occur: the Self-Timer function is counting down, the camera attains focus in S (Single-Servo) autofocus with [Focus] selected at CS-a2 [AF-S priority selection], when focus locks in Live View, when the release timer is counting down in Self-Timer and delayed release modes, when a photograph is taken in Quick-Response Remote or Mᴜᴘ Mirror-Up mode, or when the card is locked and you attempt to take a picture. The beep will not sound during video recording, if [Q] Quiet Shutter Release is selected, or if [Release] is selected at CS-a2. The options are:

- O [Volume]: Off (default), 1 (low), 2 (medium), or 3 (high)
- O [Pitch]: Choose high (default), or low

d2: Viewfinder Grid Display: A pattern of gridlines can be displayed in the viewfinder to aid in composition. The options are:

○ **[On]**
○ **[Off]** (default)

HINT: This is a very useful feature for any photography that requires precise alignment of elements in the picture, such as a horizon, surface of water, or buildings. I keep this item in **[My menu]**, so that it can be accessed quickly.

---

d3: ISO Display and Adjustment: This item determines how the camera will display the number of exposures remaining, or the ISO sensitivity. The options are:

○ **[Show ISO sensitivity]**: The ISO value is shown in place of the number of exposures remaining in the viewfinder and control panel.
○ **[Show ISO/Easy ISO]**: The ISO value is shown in place of the number of exposures remaining in the viewfinder and control panel, plus ISO value can be set in the **P** and **S** modes by rotating the Sub-Command dial, or in **A** mode by rotating the Main Command dial.
○ **[Show frame count]** (default): The number of exposures remaining in the viewfinder and control panel.

d4: Viewfinder Warning Display: At the default setting of **[On]**, the camera will display a warning in the viewfinder to indicate the following: a low battery, Monochrome Picture Control is selected, or no memory card is inserted in the camera: The options are:

○ **[On]** (default)
○ **[Off]**

d5: Screen Tips: At the default setting of **[On]**, the camera will display tips on items selected in the Information Display. The options are:

○ **[On]** (default)
○ **[Off]**

d6: CL Mode Shooting Speed: This item determines the frame rate of the camera when the release mode is set to Continuous-Low (CL) shooting. The options are as follows:

- O **[1]:** 1 frame per second (fps)
- O **[2]:** 2 fps
- O **[3]** (default): 3 fps
- O **[4]:** 4 fps
- O **[5]:** 5 fps

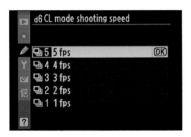

HINT: I rarely use the CL shooting mode, as I prefer to have the camera shoot at its fastest rate when necessary, or control shooting by taking individual frames in rapid succession in Continuous-High (CH) shooting mode. Your own specific shooting requirements will determine the choice you make for this item. If you expect to shoot a moving subject using autofocus, it can be beneficial to select 5 fps, as this will give the camera a little more time to process data compared with using the fastest frame rate.

d7: Maximum Continuous Release: Determines the maximum number of pictures that can be shot in a single sequence (burst). Your options are any numbers between 1 and 100 (default).

d8: File Number Sequence: Controls whether file numbering continues in a consecutive sequence from the last number used or is reset when a memory card is formatted, a new folder is created, or a new memory card is inserted. The options are:

○ **[On]** (default): Whenever a memory card is formatted or a new memory card is inserted in the camera, file numbering continues consecutively from the last number used or from the largest number in the current folder, whichever is higher. If the current folder contains a photograph numbered 9999, a new folder will be created automatically, and numbering is reset to 0001.

○ **[Off]**: File numbering is reset to 0001 whenever a memory card is formatted, a new folder is created, or a new memory card is inserted in the camera.

○ **[Reset]**: The same as for **[On]**, except that the file number for the next exposure is assigned by adding one to the largest file number in the current folder, so if the folder is empty, the file number is reset to 0001.

HINT: If you expect to shoot pictures using more than one memory card, I strongly suggest that you use the **[On]** option; otherwise, which could become very confusing once images are saved to your computer.

---

d9: Information Display: Determines the nature of the shooting info display that is shown when the ▣ button is pressed. The options are:

○ **[Auto]**: (default) The display will change automatically from black on white to white on black to maintain best contrast with the background.

○ **[Manual]**: Select **[B]** (black) for dark characters on a light background, or **[W]** for white characters on a dark background; the monitor brightness adjusts automatically for maximum contrast.

HINT: Very much a personal preference, I have found the manual **[W]** setting useful when shooting in low-light, as the monitor screen emits far less light compared with the **[B]** option and is thus less distracting. Conversely, the **[B]** setting is probably easier to read in bright conditions.

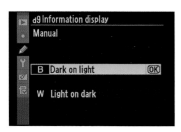
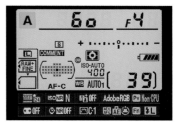

^ The nature of the Information Display can be adjusted to suit the shooting conditions; dark on light (shown above) works well in brighter ambient light.

d10: LCD Illumination: Controls operation of the backlight in the LCD display of the control panel. The options are:

- **[On]:** The backlight remains on while the exposure meter is active.
- **[Off]** (default): The illumination is only on when the power switch is rotated past the ON position (to ☼) and released.

d11: Exposure Delay Mode: This item enables the camera to delay the release of the shutter by approximately one second after the shutter release button is pressed and the reflex mirror has been raised. Its purpose is to help reduce the risk of camera vibration, which might affect the sharpness of a picture. This only has two options:

- **[On]**
- **[Off]** (default)

> **HINT:** Since the camera has a proper Mirror Lock-Up facility that can be used in conjunction with a remote shutter release, I see little value in using this item for still pictures, unless you do not have the optional MC-DC2 or ML-L3 remote release accessory.

d13: Flash Warning: This item controls the display of the ⚡ Flash-Ready indicator, which will blink in the viewfinder if the D7000 determines that the flash is required to produce a proper exposure. This only has two options:

- O **[On]** (default)
- O **[Off]**

d13: MB-D11 Battery Type: To ensure efficient and proper operation of the MB-D11 battery pack when fitted with AA / LR6 size batteries, use this item to select the type of battery inserted in the MS-D11 battery holder. The options are:

- O **[LR6]**: Alkaline
- O **[HR6]**: NiMH
- O **[FR6]**: Lithium

HINT: Although I would suggest that use of AA batteries in the MB-D11 battery pack should only be considered as an emergency measure, if you have to resort to using such batteries, ensure the correct type is selected here at CS-d13.

d14: Battery Order: Use this item to select the order in which the batteries are used when the camera is fitted with the MB-D11 battery pack. The options are as follows:

- O ▨▨◨▥▥▥ (default): The battery or batteries in the MB-D11 will be used first; the type of battery inserted in the MB-D11 is displayed in the Information Display.
- O ▨▨◨▥▥▥: The EN-EL15 battery in the camera is used first.

HINT: Access to the battery or batteries in the MB-D11 is far easier when it is attached to the camera, making it easier to replace them, so I recommend the default setting.

BRACKETING / FLASH (e)

e1: Flash Sync Speed: Use this item to select the flash synchronization speed. Your options include shutter speeds between **[1/250s – 1/60s]**, plus:

O **[1/250s (Auto FP)]** (default)

O **[1/320s (Auto FP)]**

NOTE: 1/250s (Auto FP) and 1/320s (Auto FP) options are only supported when using an external Speedlight compatible with the Nikon Creative Lighting System; currently, this includes the SB-900, SB-800, SB-700, SB-600, and SB-R200.

---

e2: Flash Shutter Speed: Use this item to select the slowest flash synchronization speed in **A** (Aperture-Priority) and **P** (Programmed-Auto) exposure modes when using Front- or Rear-Curtain sync, or Red-Eye Reduction. You can choose from shutter speeds between 1/60 second (default) and 30 seconds.

HINT: I recommend using a shutter speed at which you are confident you can hold the camera steady, otherwise there is a risk that any part of the picture illuminated by ambient light will not be sharp due to the effects of camera shake. For most practical purposes with a short focal length lens (i.e., < 35mm) this will be around 1/30 to 1/15 second. At longer shutter speeds, use a tripod or some other form of camera support.

---

e3: Flash Control for Built-In Flash: Use this item to select the flash mode for the built-in Speedlight of the D7000.The options are:

O TTL⚡ **[TTL]** (default): The camera uses its 2016-segment RGB sensor (the same sensor used for Matrix metering) to control flash output automatically; it performs i-TTL balanced fill-flash (monitor pre-flashes are used), and distance information is included if you're using a D- or G-type lens. Standard TTL flash is used if the camera is set to Spot metering.

O M⚡ **[Manual]**: The flash can be set to deliver a specific amount of light, between its maximum output and 1/128 of its maximum output.

O RPT⚡ **[Repeating flash]**: The flash can be set to emit a sequence of outputs during a single exposure to produce a strobe-light effect. This item has three options:

  ● **[Output]**: Similar to Manual flash, the output of the flash is set to a specific level between 1/4 and 1/128 power.

  ● **[Times]**: Choose the number of times the flash fires (this is dependent on the shutter speed used and frequency for flash outputs).

  ● **[Frequency]**: Used to set the frequency of flash outputs.

> The ability to use the built-in Speedlight to control a compatible remote external flash (such as the SB-700) wirelessly expands the creative possibilities for lighting your subject.

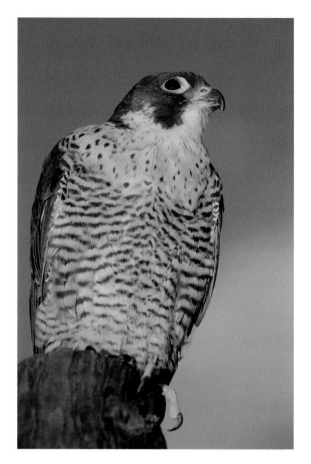

o CMD⚡ [Commander mode]: This item allows you to use the built-in Speedlight as a master / commander flash to control one or more remote Speedlights in up to two separate groups. All Speedlights must be compatible with the Advanced Wireless Lighting system (at the time of writing, the only external Speedlights that support this are the SB-900, SB-800, SB-700, SB-600, and SB-R200).

HINT: The options available within this item provide a variety of ways for using the built-in Speedlight. See pages 284-290, for a full explanation of the flash modes available here.

The options for each of the items in CS-e3 are explained in the chart below.

OPTION	DESCRIPTION
Built-in flash	Choose a flash mode for the built-in flash (commander flash).
TTL	This is i-TTL mode. Choose Flash Exposure Compensation from values between +3.0 and -3.0 EV in increments of 0.3 EV.
M	Choose the flash level from values between 1/1 and 1/128 (of full power).
– –	The built-in flash will not fire, although remote flash units do. The built-in flash must be raised so that it can emit monitor pre-flashes.
Group A	Choose a flash mode for all flash units in group A.
TTL	This is i-TTL mode. Choose Flash Exposure Compensation from values between +3.0 and -3.0 EV in increments of 0.3 EV.
AA	Auto Aperture (available only with SB-900 and SB-800 flash units). Choose Flash Exposure Compensation from values between +3.0 and -3.0 EV in increments of 0.3 EV.
M	Choose the flash level from values between 1/1 and 1/128 (of full power).
– –	The flash units in this group will not fire.
Group B	Choose a flash mode for all flash units in group B. The options available are the same as those listed for Group A, above.
TTL	This is i-TTL mode. Choose Flash Exposure Compensation from values between +3.0 and -3.0 EV in increments of 0.3 EV.
AA	Auto Aperture (available only with SB-900 and SB-800 flash units). Choose Flash Exposure Compensation from values between +3.0 and -3.0 EV in increments of 0.3 EV.
M	Choose the flash level from values between 1/1 and 1/128 (of full power).
– –	The flash units in this group will not fire.
Channel	Choose from channels 1–4. All flash units in both groups must be set to the same channel.

NOTE: If the SB-400 Speedlight is attached to the D7000 and turned on, CS-e3 changes to [Optional flash], which allows the flash control mode for the SB-400 to be set to [TTL] or [Manual]; the [Repeating flash] and [Commander mode] options are not available.

e4: Modeling Flash: Pressing the (Depth-of-Field) Preview button will cause either the built-in flash or an external flash unit (currently the SB-900, SB-800, SB-700, SB-600, or SB-R200) to emit a very rapid series of low-intensity light pulses that act as a modeling light, so you can assess the effect of the flash illumination. The options are:

- O **[On]** (default): The modeling light function operates when the Preview button is pressed.
- O **[Off]**: No light will be emitted.

HINT: Due to low intensity, and brevity of the light pulses emitted by this feature, it is only really useful at short flash shooting distances. However, if you take an external Speedlight off the camera using a dedicated TTL flash cord, such as the SC-28, it can be helpful in assessing the position and nature of shadows cast by the flash.

---

e5: Auto Bracketing Set: This item allows you to decide which features are affected when the Auto Bracketing feature is used. Choose from the following:

- O **[AE & Flash]** (default): The camera brackets the exposure for both ambient light and flash output.
- O **[AE only]**: The camera only brackets the ambient light exposure.
- O **[Flash only]**: The camera only brackets the flash output level.
- O **[WB bracketing]**: The camera brackets the White Balance value when recording pictures in the JPEG format (this feature is not available for the NEF or NEF + JPEG options).
- O **[ADL bracketing]**: The camera brackets exposures using the Active D-Lighting controls.

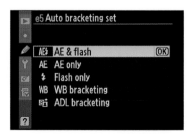

e6: Bracketing Order: This item allows you to select the order in which the camera makes exposures in a bracketing sequence. The options are as follows:

- O **[MTR>Under>Over]** (default): The metered exposure is followed by any underexposed frames, and then the overexposed frames.
- O **[Under>MTR>Over]**: Underexposed frames are taken first, followed by the metered, and then the overexposed frames.

CONTROLS (f)

f1: Switch: This item selects what happens when the collar of the power switch is rotated to the ☀ position. The options are:

- O ☀ **[LCD backlight]** (default): The control panel backlight illuminates for six seconds.
- O ☀🈔 **[☀ and information display]**: The control panel backlight illuminates, and the Information Display opens in the monitor.

f2: OK Button (Shooting Mode): Pressing the center button of the Multi Selector can be used to select a variety of camera operations. Your options in the Shooting mode are:

- O **[Select center AF point]** (default): Pressing the center button of the Multi Selector selects the center AF point.
- O **[Highlight active AF point]**: Pressing the center button of the Multi Selector illuminates the active AF point.
- O **[Not used]**: Pressing the center button of the Multi Selector button has no effect when the camera is in the Shooting mode.

f3: Assign Fn Function Button: The **Fn** button, located on the front of the camera below the shutter release button can be assigned a variety of functions. The options available are as follows:

○ **[Preview]:** Pressing the **Fn** button activates Depth-of-Field Preview.

○ 🔒 **[FV lock]** (default): Pressing the **Fn** button once will activate Flash Value Lock; pressing it again will cancel it (this applies only to the built-in flash and the SB-900, SB-800, SB-700, SB-600, SB-400, and SB-R200 Speedlights).

○ 🔒 **[AE/AF lock]:** Press the **Fn** button to lock autoexposure and autofocus.

○ 🔒 **[AE lock only]:** Press the **Fn** button to lock autoexposure only.

○ 🔒 **[AE lock (hold)]:** Same as **[AE lock only]**, except that AE Lock is active once the button has been pressed and released until the camera or light meter is turned off, or you press the **Fn** button a second time.

○ 🔒 **[AF lock only]:** Press the **Fn** button to lock autofocus.

○ 🔒 **[Flash off]:** Press and hold the **Fn** button to take a photo without flash while a flash is activated.

○ **BKT [Bracketing burst]:** Press the **Fn** button while the camera is set to either **S** Single-Frame or **Q** Quiet Shutter Release mode to have all shots in the currently set bracketing sequence fire each time you press the shutter release. If a White Balance Bracketing sequence is set or the release mode is set to **CH** Continuous High or **CL** Continuous Low, the camera will repeat the bracketing burst as long as you hold down the shutter release button. In this latter scenario, if the release mode is set to **S** Single-Frame rather than a Continuous mode, the frame rate will default to that of **CH** Continuous High.

○ 🔲**[Active D-Lighting]:** Press the **Fn** button and rotate the Main Command dial to choose Active D-Lighting.

○ +RAW **[+NEF (RAW)]:** Press the **Fn** button to record an NEF image file in addition to a JPEG (if the camera is set to record JPEG). This function will be deactivated once you release the shutter release button, so if you want to continue recording an NEF with each JPEG using this feature, do not completely let go of the shutter release button; rather, keep it halfway depressed between shots. To cancel **[+NEF (RAW)]** before having taken any frames, simply press the **Fn** button a second time.

○ ⬛ **[Matrix metering]:** Press the **Fn** button to quickly activate Matrix metering, which will remain active as long as the **Fn** button is held down.

○ ⬛ **[Center-weighted metering]:** Press the **Fn** button to quickly activate Center-Weighted metering, which will remain active as long as the **Fn** button is held down.

- ⊡ **[Spot metering]**: Press the **Fn** button to quickly activate Spot metering, which will remain active as long as the **Fn** button is held down.

- ⊞ **[Framing grid]**: Press the **Fn** button and rotate the Main Command dial to turn the viewfinder-framing grid on or off.

- **[Viewfinder virtual horizon]**: Press the **Fn** button to show or hide the Virtual Horizon indicator in the viewfinder.

- ⬚ **[Access top item in My menu]**: Press the **Fn** button for quick access to the top item listed under My Menu.

- **[1 step/spd aperture]**: Pressing the **Fn** button while rotating the Command dials to change shutter speed (**S** and **M** modes) and aperture (**A** and **M** modes) will cause both to change in increments of 1.0 EV, regardless of the step value set at CS-b2 **[EV steps for exposure control]**.

- non-CPU **[Choose non-CPU lens number]**: Press the **Fn** button and rotate a Command dial to choose among non-CPU lenses already programmed via **[Non-CPU lens data]** in the Setup menu.

- **[Playback]**: Press the **Fn** button to enter the Playback mode.

- REC **[Start recording movie]**

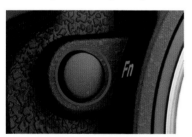

< The **Fn** button is located on the front of the camera next to the lens mount, below the shutter release button.

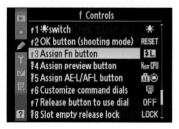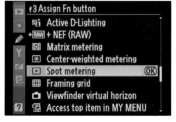

∧ **[Spot metering]** is one of the many different roles that can be assigned to the **Fn** button.

HINT: What you choose for this item will be a matter of personal preference based on the specific shooting situation. When using flash, the FV Lock is useful, and when shooting in ambient light, I find the ability to select Spot metering at the press of this button (instead of the Matrix metering I normally use) very useful.

f4: Assign Preview Button: The Preview button, located on the front of the camera below the **Fn** button, can be assigned a variety of functions. The options are the same as for the [Assign **Fn** button] except that the default is [Preview].

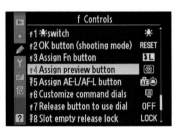
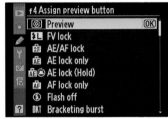

⌃ [Preview] is the default setting for CS-f4.

f5: Assign ▓ Button: The ▓ button, located on the rear of the camera beside the viewfinder eyepiece, can also be assigned a variety of functions. The options are as follows:

o ▓ **[AE/AF lock]:** Press the ▓ button to lock autoexposure and autofocus.

o ▓ **[AE lock only]:** Press the ▓ button to lock autoexposure only.

o ▓ **[AF lock only]:** Press the ▓ button to lock autofocus only.

o ▓ **[AE lock (hold)]:** Same as [AE lock only], except that AE Lock is active once the button has been pressed and released, until the camera or light meter is turned off or you press the ▓ button a second time.

o ▓ **[AF-ON]:** Press the ▓ button to activate autofocus; the shutter release button cannot be used to initiate autofocus.

o ▓ **[FV lock]:** Pressing the ▓ button once will activate Flash Value Lock; pressing it again will cancel it (this applies only to the built-in flash and the SB-900, SB-800, SB-700, SB-600, SB-400, and SB-R200 Speedlights).

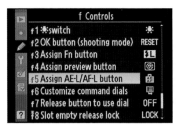
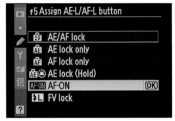

∧ **AF-ON** is one of several roles that can be assigned to the AE-L/AF-L button.

f6: Customize Command Dials: This item provides additional functionality to the Main and Sub-Command dials. The options are:

○ **[Reverse rotation]**: Set **[No]** (default) to have the Command dials operate in the direction as described in this book. Set **[Yes]** if you wish to have the Command dials operate in the reverse direction.

○ **[Change main/sub]**: Set **[Off]** (default) to have the Main Command dial control the shutter speed and the Sub-Command dial the aperture. Set **[On]** to reverse this selection, or **[On (Mode A)]** to use the Main Command dial to select the aperture in **A** exposure mode (settings apply to Command dials of the MB-D11 as well).

○ **[Aperture setting]**: Use this item to select a method of changing aperture.

● **[Sub-command dial]** (default): The aperture can only be adjusted using the Sub-Command dial (or Main Command dial if **[On]** is selected at **[Change main/sub]**).

● **[Aperture ring]**: The aperture can only be adjusted using the lens aperture ring, and the camera aperture display will show aperture increments of 1.0 EV. (Aperture for G-type Nikkor lenses, which do not feature aperture rings, is still set via the Sub-Command dial.) Live View is not available when **[Aperture ring]** is selected and a CPU lens with an aperture ring is mounted on the camera. Regardless of the option chosen, the aperture ring must be used to adjust aperture when a non-CPU lens is used.

○ **[Menus and playback]**: Set **[Off]** (default) to use the Multi Selector to select an image for display, highlight thumbnails, and navigate through menus. Set **[On]** or **[On (image review excluded)]** to have the Main Command dial perform the same function as pressing the Multi Selector to the left or right, and have the Sub-Command dial perform the same function as pressing the Multi Selector up or down. Select **[On (image review excluded)]** to prevent the Command dials from being used for Playback during Image Review. When you're using the Command dials to navigate a menu, press ▶ or the ⊛ button to make a selection.

f9: Release Button to Use Dial: Normally, to make a range of adjustments to the D7000 requires a button to be pressed and held down while rotating a Command dial. This item allows you to make the same adjustment by pressing and releasing the appropriate button and then rotating the appropriate Command dial. The options are:

- O **[No]** (default): Make adjustments to settings by pressing and holding the appropriate button while rotating the appropriate Command dial.
- O **[Yes]**: Make adjustments to settings by pressing and releasing the appropriate button (, , , ISO, QUAL, WB, AF-mode, or BKT), and then rotating the appropriate Command dial (also applied to the Fn and Preview buttons when they have been assigned Active D-Lighting via CS-f3 and CS-f4, respectively). To end the setting, press the button again or press the shutter release halfway. Except when **[No limit]** is selected at CS-c2, the settings will end when the exposure meter turns off.

f8: Slot Empty Release Lock: This item allows the shutter to operate without a memory card being installed in the camera. The options for this item are:

- O **[Release locked]** (default): The shutter release is disabled if no memory card is installed in the camera.
- O **[Enable release]:** The shutter release operates if no memory card is installed in the camera. The camera stores no picture; however, the last recorded image is displayed on the monitor as a DEMO image

HINT: Potential disaster looms with this item unless it is set to the default—you do not want the camera to operate as though it is recording pictures when in fact there is no memory card installed.

f9: Reverse Indicators: At the default setting, the exposure indicator display shown in the control panel, viewfinder, and Information Display are shown with positive values to the left and negative values to the right. The display can be reversed using this item.

- O **[+ 0 -]** (default): Positive values are shown to the left and negative values to the right.
- O **[- 0 +]**: Reverses the exposure indicator display; positive values are shown to the right and negative values to the left.

f10: Assign MB-D11 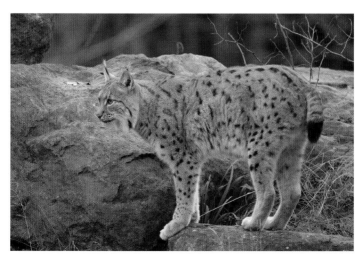AE-L/AF-L button: The AE-L/AF-L button, located on the rear of the optional MB-D11 battery pack, can be assigned a variety of functions. The options are as follows:

- ○ 🔲 **[AE/AF lock]** (default): Press the AE-L/AF-L button to lock autoexposure and autofocus.
- ○ 🔲 **[AE lock only]**: Press the AE-L/AF-L button to lock autoexposure only.
- ○ 🔲 **[AF lock only]**: Press the AE-L/AF-L button to lock autofocus only.
- ○ 🔲 **[AE lock (hold)]**: Same as **[AE lock only]**, except that AE Lock is active once the button has been pressed and released, until the camera or light meter is turned off or you press the AE-L/AF-L button a second time.
- ○ **AF-ON [AF-ON]**: Press the AE-L/AF-L button to activate autofocus; the shutter release button cannot be used to initiate autofocus.
- ○ 🔲 **[FV lock]**: Pressing the AE-L/AF-L button once will activate Flash Value Lock; pressing it again will cancel it (this applies only to the built-in flash and the SB-900, SB-800, SB-700, SB-600, SB-400, and SB-R200 Speedlights).
- ○ **Fn [Same as Fn button]**: Pressing the AE-L/AF-L button performs the same function as assigned to the Fn button under CS-f3.

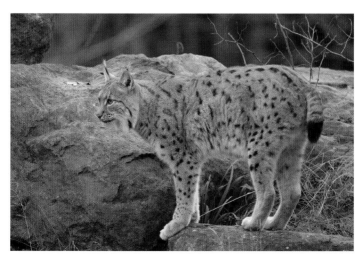

^ When photographing a subject that can move at any moment, it is often useful to assign the AE-L/AF-L button the AF-ON function, in combination with setting AF-C (Continuous-Servo AF) mode.

The Setup menu is used to establish the basic configuration of the camera; once the settings for most of the items in this menu are made, generally, they will not be changed very frequently.

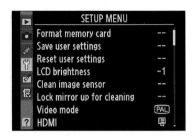

FORMAT MEMORY CARD

A new memory card should always be formatted when it is first placed into the D7000. It is also good practice to format any memory card whenever you insert it into the camera, even if the card has been formatted using a computer. This is particularly important if you use your memory cards between different camera bodies. Before you format any card, ensure that any image files stored on it have been saved to another storage device.

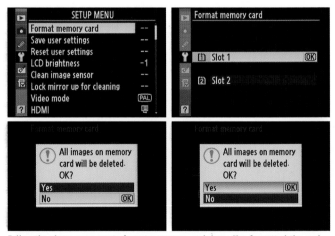

Follow the above sequence to format a memory card; here, I've formatted the card in Slot 1.

The most convenient way to format a card is to use the two-button method (see pages 146-148 for full details). However, the [Format] item in the Setup menu can also be used. Highlight [Format] and press ▶ and then select the appropriate card slot and press ▶ again. Highlight [Yes] and press ⊛ to begin the format process.

SAVE USER SETTINGS

This item allows you to save a number of settings that cover exposure and focusing, plus settings in the Shooting and Custom Settings menus and assign them as a group to the **U1** and **U2** positions of the Mode dial, allowing you to configure the camera for a specific shooting situation and recall those settings by rotating the Mode dial to the appropriate position. The following parameters can be stored by the D7000: Flexible Program (**P** mode), shutter speed (**S** and **M** modes), aperture (**A** and **M** modes), Exposure and Flash Compensation, flash mode, focus point, metering, AF and AF-Area modes (does not apply to Live View / D-Movie modes), Bracketing, and Shooting and Custom Settings menus (except Storage Folder, File Naming, Manage Picture Control, Multiple Exposure, and Interval Timer shooting).

1. Adjust settings as required for the parameters listed above.
2. Highlight [Save user settings] in the Setup menu and press ▶.
3. Highlight [U1] or [U2] and press ▶.
4. Highlight [Save settings] and press the ⊛ button to assign the settings to the current Mode dial position.
5. To recall the settings, simply rotate the Mode dial to the appropriate User Settings mode.

HINT: This item represents a quick and very efficient way to set up the D7000 for a specific type of subject or style of shooting—for example, you might configure **U1** with settings for sport / action photography, and **U2** with settings for portrait or flash photography.

RESET USER SETTINGS

This item allows you manage the User Settings by resetting all the parameters selected for **U1** and **U2** to their default settings.

1. Highlight **[Reset user settings]** in the Setup menu and press ▶.
2. Highlight **[U1]** or **[U2]** and press ▶.
3. Highlight **[Reset]** and press the ⊛ button.

LCD BRIGHTNESS

The brightness of the LCD monitor on the back of the camera is set to a default value. However, this can be adjusted to help improve the visibility of any displayed image or page of information. To adjust LCD brightness:

1. Highlight the **[LCD brightness]** item in the Setup menu and press ▶.
2. Adjust the brightness value up or down by pressing ▲ or ▼.
3. Press the ⊛ button to confirm the screen brightness value.

A negative value reduces screen brightness, while a positive value increases screen brightness. The screen displays a grayscale to help you judge the brightness effect on the full tonal range present in your images.

NOTE: I consider the default value for the screen brightness level to be too high, and for a more accurate assessment of images, I suggest setting screen brightness to -1.

CLEAN IMAGE SENSOR

This item is used to automatically clean the optical low-pass filter of the D7000 by vibrating it at high frequencies. It is effective in removing loose, dry particles that have settled on the filter surface, but will not remove smear marks caused by liquids or grease; these will require cleaning with an appropriate fluid and swabs (see pages 354-360 for full details on cleaning the OLPF).

LOCK UP MIRROR FOR CLEANING

This item is used for cleaning or inspecting the optical low-pass filter manually; it should not be confused with the Mirror Up (Mᴜᴘ) option available in the camera's release modes (see pages 101-102 for full details).

VIDEO MODE

Video mode allows you to select the type of signal used by any video equipment, such as a VCR or television, to which you may connect your camera. This should be set before connecting your camera to the device with the supplied EG-D2 A/V cord (see pages 340-341 for full details).

HDMI (HIGH DEFINITION MEDIA INTERFACE)

The D7000 has an HDMI (High Definition Media Interface) connector located under the larger rubber port door on the left side of the camera. It allows pictures to be played back on high definition televisions and monitors using a mini type-C HDMI cable. The HDMI [Output resolution] item in the Setup menu allows you to select one of five HDMI formats. Ensure you select the required format before connecting the camera to the HDMI device. The camera monitor will turn off automatically when an HDMI device is connected.

OPTION	DESCRIPTION
Auto	The D7000 selects the appropriate format automatically.
480p (progressive)	640 x 480 (progressive) format
576p (progressive)	720 x 576 (progressive) format
720p (progressive)	1280 x 720 (progressive) format
1080i (interlaced)	1920 x 1080 (interlaced) format

If [On] is selected for [HDMI] > [Device control] in the Setup menu when the camera is connected to a device that supports the HDMI-CEC, and both the camera and device are switched on, it is possible to use the remote control for the device in place of the Multi Selector button of the D7000 camera to perform Playback and Slide Show functions.

FLICKER REDUCTION

The frequency of AC power used with certain types of fluorescent light can cause flickering and / or banding patterns to appear in the Live View display or during video recording in D-Movie mode. Use this item to set a frequency to match that of the AC power supply.

TIME ZONE AND DATE

Time zone and date enables you to set and change the date and time recorded by the camera's internal clock, and also how it is displayed (see page 34 for full details).

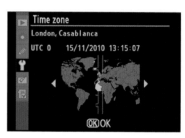

LANGUAGE

The [Language] item in the Setup menu of the D7000 allows you to select one of 24 languages for the camera to use when displaying menus and messages (see page 34 for full details).

IMAGE COMMENT

The [Image comment] feature of the Setup menu allows you to attach a short note or reference to an image file. Comments can be up to 36 characters long and may contain letters and / or numbers. Since the process requires each character to be input individually, this is not a feature you will use for each separate picture; however, as a way of assigning a general comment (e.g., the name of a location / venue / event) it is very useful. To attach an image comment:

1. Highlight the [Image comment] item in the Setup menu and press ▶.
2. Highlight [Input comment] from the listed options and press ▶.

3. To enter your comment, highlight the character you wish to input using the Multi Selector and press its center button to select it. If you accidentally enter the wrong character, use the ⊞ button in combination with the Multi Selector to move the cursor over the unwanted character and press the 🗑 button to erase it.

4. Press the ⓞ button to save the comment and return to the [Image comment] options list.

5. To actually attach the comment to your photographs, scroll down to the [Attach comment] option to highlight [Set] and press ▶. A small check mark will appear in the box to the left of the option.

6. Finally, highlight [Done] and press the ⓞ button to confirm the selection.

7. If you wish to exit this process at any time prior to Step 5 without attaching the comment, simply press the MENU button.

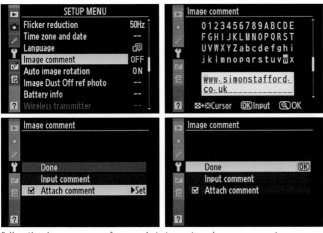

Follow the above sequence of screen shots to create and save a comment.

When the check mark is present in the [Attach Comment] option of the [Image comment] item, the saved comment will be attached to all subsequent images shot on the camera. To prevent the comment from being attached to subsequent images, simply return to the [Image comment] menu and uncheck the [Attach comment] box. The image comment will remain stored in the camera's memory and can be attached to future images by rechecking the [Attach comment] box. The comment will be displayed on the third page of the photo Information Display available via the single-image Playback option. It can also be viewed in Nikon View NX2 or Capture NX2 software.

AUTO IMAGE ROTATION

The D7000 automatically recognizes the orientation of the camera as it records an image (i.e., horizontal, vertical 90° clockwise, or vertical 90° counter-clockwise). At its default setting, the camera stores this information so the image can be automatically rotated during image Playback, or when viewing images on the computer with compatible software. If you do not want the camera to record the shooting orientation, the [Auto image rotation] feature can be switched off. The [Rotate tall] item must be turned on in the Playback menu for the image to be viewed on the camera's monitor in the orientation in which it was originally taken. To set [Auto image rotation]:

1. Highlight [Auto image rotation] in the Setup menu and press ▶.
2. Highlight [On] or [Off] as required.
3. Press ® to confirm the selection.

NOTE: If you shoot with the camera tilted up or down, it may not record its orientation correctly. In this case, it is probably easier to select off and rotate pictures in appropriate software such as Nikon View NX2 or Nikon Capture NX2.

IMAGE DUST OFF REF PHOTO

The [Image Dust Off ref photo] item in the Setup menu is designed specifically for use with the Image Dust Off function in Nikon Capture NX2 (version 2.2.6 or later is required for the D7000). The image file created by this function creates a mask that is overlaid electronically on an image file to enable the software to reduce or remove the effects of shadows that are cast by dust particles on the surface of the optical low-pass filter. To obtain a reference image for the Image Dust Off function you must use a CPU-type lens, preferably with a focal length of 50mm or more. To use [Image Dust Off ref photo]:

1. Highlight [Image Dust Off ref photo] in the Setup menu and press ▶.
2. [Start] will be displayed and highlighted on the monitor. Press ▶ to begin the process. A message instructing you to take a picture of a bright, featureless white object 10 cm (3.9 inches) from the lens will be displayed on the monitor.

3. Frame the target accordingly, and press the shutter release button down all the way (focus will be set automatically to infinity).

Once you have recorded the Image Dust Off reference photograph, it can be displayed on the camera; it can be identified by its file extension, which is NDF. These files cannot be viewed using a computer.

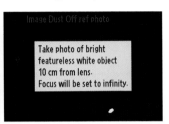

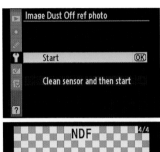

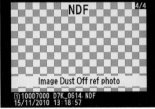

Follow the above sequence to create an [Image Dust Off ref photo].

> A warning is displayed if the camera cannot record a reference image.

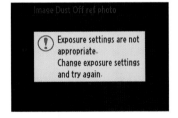

BATTERY INFO

The EN-EL15 rechargeable battery has an electronic chip in its circuitry that allows the D7000 to report detailed information regarding the status of the battery. To access this information, select [Battery info] from the Setup menu and press ▶; parameters concerning the battery will be displayed on the monitor. If the MB-D11 battery pack is fitted to the D7000, the [Battery info] display will show information for each battery separately (see page 39 for full details).

WIRELESS TRANSMITTER

Using the optional Nikon WT-4 / WT-4a wireless transmitter, it is possible to transfer or print photographs over wireless or Ethernet networks. Furthermore, the D700 can be controlled from a network computer(s) running Nikon Camera Control Pro 2 with Nikon View NX2 software (see pages 330-331 for full details).

COPYRIGHT INFORMATION

The [Copyright information] item works in the same way as the [Image comment] item except it has different titles for the text fields. It allows the name of the photographer to be entered under the [Artist] option and the name of the copyright holder to be entered under the [Copyright] option. The [Artist] option permits a maximum of 36 characters to be used, while the [Copyright] option can have up to 54 characters.

As with the [Image comment] item, ensure that a check mark appears in the check box for [Attach copyright information] by highlighting it and pressing ▶; then, highlight [Done] and press ⊛ to complete the process. Copyright Information is displayed on the fourth page of the photo information pages in single-image Playback, or can be viewed in Nikon View NX2 or Capture NX2 software; however, it is important to understand that the information recorded with this feature is not saved in standard XMP / IPTC format, but a proprietary Nikon format.

SAVE / LOAD SETTINGS

It is possible to save most menu settings to the memory card installed in Slot 1 of the D7000 using the [Save/load settings] item in the Setup menu. These settings can then be restored to the same camera subsequently, or to another D7000 by using the [Load settings] option. Saved settings are stored in a file named NCSETUP7; if the file name is changed, the D7000 will not be able to load the settings. The following settings can be saved to a memory card:

MENU	OPTION
Playback menu	Display Mode
	Image Review
	After Delete
	Rotate Tall
Shooting menu	File Naming
	Role Played by Card in Slot 2
	Image Quality
	Image Size
	JPEG Compression
	NEF (RAW) Recording
	White Balance with Fine-Tuning & Presets
	Set Picture Control
	Auto Distortion Control
	Color Space
	Active D-Lighting
	Long Exp. NR
	High ISO NR
	ISO Sensitivity
	Movie Settings
	Remote Control mode
Custom settings	All Custom Settings except Reset
Setup menu	Clean Image Sensor
	Video Mode
	HDMI
	Flicker Reduction
	Time Zone & Date (except Date and Time)
	Language
	Image Comment
	Auto Image Rotation
	Copyright Information
	GPS
	Non-CPU Lens Data
My Menu / Recent Settings	All My Menu items
	All Recent Settings
	Choose Tab

Using the dedicated Nikon GP-1 GPS unit connected to the accessory terminal of the D7000, it is possible for the camera to record GPS information when a picture is taken.

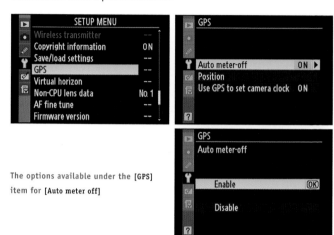

The options available under the [GPS] item for [Auto meter off]

As soon as the camera confirms communication with the connected GPS device, GPS will be displayed in the Information Display; if the GPS icon is shown blinking, it means the GP-1 is still searching for a GPS signal and any picture taken will not include GPS data. If the GPS icon is not displayed, it means the camera has received no new GPS data from the GP-1 for at least 2 seconds, and again, no GPS data will be recorded if a picture is taken. The information recorded when an exposure is made with the GPS icon displayed includes current latitude, longitude, altitude, time, and heading (see note below). The time provided by the GPS device uses the Universal Time Coordinated (UTC) and is independent of the camera's internal clock. To view GPS data, open an image in single-image Playback, and then use the Multi Selector button to scroll through the photo information pages until the GPS Data page is displayed. The [GPS] item in the Setup menu has two options:

O [Auto meter off]: Allows you to choose whether or not the exposure meters will turn off automatically when a GPS unit is attached. Highlight [Auto meter off] and press ▶ to display the two sub-options:

- **[Enable]** (default): If no camera operation is performed for the period selected at **[Auto off timers]** in the Setup menu, the exposure meter will turn off automatically. While this reduces drain on the camera's battery, it may prevent GPS data from being recorded, because if the camera's meter is turned off, the GPS device may also switch off or go into a standby mode. If the shutter release is then pressed all the way down without pausing to record an exposure, there may be insufficient time for the GPS device to reactivate.

- **[Disable]**: The camera's exposure meter will not turn off automatically while the GP-1 GPS device is connected; GPS data will always be recorded, as the GP-1 device also remains active.

O **[Position]**: Only available if a GP-1 device is connected and GPS communication is confirmed; if not, the **[Position]** item is grayed out in the menu. When communication is established with the GP-1, the camera displays current latitude, longitude, altitude, and date / time (UTC code).

O **[Use GPS to set camera clock]**: Select **[Yes]** to synchronize the camera clock with the UTC time code reported by the GP-1 GPS device.

VIRTUAL HORIZON

The **[Virtual horizon]** item enables a display that shows the orientation of the camera relative to a virtual horizon. It only operates along one plane, but can be useful in situations where it is important to ensure the camera is level to a natural horizon or some other feature in the scene being photographed. It is not as effective, however, as a small bubble (spirit) level attached to the camera's accessory shoe. When the camera's built-in orientation sensor determines the camera is level, the Virtual Horizon line and the arrowhead above the camera icon in the display will change from yellow to green.

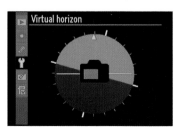

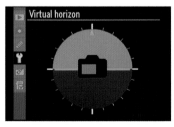

⌃ The **[Virtual horizon]** item, camera tilted   ⌃ The **[Virtual horizon]** item, camera level

NON-CPU LENS DATA

The D7000 can be used with older, non-CPU-type lenses. If you register the details of the lens (focal length and maximum aperture) in the [Non-CPU lens data] feature of the Setup menu, the functionality of many of the options and settings available with CPU-type lenses are also available with non-CPU lenses. This enables the use of Color Matrix metering, the display of aperture value, control of flash output for balanced fill-flash, and inclusion of information about the lens in the shooting data recorded by the camera (see pages 317-318 for full details).

AF FINE TUNE

The phase-detection autofocus system used by the D7000 (as in all other Nikon DSLR cameras) assumes all Nikkor AF lenses will behave alike when the AF system adjusts the focus point. As soon as the camera assesses the current level of defocus and the direction of the focus error (i.e., it is in front of or behind the point where it calculates the focus point should be), it signals the lens to move by what it considers to be the required amount. Once focus is set, provided that any new calculated focus error falls within a preset tolerance, the AF system will not refocus. When you are using a wide-angle lens at long focus distances, the very fine tolerances are of no consequence; however, at very close focus distances, with a lens that has both a long focal length and wide maximum aperture, those tolerance levels become far more critical. Sometimes, a specific camera body and lens combination produces a consistent focus error, which results in either "back focus," where the focus point falls behind the intended point of focus, or "front focus," where it falls in front of it. Since the focus error for a particular combination tends to be constant, (due to the errors in the assessment and signaling to the lens when setting focus being consistent) it is usually possible to address the problem by setting a constant level of adjustment. This is the purpose of the [AF fine tune] item in the Setup menu, which allows the AF system to be tweaked for up to twelve specific lenses when used on a specific D7000 camera.

It is important to test your own equipment extensively and exhaustively to establish that there is a "back-focus" or "front-focus" problem. If you determine this is the case, only then should you use the [AF fine tune] item.

○ **[AF fine tune (On/Off)]**
  ● **[On]**: Turn AF Fine Tune on.
  ● **[Off]** (default): Turn AF Fine-Tune off.
○ **[Saved value]**: Tune AF for the lens currently mounted on the camera. Press ▲ or ▼ to select a value between +20 and -20. A positive value moves the focus point away from the camera; a negative value has the opposite effect. Values for up to 12 types of lenses can be stored, but only one value for each lens type can be stored (i.e., if you have two Nikkor lenses of the same type, the D7000 will apply the same fine-tuning adjustment to both).
○ **[Default]**: If no AF tuning value is saved for the current lens, use this option to set a value. Adjustment operates in the same way as described above.
○ **[List saved values]**: Previously saved values for AF fine-tuning are listed. To delete a setting, highlight the required lens and press 🗑. To change the lens number used to identify a particular lens, highlight the required lens and press ▶. Use ▲ or ▼ to select a two-digit number. Press ⑳ to save any changes and return to the Setup menu.

EYE-FI UPLOAD

This item is only available when a dedicated Eye-Fi memory card is installed in the D7000. The wireless-communication-enabled Eye-Fi memory cards must be used according to the laws and regulations that apply in the shooting location. To upload JPEG files directly from the camera to the predetermined destination, select **[Enabled]**. If the Wi-Fi signal is not sufficiently strong, image upload will not take place. In areas where Wi-Fi is unavailable or wireless devices are prohibited, ensure that the **[Disable]** option is selected.

When [Firmware version] is selected from the Setup menu, the current version of the firmware installed on the camera is displayed on the monitor. To check the current firmware installed on your camera, highlight the [Firmware version] item in the Setup menu and press ▶; the details of the firmware are displayed on the next page. Press the ⊛ button to return to the Setup menu. At the time of writing, the current firmware versions for the D7000 are: A 1.00, B 1.00, and L 1.002. Firmware updates can be downloaded from any of the Nikon technical support web sites, visit: www.nikon.com.

☑ *RETOUCH MENU*

The Retouch menu enables you to create retouched, cropped, or resized versions of the image files saved on a memory card installed in the camera. When the features in this menu are applied to an image, a new copy of the file is created and stored on the same memory card. The original image file remains on the card in its unmodified form.

While I feel options available in the Retouch menu are a useful aspect of camera control, I believe it is important to keep them in perspective. The items available in this menu cannot be considered anywhere near as sophisticated as their equivalent adjustments in any good digital imaging software. They are intended to provide a quick, convenient, and largely automated method of producing a modified version of the original image without the use of a computer. As such, they offer an unprecedented level of control when using in-camera processing to produce a finished picture directly from the camera.

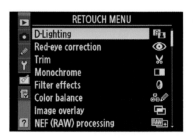

To select an image directly from the Retouch menu, open the Retouch menu, highlight the desired function, and press ▶ to display thumbnail images on the monitor. Depending on the item selected, a further menu of options may be displayed before the thumbnail images; if so, highlight the required option and press ▶ again. Use the Multi Selector to scroll through the thumbnail images; a yellow border will frame the currently selected picture (to view images stored in another location—another memory card or folder—hold down the BKT button and press ▲). To view an image full-frame, press and hold the ⊕ button. Once you have selected the picture to be modified and copied, press the ⊛ button to display the retouch options (see details below for each Retouch menu item). To cancel the process, press the MENU button. To apply the retouch option and save the new copy image, press the ⊛ button.

Alternatively, it is possible to access the Retouch menu directly from full-frame Playback. Display the picture to be modified and press the ⊛ button. The Retouch menu will be displayed (the [Image overlay] item is not accessible via this route); select the required item by using ▲ or ▼ and press ⊛ to open the options for that item. To return to full-frame Playback, press the ▶ button. Press ⊛ to create the retouched copy. An ◺ icon identifies the retouched copy file.

IMAGE QUALITY AND SIZE

The image quality and size settings of the copy image created by the Retouch menu will depend on that of the original image file(s), though the selected option within the Retouch menu may also affect image size and quality. Except in the case of [Trim], [Image overlay], [NEF (RAW) processing], and [Resize] the following apply:

- Copies created from JPEG images are the same size and quality as the original file.
- Copies of NEF files are saved as a JPEG files with [Large] and [Fine] selected for size and quality.
- The copy the [Image Overlay] option creates is always saved at the image quality and size currently set on the camera, regardless of the fact that this option is only available with NEF images. If you wish to save the copy image as an NEF file, ensure the image quality on the camera is set to NEF before you apply this option.

⌘ *D-LIGHTING*

The D-Lighting feature of the Retouch menu brightens shadow areas to reveal more detail. It is not an overall brightness control, its application is selective; by modifying the tone curve applied to the image, it only affects the shadow areas of the recorded image and preserves the mid and highlight tones.

Select the image (as described above) and press the ⊛ button to display two thumbnail images; one unmodified (left) and the other modified (right). You can select three levels of D-Lighting: low, normal, or high, using ▲ or ▼. To view the preview image full-frame, press and hold the ⊛ button. Once you have decided which level is most appropriate, press the ⊛ button to apply the change and create the copy image. You can press the ▶ button to cancel the function without making any changes.

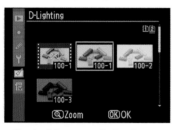

^ Thumbnail images are displayed so you can select of the picture to which D-Lighting will be applied; the feature applies a post-exposure adjustment to brighten shadow areas.

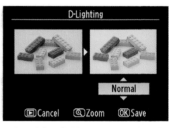

^ The original (left) and modified (right) picture can be viewed on the monitor.

👁 *RED-EYE REDUCTION*

This option is only available with pictures taken using either the built-in Speedlight of the D7000 or an external Nikon Speedlight. Select the image and press the ⊛ button. If no flash was used for the chosen exposure, a small yellow box containing a cross is displayed over the thumbnail image, and the image cannot be selected. If flash was used, but the camera cannot detect the presence of red eye, a message stating, "Unable to detect red eye in selected image," will be displayed.

If the D7000 detects what it considers to be a red-eye effect, the image will be displayed with a small navigation window; press and hold the ⊕ button to zoom into the image. You can navigate around the image to view other areas of the picture using the Multi Selector; the area currently displayed on the monitor is shown with a yellow border in a navigation window. To scroll rapidly to another area of the picture, press and hold the Multi Selector down.

If you can see the effects of red eye in the selected picture, press the ⊛ button to cancel the zoom control and return to the full-frame Playback, and then press ⊛ again. The D7000 will then create a copy image automatically, using processed image data, to reduce the red-eye effect.

> **NOTE:** Since this is a completely automated process, it is possible for the camera to inadvertently select an image not affected by red-eye but an area of the image that looks like red eye, which is why it is important to double check the preview image before confirming the operation of the process.

✂ TRIM

The **[Trim]** option enables you to crop the original image to exclude unwanted areas. Highlight the **[Trim]** option in the Retouch menu and press ▶ to display a set of thumbnail images. Select the image and press the ⊛ button.

The selected image is displayed on the LCD monitor, along with a yellow frame to show the crop area; you can move the crop frame around the image using the Multi Selector button. Press the ⊞ button to reduce the size of the crop area. Use the ⊕ button to increase the size of crop area; the crop size is displayed in the top-left corner of the image in pixel dimensions (width x height). It is also possible to adjust the aspect ratio of the cropped area; rotating the Main Command dial allows you to switch between 3:2, 4:3, 5:4, 1:1, and 16:9.

Once you have decided on the location, size, and aspect ratio of the crop area, press the ⊛ button to create the cropped copy. The new copy image will be displayed on the LCD monitor. Press the MENU button to return to the Retouch menu display.

▢▪ *MONOCHROME*

This item allows you to save the copied image in one of three monochrome effects: **[Black-and-white]** (grayscale), **[Sepia]** (brown tones), or **[Cyanotype]** (blue-and-white tones). In all three cases, the image data is converted to black and white using an algorithm dedicated to this feature; it is a different algorithm than the one used for the **[Monochrome]** option in the Picture Controls. The image data for the black-and-white copy is still saved as an RGB file (i.e., it retains its color information).

Select the image as described above. With this item, you must select the option before the thumbnail images are displayed. If you select either the **[Sepia]** or **[Cyanotype]** option, the degree of the color shift can be adjusted using ▲ to increase and ▼ to decrease the effect. Once you are satisfied with the preview image, press the ⊛ button to save the copy picture. Press the MENU button to return to the Retouch menu display.

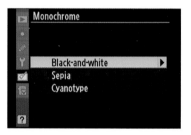

◑ *FILTER EFFECTS*

The **[Filter Effects]** option in the Retouch menu offers two choices that simulate the effects of a skylight or color correction (warm) filter. Select the image as described above; with this item you must select the option before the thumbnail images are displayed.

- **[Skylight]**: Nikon describes this option as emulating the effect of a Skylight filter. The effect is very subtle, reducing the amount of blue in the image by a very modest amount.

- **[Warm tone]**: This effect increases the amount of red in the image and produces results similar to that of a Wratten 81-series color-correction filter. Again, the effect is subtle, and proper White Balance control should eliminate the need to use it.

- **[Red intensifier]**: Intensifies red; use the Multi Selector to select one of three levels: ▲ to increase, and ▼ to decrease the effect.

○ **[Green intensifier]**: Intensifies green; use the Multi Selector button to select one of three levels: ▲ to increase, and ▼ to decrease the effect.

○ **[Blue intensifier]**: Intensifies blue; use the Multi Selector button to select one of three levels: ▲ to increase, and ▼ to decrease the effect.

○ **[Cross screen]**: This filter effect adds a star-point effect to point light sources in the image.

- **[Number of points]**: Select from 4, 6, or 8.
- **[Filter amount]**: Choose the brightness of the light sources affected.
- **[Filter angle]**: Set the angle of the star points.
- **[Length of points]**: Set the length of the star points.
- **[Confirm]**: Use to preview the effects of the filter (to preview in full-frame, press the ⊕ button).
- **[Save]**: Create the retouch copy.

○ **[Soft]**: This filter adds a soft effect; use the Multi Selector button to select one of three levels: High, Medium, or Low.

In all cases, a preview image is displayed. After selecting the filter effect, press the ⊛ button to apply it and create the copy image.

COLOR BALANCE

The **[Color balance]** item is used to produce a copy image with a modified color balance from the original file. Select the image (as described above) and press the ⊛ button to display to control options. A thumbnail image of the selected picture is displayed alongside histograms for the composite RGB, red, green, and blue channels. Below the thumbnail is a two-dimensional CIE color space map with vertical and horizontal axes aligned on its center. The central point of the color space map represents the color balance of the original file. Press the Multi Selector up to increase the level of green and down to increase the level of magenta. Press it to the left to increase blue and to the right to increase amber. The black square cursor will shift position accordingly, the histograms will reflect the altered color distribution, and the thumbnail image can be used to preview the effect.

To magnify a section of the preview image, press the ⊕ button; the histograms are updated to represent only the displayed portion of the image. When the preview image is enlarged, press the ?/o-n button to switch back and forth between the magnifying function and the Color Balance control. When zoomed in, you can use ⊖ to zoom out. To move around the magnified image, use the Multi Selector button. Once you are satisfied with the adjustment, press the ⊛ button to apply the color shift and save a copy of the image.

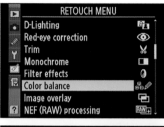

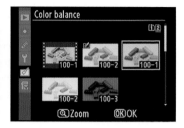

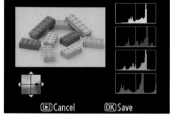

Color balance can be adjusted in the D7000, but it is no match for post-processing using a computer.

THE MENU SYSTEM

258

🖼 IMAGE OVERLAY

The [Image overlay] item enables the combination of a pair of NEF files, combining them to form a single, new image (the original image files are not affected by this process). The images do not have to be taken in consecutive order, but must have been recorded by a D7000 and be stored on the same memory card. To use Image Overlay:

1. Highlight the [Image overlay] option in the Retouch menu and press the ▶ button.
2. The [Image overlay] page will open with [Image 1] highlighted.
3. To select the first picture, press the ⊛ button; a thumbnail view of all NEF files stored on the memory card will be displayed. Scroll through the images using the Multi Selector to highlight the image you wish to select.
4. Press ⊛ and the selected image will appear in the [Image 1] box and the [Preview] box.

5. Adjust the gain value of **[Image 1]** by pressing ▲ or ▼. The effect of the gain control can be observed in the **[Preview]** box (the default value is x1.0; x0.5 cuts the gain in half, while selecting x2.0 doubles the gain).

6. Highlight the **[Image 2]** box and repeat Steps 2 – 5 above.

7. Once you have adjusted the gain of both images to achieve the desired effect, highlight the **[Preview]** box by pressing ◀ or ▶. Highlight **[Overlay]** using ▲ or ▼ and press ⓞⓚ to display a preview of the combined images. If the result is satisfactory, press the ⓞⓚ button to save the new image; otherwise, press ⚏ to return to the previous step.

8. To save the image without displaying a preview, highlight **[Save]** at Step 7 above instead of **[Overlay]**, and press the ⓞⓚ button. The new image will be displayed full-frame.

Image attributes such as White Balance, sharpening, color space, saturation, and hue will be copied from the image selected as **[Image 1]**. The shooting data is also copied from **[Image 1]**. Image Overlays saved as NEF files use the same compression and bit depth as the original files; JPEG overlays are saved using size-priority compression.

📷 *NEF (RAW) PROCESSING*

This item can be used to create JPEG format copies of pictures saved and stored on the installed memory card at an image quality of NEF (RAW) or NEF (RAW) + JPEG. To use **[NEF (RAW) processing]**:

1. Highlight **[NEF (RAW) processing]** in the Retouch menu and press ▶.

2. Select the required NEF picture from the displayed thumbnail pictures by pressing the Multi Selector button. Note that only NEF pictures will be displayed. Press the ⓞⓚ button to select the highlighted picture.

3. A preview image is now displayed next to a menu of options:

   • **[Image quality]**: Choose Image Quality from JPEG Fine, JPEG Normal, or JPEG Basic.

   • **[Image size]**: Choose image size from Large, Medium, or Small.

   • **[White balance]**: Choose White Balance settings, specify fluorescent lighting type, apply White Balance Fine-Tuning (including photographs taken at a WB setting of Preset manual, but these can only be fine-tuned from the Preset Manual White Balance option). The Preset Manual option is only available for pictures taken at this White Balance setting. If **[Auto]** is selected, WB will be set to whichever of **[Normal]** and **[Keep warm lighting colors]** was in effect when the picture was taken.

- **[Exposure compensation]**: Adjust the exposure level ±2 EV.

- **[Picture Control]**: Choose a Picture Control option.

- **[High ISO NR]**: Adjust level of ISO Noise Reduction

- **[Color space]**: Choose sRGB or Adobe RGB.

- **[D-Lighting]**: Set D-Lighting level.

4. Highlight any that you want to change from their current settings and press ▶. Select the desired setting and press the ⊗ button to return to the preview image and menu display. Repeat the selection process for any other options to be used.

5. Once all settings have been adjusted, highlight **[EXE]**.

6. Press ⊗ to create and save a JPEG format copy and return to full-frame Playback.

7. Press the MENU button to return to full-frame Playback without creating a copy image.

RESIZE

The **[Resize]** item offers options to reduce the resolution of the original image to create a copy that has a smaller file size:

OPTION	SIZE (PIXELS)
[2.5 M]	1920 x 1280
[1.1 M]	1280 x 856
[0.6 M]	960 x 640
[0.3 M]	640 x 424
[0.1 M]	320 x 216

The direct selection of a picture from single-image Playback for processing using this menu item is as described on page 253. However, if the **[Resize]** item is selected from the **[Retouch menu]**, the method of selecting an image and size differs from the method used when the **[Resize]** item is accessed directly from single-image Playback. It is necessary to select the Image Size and destination of the copy image before selecting the picture to which the process will be applied. Using the Retouch menu route, proceed as follows:

1. Open the Retouch menu, highlight **[Resize]** and press ▶ to display three options: **[Select image]**, **[Choose destination]** (only displayed if two memory cards are installed) and **[Choose size]**.

2. Highlight [Choose size], and then press ▶ to display the size options (listed above), and highlight the required size. Press the ⓞⓚ button to confirm your choice and return to the previous page.

3. Highlight [Destination], and then press ▶ to display Slot 1 and Slot 2. Highlight the required slot. Press the ⓞⓚ button to confirm your choice and return to the previous page.

4. Highlight [Select picture] and press ▶ to display thumbnail images. The currently selected image is shown framed by a yellow border.

5. Use the Multi Selector to highlight a desired image (the yellow border will shift accordingly), and then press the center button of the multi selector to select it (▣ appears in the top right corner of the thumbnail to indicate it has been selected). Press and hold ⊕ to view an enlarged picture. To select images stored in another location, hold down the **BKT** button and press ▲. Select the memory cad and folder accordingly.

6. Repeat as required; once you have selected all the images you want to reduce in size, press the ⓞⓚ button. A confirmation page will be displayed indicating how many images are to be processed.

7. Select [Yes] to proceed with the process or [No] to return to the previous page. If you select [Yes], press the ⓞⓚ button to apply the effect and save the copy picture(s).

⊏⊀ QUICK RETOUCH

This item can be used to make a rapid enhancement to color saturation and contrast; the D7000 will apply D-Lighting accordingly to increase the brightness of strongly backlit subjects. Select an image as described above and press ⓞⓚ to display the image alongside a preview image. Use ▲ or ▼ to select one of three values: [Low], [Normal], or [High]. Press and hold ⊕ to view the preview image full-frame, and press ⓞⓚ to make the copy image. To return to the normal full-frame Playback, press the ▶ button, or press the MENU button to return to the Retouch menu.

HINT: This is about as "quick and dirty" as it gets as far as image adjustment goes; this item should only be considered when the need to expedite an image with adjusted color saturation and contrast is immediate and imperative!

⌐ *STRAIGHTEN*

If you shoot a picture and then find that it is not aligned as it should be—for example, a horizon line slopes to one side—this item can be used to straighten the image. The image can be rotated by up to five degrees in steps of approximately 0.25 degree by pressing ▶ to turn the image clockwise, or pressing ◀ to turn the image counterclockwise; a pattern of gridlines is displayed on the monitor screen to assist in aligning the image. The edge of the image will be trimmed to produce a square copy. Press ⊛ to copy the picture once you have rotated the image as required. To return to the normal full-frame Playback without copying the image, press the ▶ button.

⊕ *DISTORTION CONTROL*

Optical distortion of a lens can result in straight lines close to the edge of the frame appearing to be bowed. Typically, wide-angle lenses produce barrel distortion that causes lines to bend outward away from the center of the image, while long lenses can cause pincushion distortion, where lines bend inward toward the center of the image. This item corrects such optical distortion; the [Auto] option applies correction automatically, and then you can refine the correction using the Multi Selector button. The [Auto] option is not available if the [Auto distortion control] item in the Shooting menu is set to [On]. Alternatively, you can select the [Manual] option and press ▶ to reduce barrel distortion, or press ◀ to reduce pincushion distortion. The greater the degree of correction, the more the peripheral area of the original frame will be cropped. Press ⊛ to copy the picture. To return to the normal full-frame playback without copying the image, press the ▶ button.

⊞ *FISHEYE*

This item modifies an image to emulate the appearance of a picture taken using a fisheye lens. This type of lens is not corrected to render straight lines as straight but with an increasing amount of distortion the further the line is from the center of the frame. Select [Fishetye] and press ▶ to display thumbnail images. Select the required image and press ⊛. Press ▶ to increase the (barrel) distortion, which will result in more of the image being cropped at the edges, or press ◀ to reduce the effect. Press ⊛ to copy the picture. To return to the normal full-frame Playback without copying the image, press the ▶ button.

▧ COLOR OUTLINE

This item converts a conventional color picture to an outline image that can be used as a starting point for a drawing or painting. Select [Color outline] and press ▶ to display thumbnail images. Select the required image and press ⊛. The image is displayed as a monochrome line drawing. Press ⊛ to save the copy image. To cancel the process and return to the normal full-frame Playback, press the ▶ button.

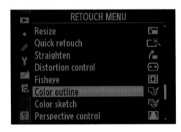
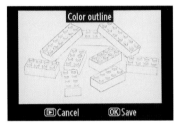

▧ COLOR SKETCH

This item converts a conventional color picture to an image that emulates the effect of a sketch created with colored pencils. Press ▲ and ▼ to highlight [Vividness] or [Outlines] and press ◀ and ▶ to apply adjustments, using the scales displayed at the right side of the screen as guide. Vividness alters the color saturation, while outlines can be made more or less prominent. Press ⊛ to save the copy image. To cancel the process and return to the normal full-frame Playback, press the ▶ button.

▨ PERSPECTIVE CONTROL

This item is used to correct the perspective of an image—for example, the converging vertical lines that occur when shooting a picture of a tall building with the camera tilted upward to include the entire subject in the frame. Select [Perspective control] and press ▶ to display thumbnail images. Select the required image and press ⊛. Use the Multi Selector button to adjust the image as required, using the scales displayed along the bottom and left side of the LCD monitor screen as a guide. Press ⊛ to save the copy image. To cancel the process and return to the normal full-frame Playback, press the ▶ button.

MINIATURE EFFECT

This option is intended to emulate the effect of using a Nikkor PC-E Tilt / Shift lens when shooting pictures with a tilt movement applied. This effect alters the focus characteristics by reducing the depth of field to a very narrow region, thereby creating an effect as though the viewer is looking at a tiny model of the scene. For the best results, shoot pictures to be converted with this item from a high vantage point.

Select [Miniature effect] and press ▶ to display thumbnail images. Select the required image and press ⓞ. The image is displayed full-frame with a narrow oblong box marked with a yellow outline—this is the approximate plane of focus. If the picture is in a horizontal (wide) format, press ▲ and ▼ to choose within the area of the yellow box. Press ◀ and ▶ to position the area of focus if the picture is in a vertical (tall) format. Press and hold ⊕ to view the preview image full-frame. Press ⓞ to save the copy image. To cancel the process and return to the normal full-frame Playback, press the ▶ button.

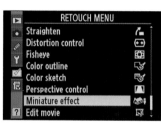

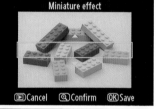

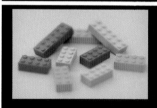

The [Miniature effect] item allows you to create a copy image with altered depth-of-field characteristics, emulating the effect achieved by a tilt / shift type lens.

EDIT MOVIE

This item allows you to trim video clips recorded in the D-Movie mode, or to save a selected frame from a video clip as a JPEG file picture. To edit a movie clip from the Retouch menu:

1. Select [Edit movie] and press ▶ to display the options.
2. Select [Choose start point] and press ▶ to display a thumbnail of the movie clips stored on the memory card.

3. Select the required movie clip and press ⊛. The first frame of the movie is displayed on the monitor screen. Press ⊛ to begin Playback.

4. Press ▲ to pause the clip and display [Proceed] and select [Yes] to delete all frames prior to the displayed frame and save a new trimmed copy of the video clip.

5. Select [Edit movie] and press ▶ to display the options.

6. Select [Choose end point] and press ▶ to display a thumbnail of the movie clips stored on the memory card.

7. Select the required movie clip and press ⊛. The first frame of the movie is displayed on the monitor screen. Press ⊛ to begin Playback.

8. Press ▲ to pause the clip and display [Proceed], and select [Yes] to delete all frames after the displayed frame and save a new trimmed copy of the video clip.

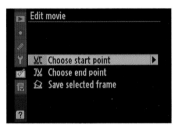
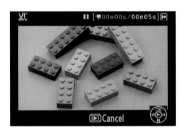

To save a selected frame using the Retouch menu:

1. To select an individual frame and save it as a JPEG picture, select [Edit movie] and then press ▶ to display the options. Select [Save selected frame] and press ▶ to display a thumbnail of the movie clips stored on the memory card. Select the required movie clip and press ⊛.

2. Press ⊛ again and the clip will begin to play back.

3. Press ▼ to pause the playback.

4. To save the currently displayed frame, press ▲, and then highlight [Yes] and press ⊛ to create a JPEG picture.

■◆□ *SIDE-BY-SIDE COMPARISON*

Use this item to compare a retouched copy with the original (source) file, as follows:

1. Select either a picture that has been retouched or a retouched copy (indicated by the ☑ icon) for **[Side-by-side comparison]**.
2. Press the ⊛ button to display the original source image to the left and the retouched copy on the right. The options used to create the copy are displayed above the two images.
3. Use ◀ and ▶ to switch between the two images; the selected version is shown with a yellow border. Press and hold ⊕ to view an enlarged view of the selected image.
4. If the image was created using the **[Image overlay]** option, use ▲ or ▼ to view the second source image.
5. Press the ▣ button to return to the Playback mode.
6. To return to Playback mode with the selected image displayed, press ⊛.

▤ *RECENT SETTINGS /* ▩ *MY MENU*

The last tab on the left-hand side of the root menu page is for both My Menu and Recent Settings. By default, it is My Menu, but you can toggle between the two using the **[Choose tab]** item, selectable from either menu. To toggle from one to the other, highlight **[Choose tab]** and press ▶ to display the two options: **[My menu]** and **[Recent settings]**. Highlight the one you want and press the ⊛ button.

[My menu] allows you create a customized menu from practically any combination of items in the Playback, Shooting, Custom Setting, Setup, or Retouch menus. Items can be added, deleted, and reordered at any time. Given the complexity and size of the menu system, this useful feature allows those menu items that you frequently use to be located in a single menu. Up to four items can be added to the **[My menu]** list of items before it becomes necessary to scroll to additional pages. The default My Menu control items, **[Add items]**, **[Remove items]**, and **[Rank items]**, are always displayed.

In **[Recent settings]**, up to 20 of the most recently used menu items will be displayed; as different menu items are used, they will be added automatically to the top of the Recent Settings menu list in chronological order. To scroll these items, use ▲ or ▼, and use ⊛ to select the highlighted item. To revert back to using My Menu, open the [Recent settings] item, highlight [Choose tab], and press ▶ to display [My menu] and [Recent settings] again. Highlight [My menu] and press the ⊛ button.

USING MY MENU

To add a menu item:

1. Open [My menu], highlight [Add items], and press ▶ to display a list of the five menus.
2. Highlight the desired menu and press ▶.
3. Highlight the item that you want to add to My Menu and press the ⊛ button.
4. To position the selected menu item in the [My menu] list, use ▲ or ▼; once it's positioned, press the ⊛ button to add the new item.

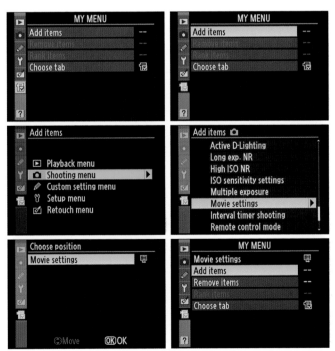

The above sequence shows adding the Movie Settings item from the Shooting menu to My Menu.

To delete a menu item:

1. Open **[My menu]**, highlight **[Remove items]**, and press ▶ to display the list of items in **[My menu]**.
2. Highlight the item to be removed and press ▶; a check mark will be shown in the box to the right of the selected menu item.
3. To confirm the deletion of the selected item, highlight **[Done]** and press the ⊛ button. A confirmation dialog box is displayed with the message "Delete selected items?" If you wish to proceed, press the ⊛ button.

To reorder the items in **[My menu]**:

1. Open **[My menu]**, highlight **[Rank items]**, and press ▶ to display the list of the menu items in **[My menu]**.
2. Highlight the item to be relocated and press ⊛.
3. To position the item in the menu list, use ▲ or ▼; a solid yellow line indicates the location for the menu item.
4. Once positioned, press the ⊛ button and the menu item will be moved.

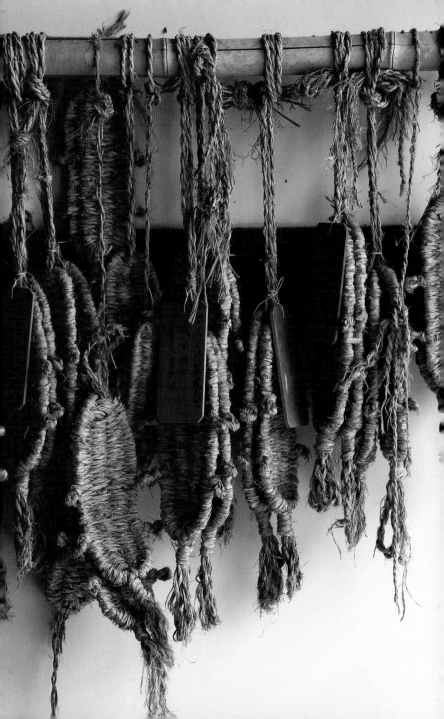

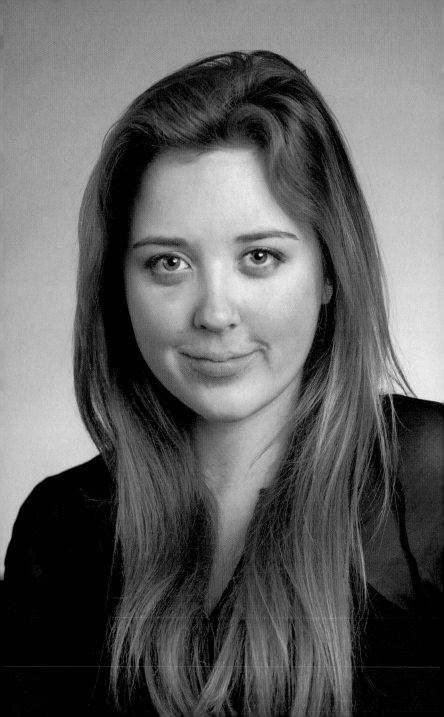

Nikon Flash Photography

THE BASICS OF FLASH

Before we take a look at the flash capabilities of the D7000, it is helpful to understand some basics about the physics of light and flash exposure. One of the most important principles to affect flash exposure is the Inverse Square Law. It states that light from a point light source, such as a flash unit, falls off as it travels over a distance by the inverse of the square of that distance. Put simply, if you double the distance from a light source, its intensity drops by a factor of four because as light travels from the source it spreads out, illuminating a wider area. So, at double the distance from the source, light covers four times the area. At four times the distance, the light covers sixteen times the area, so its intensity is reduced to one sixteenth of its intensity at the original distance.

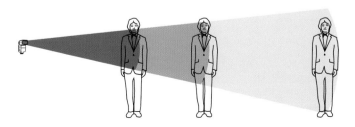

Besides being aware of Inverse Square Law, it is also essential that you appreciate how flash exposure is influenced by ISO sensitivity, lens aperture, and shutter speed. Just as when exposing for ambient light, if the ISO value is doubled, the amount of light required from the flash to maintain the same flash exposure (assuming no other factors change) is halved; and conversely, if the ISO value is halved, the flash output must be doubled. Equally, altering the lens aperture has the same effect on flash exposure as altering the ISO level. So, for example, if the aperture is changed from f/8 to f/5.6 to allow twice as much light to pass through the lens, the flash need only output half as much light to maintain the same flash exposure. If, however, the lens aperture is changed from f/8 to f/11, to allow only half as much light to pass through the lens, the flash output must be doubled to maintain the same flash exposure.

The intensity of the light produced by a given flash unit is always the same; therefore, the flash exposure is controlled by the duration of the flash output. At its maximum output of light, the duration of flash pulse from a modern Nikon Speedlight flash unit is typically about 1/1000 of a second, so as the amount of light output from the flash is reduced from its maximum level, the duration of the flash pulse becomes even briefer. Yet, the maximum normal flash synchronization (sync) speed (the briefest shutter speed at which the opening and closing of the shutter allows the light from the flash to be recorded fully by the camera) is usually 1/250 second. Hence, provided the shutter speed is set to the flash sync speed or slower, it has no effect on the flash exposure. The only time the shutter speed is of any consequence when shooting with flash is if ambient light is also being recorded as part of the overall exposure, for example, when using flash as a fill light (supplementary light) with ambient light. In this case, the ambient light exposure will be influenced by the shutter speed, but it still has no effect on the flash exposure. Exposure control can be summarized as follows:

- The flash exposure is dependent on the lens aperture, ISO, and amount of light output by the flash unit.
- The ambient light exposure is dependent on lens aperture, ISO, and shutter speed.

Because a flash unit emits a precise, fixed amount of light based principally on the flash-to-subject distance, ISO setting, and lens aperture, the light from the flash will only illuminate the subject properly at a specific distance. Therefore, any element in the scene closer to the flash than the subject (for which the flash output has been calculated) will be overexposed and anything farther away will be underexposed.

Finally, the output of an electronic flash unit, often referred to as its power, is quantified by a value known as its guide number (GN). The higher the guide number, the more powerful the flash unit. Guide numbers are quoted as a distance (usually expressed in either feet or meters) for a given ISO level and angle of view (usually expressed as a lens focal length for the camera format in use). For example, the built-in Speedlight of the D7000 has GN of 39 feet (12 m) at ISO 100, 16mm. It is essential when comparing guide numbers to make sure that the same units are used for linear measurement, ISO value, and focal length (see the section "Manual Flash Exposure Control" on pages 289-290 for details on how to use the GN value to calculate flash output manually).

> The top-of-the-line flash compatible with the D7000, the SB-900, offers a powerful range, a zoom / tilt / swivel head, wireless operation, and many other features.

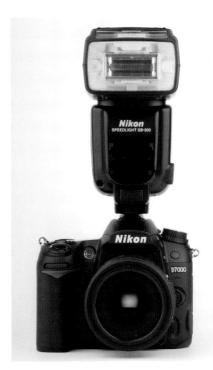

Modern electronic flash systems have moved far beyond the fundamental principles of flash exposure control, to incorporate a range of features that refine the process even further. The most advanced of these is the Nikon Creative Lighting System (CLS), which represents the most sophisticated method of flash exposure control developed by Nikon to date. It encompasses a range of attributes that are as much a part of the camera models that support the CLS, as it is of the CLS-compatible Speedlight flash units themselves. Features include: intelligent through-the-lens (i-TTL) flash exposure control; Flash Value (FV) Lock; Flash Color Information Communication; Auto FP High-Speed Sync; Wide-Area AF-Assist to improve autofocus accuracy with cameras such as the D7000, which have multiple AF points covering a large part of the frame area; and the Advanced Wireless Lighting (AWL) system, which provides wireless control of multiple Speedlights using i-TTL.

Currently, CLS compatibility encompasses the D7000, together with the D3-series, D2-series, D700, D300-series, D200, D90, D5000, D3100, D3000, D80, D70-series, D60, D50, D40-series, and F6 cameras, including the internal Speedlight units of those models that possess them. The CLS includes the following external Nikon Speedlights: SB-900, SB-800, SB-700, SB-600, SB-400, and SB-R200. However, some of the listed camera models do not support all the features of the CLS.

The D7000 supports an Auto FP High-Speed Sync feature when used with either its built-in Speedlight (to maximum flash sync speed of 1/320 second) or an external CLS Speedlight (to a maximum flash sync speed of 1/8000 second). The camera also supports the FV Lock feature with both the built-in and compatible external Speedlights. Furthermore, its built-in Speedlight has the ability to be used with manual flash output control, in a repeating flash mode (this feature is supported with compatible external units as well), and as a Commander unit for remote control of compatible Speedlights using the AWL system. All of these features are discussed in further detail later in this chapter.

When used in combination with a CPU-type lens, the D7000 supports two methods of TTL-controlled flash exposure with its built-in flash unit or a compatible external Speedlight. To select TTL flash control for the built-in Speedlight, open the Custom Settings menu and navigate to CS-e3 **[Flash cntrl for built-in flash]** and press ▶. Highlight **[TTL]** and press ⓞⓚ. When using an external Speedlight, the flash mode is selected via the controls on the Speedlight.

i-TTL BALANCED FILL FLASH
This is Nikon's third generation of TTL flash exposure control. When the D7000 is set to 3D-Color Matrix metering, a D- or G-type Nikkor lens is mounted, and the built-in Speedlight (or an external Speedlight such as the SB-600, SB-700, SB-800, or SB-900) is activated, i-TTL Balanced Fill Flash will attempt to balance the ambient light exposure to the flash output.

It is important to note that whenever you see the term "i-TTL Balanced Fill-flash," ambient (existing) light and flash are being mixed in a fully automated process to produce the final exposure. How the two light sources are mixed and in what proportion will depend on a wide variety of factors including: ISO sensitivity, lens aperture, exposure mode, Exposure Compensation value, brightness of both the ambient light and flash illumination, and the nature of the scene being photographed.

Fill Flash is a recognized lighting technique in which the flash is used to supplement the main ambient light source. The level of illumination provided by the flash is generally weaker than the ambient light, because its purpose is to provide a small amount of additional light in the shadows and other less well-lit areas of a scene to help reduce the overall level of contrast, although many photographers also use the technique when shooting portraits to put a small catch light in their subject's eyes.

When the camera is in Manual exposure mode (M), only the flash exposure is determined by the i-TTL system. However, when i-TTL is used with any of the camera's automated exposure modes, it is the D7000, not the photographer, that is in control of the exposure for both the ambient light and the flash output. The camera assesses the flash output level and the ambient light in an attempt to create a balanced

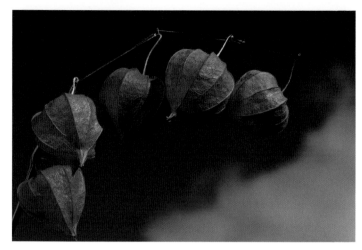

^ To ensure that you maintain full control over flash output level when using TTL flash, it is essential to use the Standard iTTL flash mode.

exposure using both light sources. To achieve this, the D7000 will often adjust the exposure for either the ambient light or the flash output, and sometimes both. Consequently, any manually applied adjustment of either the ambient light exposure or flash output level is frequently overridden (or even ignored). This often results in a picture with too much flash exposure, spoiling the fill-flash effect. The lack of user control also makes it difficult to achieve consistent, repeatable results.

STANDARD i-TTL FLASH

This flash mode differs from the i-TTL Balanced Fill-Flash mode in that the measurement of ambient light in the scene remains wholly independent of the flash output control and is not integrated in any way with the flash exposure calculations.

So, if you want to achieve consistent, repeatable results when using a true fill-flash technique, where the flash is the supplementary light, I recommend you use Standard i-TTL flash. In this case, any Flash Compensation or ambient Exposure Compensation you set will be applied without influence from the camera. Likewise, in any situation where you wish to use flash as the main source of illumination and have control over the flash output level as well as the exposure of ambient light, I also suggest you select Standard i-TTL flash.

i-TTL Balanced Fill Flash is the default flash exposure control method used with the built-in flash unit of the D7000. The only way to override this is to set the camera to Spot metering, which causes the camera to use Standard i-TTL flash control. When using the Nikon SB-400, SB-600, SB-700, SB-800, or SB-900 Speedlight, the flash exposure control method is selected directly on the flash unit. However, if you set the D7000 to Spot metering, the camera will override this selection and always use Standard i-TTL flash control.

USING i-TTL FLASH EXPOSURE CONTROL

Regardless of which of the two specific TTL flash modes just described is used, i-TTL offers the most refined method of automatic flash exposure control. Currently, the SB-900, SB-800, SB-700, SB-600, SB-400, and SB-R200 are the only external Speedlights that support i-TTL and the CLS, while the SU-800 Wireless Speedlight Commander can be used to control any of these units with the exception of the SB-400. If any other external Nikon Speedlight is attached to the D7000, no form of TTL flash exposure control is supported; this applies to all earlier Speedlights, even DX-type Speedlights such as the SB-80DX, designed for earlier Nikon digital SLR cameras. The i-TTL system works in the following way with the D7000:

o It uses fewer monitor pre-flashes than previous Nikon TTL flash control systems; however, they have a higher intensity, which improves the efficiency of obtaining a measurement from the TTL flash control sensor. Also, because it uses fewer pre-flashes, the amount of time taken to perform the assessment is reduced, which enables the camera to perform this process before lifting the reflex mirror.

o By emitting the monitor pre-flashes before the reflex mirror is lifted, the D7000 can use its 2016-pixel RGB metering sensor, which is located in the prism head of the camera, for TTL control of flash exposure. This allows the camera to integrate flash exposure control with the attributes of the Scene Recognition System, together with assessment of and subsequent exposure control for, the ambient light.

o The i-TTL system of the D7000 is designed to work with ISO sensitivities between 200 and 6400; Nikon states that outside of this range, flash exposure control may be less accurate.

The following is a summary of the sequence of events used to calculate flash output by the D7000, when it is used with either its built-in Speedlight or an external CLS Speedlight set to one of the two i-TTL modes described above, and a D- or G-type Nikkor lens:

1. Once the shutter release is pressed, the camera reads the focus distance from the D- or G-type lens.

2. The camera sends a signal to the Speedlight to initiate the pre-flash system, which then emits the monitor pre-flashes (pulses of light) from the Speedlight(s).

3. The light from these pre-flashes is bounced back through the lens and onto the 2016-pixel RGB metering sensor via the reflex mirror.

4. The information from the pre-flashes, gathered by the 2016-pixel RGB metering sensor, is analyzed along with measurements of the ambient light in the scene and information supplied by the focusing system. The camera determines the amount of light required from the Speedlight(s) and sets the duration of the flash discharge accordingly.

5. The reflex mirror lifts up out of the light path and the shutter opens.

6. The camera sends a signal to the Speedlight(s) to initiate the main flash discharge, which is quenched the instant the amount of light predetermined in Step 4 has been emitted.

7. The shutter closes at the end of the predetermined shutter speed duration, and the reflex mirror is lowered to its normal position.

NOTE: The emission of the monitor pre-flashes occurs immediately before the reflex mirror is raised. However, during the split-second delay between the mirror being lifted and the shutter opening, the pre-flash may cause some subjects to blink; you will not be able to see this through the viewfinder, as it will be blacked out. Using the FV Lock feature can help in this situation, as once the flash output level is locked, no further pre-flashes are emitted for subsequent exposures.

NOTE: Due to its design, the SB-R200 cannot be mounted on the accessory shoe of a camera; it can only be used as a wireless remote flash controlled by either the SU-800 Commander unit, an SB-800 Speedlight, or the SB-900 Speedlight.

The crucial phase in the sequence described above is Step 4, which is the point when the required output from the flash is calculated. As stated previously, this is accomplished using the 2016-pixel RGB metering sensor that is positioned in the viewfinder head of the D7000. The ability of this sensor is enhanced by the Scene Recognition System (SRS), which made its debut in the original D300 in mid-2007. A diffraction grating located immediately in front of the metering sensor separates the light falling on it, from both the reflected monitor pre-flash illumination and the ambient light, into its component colors. This enables the sensor to recognize shapes and objects by the distribution of color and contrast, so it can work more effectively and efficiently. The Scene Recognition System only operates with Matrix metering and is particularly sensitive to skin tones; however, if Center-Weighted or Spot metering is selected, the D7000 uses a simple grayscale metering system—in other words, it is not sensitive to color.

When Matrix metering is used, this evaluation of the shape and color of elements in the scene is performed together with conventional assessments of the overall levels of brightness and the level of contrast. This information is then combined with information from the autofocus (AF) system. The camera assesses the brightness of each of the 2016 pixels on the RGB metering sensor, and then compares them relative to each other to establish scene contrast, while it looks for patterns, such as a distribution of bright pixels in the upper and darker pixels in the lower part of a frame, which might indicate a light sky area above a subject. The metering system assumes the subject is covered by the active AF point(s), so by checking which AF point(s) reports focus, it can determine the location of the subject within the frame. Provided a D- or G-type Nikkor lens or a third-party lens that supports communication of focus distance is mounted on the camera, the metering system will also integrate the approximate subject distance into the calculations for flash output.

Once the camera has collected all the information pertaining to the shapes, colors, brightness, and the contrast pattern in the scene, it compares these values, principally the brightness patterns against information held in the camera's database, which is derived from over 30,000 sample exposures, covering an enormous range of lighting conditions. If the first comparison generates an evaluation that conflicts with the stored exposure data, the pattern of pixels may be reassessed and then a further analysis performed. For example, if any group of pixels reports an abnormally high level of brightness in comparison to the others on the sensor, the metering system will usually ignore this information in its flash exposure calculations. This can occur if there is a highly reflective surface, such as glass or water in a part of the scene, which could result in a bright reflection of the light from the flash that would otherwise cause the metering system to underexpose the picture.

FOCUS INFORMATION

As described above, when using Matrix metering and a D- or G-type Nikkor lens, focus information is provided to the metering system in two forms: camera-to-subject distance and the level of focus / defocus at each AF point.

The basic strategy of the Matrix metering system is to optimize flash output while avoiding overexposure; therefore, in most cases, the focus distance information will influence which pixels of the RGB metering sensor affect ambient exposure and flash output calculations.

For example, if the subject is positioned in the center of the frame, and the lens is focused at a middle to long distance, the camera will assess all the pixels on the sensor but place slightly more emphasis on those at the center of the frame. In this situation, if flash is the main source of illumination and the background is much farther away from the flash than the subject, it is likely to result in a typical "party picture," with the subject lit well by the flash but set against a completely black background (due to flash fall-off according to the inverse square law), as the camera will bias flash output for the subject.

Conversely, assuming the subject is positioned in the center of the frame, the lens is focused at a short distance, and the level of illumination is fairly even across the frame area, the camera will generally place slightly more emphasis on those pixels that cover the outer part of the frame area and slightly less on the central ones, as it attempts to prevent loss of highlight detail in the subject. However, an exception to this occurs if the camera detects a very high level of contrast between the central and outer areas of the frame; in this situation, the metering system may, and often does, reverse the emphasis and weights the exposure calculations according to the information received from pixels at the center of the frame area to ensure exposure accuracy in this region.

Essentially, what the camera is trying to do in both cases is prevent overexposure of the subject, which it assumes is in the center of the frame, because individual focus point information is integrated with focus distance information, as each AF point is checked for its degree of focus. This provides the camera with information about the probable location of the subject within the area of the scene. Using the examples given above, the metering system knows that the central AF point has acquired focus while the other AF points each report varying levels of defocus. Therefore, exposure is calculated on the assumption that the subject is in the center of the frame, and the camera biases its computations according to the focus distance information it receives from the lens.

It is important to understand that other twists occur in this story of interaction between exposure calculation and focus information. For example, when you acquire and lock focus on a subject using the center AF point and then recompose the shot so that the subject is located elsewhere in the frame (the central AF point consequently no longer detects focus), the camera will generally use the exposure value it calculated when it first acquired focus. However, if the level of brightness detected by the pixels at the center of the frame is assessed to have changed significantly from the level when focus was first acquired with the subject at that position, the camera can and often does adjust its flash exposure calculations— sometimes not necessarily for the better. To help improve flash exposure accuracy in situations when you wish to compose a picture with the subject close to the periphery of the frame, I recommend you use the Flash Value (FV) Lock feature (see pages 299-301 for a full description).

HINT: To avoid dark or black background when shooting in low ambient light conditions with flash, use Slow Sync with either Aperture-Priority or Programmed autoexposure mode, or set an appropriate shutter speed to achieve an exposure for the ambient light in Manual or Shutter-Priority exposure modes.

The built-in Speedlight of the D7000 has a guide number of 39 feet (12 m) at ISO 100, 68°F (20°C). The maximum normal flash synchronization speed in all exposure modes is 1/250 second; this can be raised to 1/320 second, as the built-in Speedlight supports the automatic FP high-speed flash sync feature of the CLS. The minimum flash shooting distance is 2 feet (0.6m), below which the camera will not necessarily calculate a correct flash exposure.

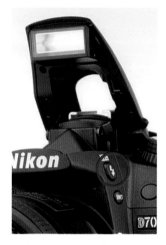

> The built-in Speedlight of the D7000 has a guide number (GN) of 39 feet (12m) at ISO 100, a relatively low guide number compared with that of the optional accessory Speedlights, such as the SB-700. The 5 Flash Mode button is located on the front of the camera, just below the flash housing.

The built-in Speedlight is switched on by pressing the flash release button that is located immediately above the ⚡ flash mode button. The unit draws its power from the main camera battery, so extended use of the flash will have a direct effect on battery life. As soon as the flash pops up, it begins to charge. The flash-ready symbol (⚡) appears in the viewfinder to indicate charging is complete and the flash is ready to fire. If the flash fires at its maximum output, the same flash-ready symbol will blink for approximately three seconds after the exposure has been made, as a warning of potential underexposure (see pages 298-299 for details on how to apply Flash Compensation to the built-in Speedlight). The flash-ready symbol operates in exactly the same way when an external Speedlight is attached and switched on as it does with the built-in Speedlight.

The built-in flash unit's shooting range will vary depending on the values set for lens aperture and ISO sensitivity:

APERTURE AT ISO (SENSITIVITY)							RANGE	
100	200	400	800	1600	3200	6400	METERS	FEET
1.4	2	2.8	4	5.6	8	11	0.7 – 8.5	2.3 – 27.9
2	2.8	4	5.6	8	11	16	0.6 – 6.1	2 – 20
2.8	4	5.6	8	11	16	22	0.6 – 4.2	2 – 13.75
4	5.6	8	11	16	22	32	0.6 – 3.0	2 – 9.8
5.6	8	11	16	22	32	–	0.6 – 2.1	2 – 6.9
8	11	16	22	32	–	–	0.6 – 1.5	2 – 4.9
11	16	22	32	–	–	–	0.6 – 1.1	2 – 3.6
16	22	32	–	–	–	–	0.6 – 0.8	2 – 2.6

When using flash, and the Mode dial is set to Program (P) autoexposure mode, the maximum aperture (smallest f/number) is limited according to the ISO sensitivity set on the D7000:

FLASH IN USE	MAXIMUM APERTURE AT ISO						
	100	200	400	800	1600	3200	6400
Built-In	2.8	3.5	4	5	5.6	7.1	8
External (Accessory)	4	4.8	5.6	6.7	8	9.5	11

If the value of the maximum aperture of the lens (lowest f/ number) is lower than the value in the table above, the maximum aperture of the lens will be limited to the value given in the table, for example, a lens with a maximum aperture of f/1.8 has an effective maximum aperture of f/4 in P mode with an ISO sensitivity of ISO 400.

LIMITATIONS OF THE BUILT-IN SPEEDLIGHT

While the built-in Speedlight on the D7000 is not as powerful as an external Speedlight, it can still provide a useful level of illumination at short ranges and is especially useful for fill-flash techniques, since it supports flash output level compensation. However, if you want to use this built-in unit as the main light source, you should be aware of the following:

O The guide number (GN) is limited, thus flash shooting ranges are relatively short (see the table on page 285).

O The flash head of the built-in Speedlight is physically much closer to the central lens axis than that of an external flash; hence, the likelihood of red-eye occurring is increased significantly.

O This close proximity of the built-in Speedlight to the central lens axis often means that the lens obscures the output of the flash, especially if a lens hood is in use. For example, if the camera is held in a horizontal orientation, the obstruction of the light from the flash will cause a shadow to appear on the bottom edge of the picture.

O The angle of coverage achieved by the built-in Speedlight is limited and only extends to cover the field of view of a lens with a focal length of 16mm or more. If used with a wider focal length lens, the flash will not be able to illuminate the periphery of the frame, and these areas will appear underexposed. Even at the widest limit of coverage, it is not uncommon to see a noticeable fall-off of illumination (vignetting) in the corners of the frame.

O The built-in Speedlight draws its power from the camera's battery, so extended use will deplete it quite quickly.

LENS COMPATIBILITY WITH THE BUILT-IN SPEEDLIGHT

The built-in flash can be used with CPU lenses (i.e., all AF and Ai-P types) with focal lengths between 16mm and 300mm, but always remove the lens hood to prevent light from the flash from being obscured. Regardless, the built-in flash has a minimum range of 2 feet (0.6 m); therefore, it cannot be used at the close focus distances of macro zoom lenses. Furthermore, it is not possible to use the built-in Speedlight with the AF-S 14–24mm f/2.8G ED, as light is always obscured regardless of the focal length in use. The built-in flash may be unable to illuminate the entire frame area evenly when using the following lenses at focus distances shorter than those given in the right-hand column of the following table:

LENS	FOCAL LENGTH	MINIMUM DISTANCE
AF-S DX 10–24mm f/3.5-4.5G ED	18 mm	3.25 ft / 1 m
	20 – 24 mm	No vignetting
AF-S DX 12–24mm f/4G ED	18mm	3.25 ft / 1 m
	20mm	No vignetting
AF-S 16-85mm f/4G ED VR	24 mm	6.6 ft / 2 m
	28 mm	3.25 ft / 1 m
	35 mm	No vignetting
AF-S 17–35mm f/2.8D ED	20 mm	6.6 ft / 2 m
	24 – 35 mm	No vignetting
AF-S DX 17–55mm f/2.8G ED	24mm	3.25 ft / 1 m
	28 – 55 mm	No vignetting
AF 18–35mm f/3.5–4.5D ED	18mm	3.25 ft / 1 m
	24 – 35 mm	No vignetting
AF-S DX 18-200mm f/3.5-5.6G ED (VR & VR II versions)	18mm	3.25 ft / 1 m
PC-E 24mm f/3.5D ED	24 mm	No vignetting
AF-S 24–70mm f/2.8G ED	28mm	4.9 ft / 1.5 m
	35 – 70 mm	No vignetting
AF-S 28–70mm f/2.8D ED	28 mm	3.25 ft / 1 m
	35 – 70 mm	No vignetting

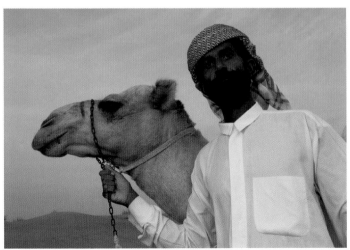

^ The built-in Speedlight may not be very powerful, but it can provide a useful amount of fill light at close range.

USING EXTERNAL NIKON SPEEDLIGHTS

The D7000 offers full i-TTL flash exposure control with five external Nikon Speedlight flash units, which are compatible with the CLS:

- SB-R200 with GN of 33 feet (10 m) at ISO 100
- SB-400 with a GN of 69 feet (21 m) at ISO 100
- SB-600 with a GN of 98 feet (30 m) at ISO 100 with the flash head set to 35mm
- SB-700 with a GN of 92 feet (28 m) at ISO 100 with the flash head set to 35mm and Standard light distribution selected
- SB-800 with a GN of 125 feet (38 m) at ISO 100 with the flash head set to 35mm
- SB-900 with a GN of 111 feet (34 m) at ISO 200 with the flash head set to 35mm and Standard light distribution selected

All models can either be attached to the camera directly or via dedicated Nikon TTL remote flash cords: SC-28, SC-29, or the discontinued SC-17, with the exception of the SB-R200. This can only be controlled as part of the Nikon Advanced Wireless Lighting (AWL) flash system via either the SU-800 commander unit, or the SB-700, SB-800, and SB-900 Speedlights when used as a master flash unit.

286

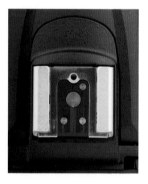

> The optional **external Speedlights can be mounted in the accessory shoe on top of the D7000 or connected to it using a dedicated TTL cord like the SC-28.**

The five Speedlights that can be attached to the accessory shoe of the D7000 offer further versatility since their flash heads can be tilted and—in the cases of the SB-600, SB-700, SB-800, and SB-900—swiveled for bounce flash. Unlike earlier Nikon Speedlights, which cancelled monitor pre-flashes if the flash head was tilted or swiveled, the SB-400, SB-600, SB-700, SB-800, and SB-900 emit pre-flashes regardless of the flash head orientation. The four latter units also have an adjustable auto zoom-head (SB-600: 24–85mm, SB-700: 24–120mm, SB-800: 24–105mm, SB-900: 17–200mm FX format and 12–200 DX format) that controls the angle of coverage. They also have a wide-angle diffuser to allow them to illuminate an even wider field of view. With the diffuser, the SB-600 and SB-800 can cover focal lengths as short as 14mm, while the SB-700 and SB-900 can cover the field of view provided by a focal length as short as 12mm on the FX format and 8mm on the DX format.

NOTE: If the SB-400 is attached to the D7000 and turned on, CS-e1 changes to **[Optional flash]**, which allows the flash control mode of the SB-400 to be chosen from either TTL or Manual.

The coverage of the SB-600 and SB-800 is set to correspond to the field of view of a lens with one of the focal lengths within the range of its zoom head. However, this is based on the assumption that the Speedlight is attached to a camera with an FX-format (24 x 36 mm) sensor. When used with the D7000, the SB-900 automatically adjusts its coverage to match the DX format (16 x 24 mm) sensor. The DX-format of the D7000 corresponds to a reduction in the angle of view for the same focal length when used on the FX-format, so the flash will illuminate a greater area with the D7000 than is necessary. Consequently, this will restrict the potential shooting range and squander flash power. In this situation, use the following table to adjust the zoom head position and thus maximize the performance of the flash unit:

FOCAL LENGTH OF LENS (MM)	ZOOM HEAD POSITION (MM)
14	20
18	24
20	28
24	35
28	50
35	50
50	70
70	85
85	105 [1]

[1] Available on SB-800 only.

The following chart illustrates which features each of the Speedlights offers.

FLASH MODE/FEATURE		SB-900 SB-800	SB-700	SB-600	SB-400	ADVANCED WIRELESS LIGHTING					
						COMMANDER			REMOTE		
						SB-900 SB-800	SB-700	SU-800[1]	SB-900 SB-800	SB-700 SB-600	SB-R200
i-TTL	i-TTL Balanced Fill-Flash for digital SLR	✓[2]	✓[3]	✓[2]	✓[3]	✓	✓	✓	✓	✓	✓
AA	Auto Aperture	✓[4]	—	—	—	✓[5]	—	✓[5]	✓[5]	—	—
A	Non-TTL Auto	✓[4]	—	—	—	✓[5]	—	—	✓[5]	—	—
GN	Distance-Priority Manual	✓	✓	—	—	—	—	—	—	—	—
M	Manual	✓	✓	✓	✓[6]	✓	✓	✓	✓	✓	✓
RPT	Repeating Flash	✓	—	—	—	✓	—	✓	✓	✓	—
Auto FP High-Speed Sync [7]		✓	✓	✓	—	✓	✓	✓	✓	✓	✓
FV Lock		✓	✓	✓	✓	✓	✓	✓	✓	✓	✓
AF-Assist for Multi-Area AF [8]		✓	✓	✓	—	✓	✓	✓	—	—	—
Flash Color Information Communication		✓	✓	✓	✓	✓	✓	—	—	—	—
REAR	Rear-Curtain Sync	✓	✓	✓	✓	✓	✓	✓	✓	✓	✓
👁	Red-Eye Reduction	✓	✓	✓	✓	✓	✓	—	—	—	—
Power zoom		✓	✓	✓	—	✓	✓	—	—	—	—

1 Only available when SU-800 is used to control other flash units.
2 Standard i-TTL flash for DSLR is used with Spot metering or when selected with flash unit.
3 Standard i-TTL flash for DSLR is used with Spot metering.
4 Selected with flash unit.
5 Auto Aperture (AA) is used regardless of mode selected with flash unit.
6 Can be selected with camera.
7 Select 1/320s (Auto FP) or 1/250s (Auto FP) for CS-e1 [Flash sync speed]
8 CPU lens required.

NON-TTL AUTOMATIC FLASH WITH SB-800 & SB-900

When using the SB-800 and SB-900 external Speedlights with the D7000, there are two additional non-TTL flash modes available; these are selected on the Speedlight via its mode button:

Auto Aperture (AA): The AA flash mode can be used in Aperture-Priority (A) or Manual (M) exposure mode. In this mode, the SB-900 and SB-800 read the ISO sensitivity setting, lens aperture, and the "command to fire the flash" signal from the camera automatically. Thereafter, the flash output level is determined using a sensor on the front panel of the Speedlight to monitor the flash exposure. As soon as this sensor detects that sufficient light has been output, the light from the flash is quenched. If, between exposures, you decide to alter the focal length or change the lens aperture, the Speedlight will adjust its output accordingly to maintain a correct flash exposure. The problem with this mode is that the coverage of the built-in flash sensor does not necessarily match the field of view of the lens, and therefore it does not "see" the same scene, which can lead to inaccuracies in flash exposure.

Automatic (A): This is the other automatic, non-TTL flash mode available with the SB-800 and SB-900 Speedlights. It can also be used in Aperture-Priority (A) or Manual (M) exposure mode. Similar to in the AA mode, a sensor on the front of the SB-800, SB-900, or DX-type Speedlight monitors flash levels and shuts off the flash when the Speedlight calculates that sufficient light has been emitted. However, the lens aperture and ISO sensitivity values must be set manually on the Speedlight to ensure that the subject is within the flash shooting range. As with the AA mode, the sensor does not necessarily cover the same angle of view as the lens, which can lead to inaccuracies in flash exposure.

MANUAL FLASH EXPOSURE CONTROL

In Manual flash mode, you set the output of the Speedlight (either built-in or external) to a fixed level. It is necessary to calculate the correct lens aperture using the flash-to-subject distance and the guide number (GN) of the Speedlight. To select Manual flash control for the built-in Speedlight, open the Custom Settings menu and navigate to CS-e3 **[Flash cntrl for built-in flash]** and press ▶. Highlight **[Manual]** and press ⊛. When using an external Speedlight, the flash mode is selected via the controls of the Speedlight.

For example, at the camera's base sensitivity of ISO 100, the built-in Speedlight of the D7000 has a guide number (GN) of 39 ft (12 m). The output level of the built-in Speedlight is determined by CS-e3 **[Flash cntrl for built-in flash]**, where a value between 1/1 (full output) and 1/128 can be selected. Since there is only one specific exposure level for any given level of sensitivity (ISO) at a particular flash-to-subject distance, it is necessary to calculate the lens aperture required to record a proper exposure. Use the following equation: Aperture = GN / Distance.

Therefore, with the built-in Speedlight of the D7000 set to 1/1 (full output) at a flash-to-subject distance of exactly 10 feet (3 m), and an ISO of 100, the lens aperture required to obtain a correct exposure of the subject will be around f/4 (39/10). Similar calculations will have to be performed when using an external Speedlight in Manual flash mode. Check the guide number (GN) for the particular Speedlight model and ensure that you conduct the calculations using the same unit of distance (feet or meters) throughout.

REPEATING FLASH

Another form of manual flash control is the Repeating Flash function, which is available with both the built-in Speedlight and compatible external Speedlights. For the built-in Speedlight of the D7000, this is selected and set via CS-e3 **[Flash cntrl for built-in flash]**. In this mode, the flash will fire repeatedly while the shutter is open to produce a strobe-lighting effect. Press ◄ or ► to select one of the three options that must be set, then use ▲ or ▼ to select the required value. Press ⊛ to return to the Custom Setting menu once all the required settings have been made. The options are as follows:

OPTION	DESCRIPTION
Output	Select the required flash output (it is expressed as a fraction of the maximum output).
Times	Select the number of times the flash will fire at the selected output level. Depending on the shutter speed used and the value selected for frequency, the actual number of flash outputs may be less than selected.
Frequency	Select how often the flash fires per second (1Hz = 1 per second).

The values available for **[Times]** is dependent on the output level of the flash, as shown in the table below:

OUTPUT	TIMES (NUMBER OF TIMES THE FLASH WILL FIRE)
1/4	2
1/8	2-5
1/16	2-10
1/32	2-10, 15
1/64	2-10, 15, 20, 25
1/128	2-10, 15, 20, 25, 30, 35

FLASH CONTROL MODES

The Information Display shows the flash control mode for the built-in flash and for external Speedlights attached via the accessory shoe or TTL flash cord using the following symbols:

BUILT-IN FLASH	FLASH SYNC	AUTO FP
i-TTL	⌐TTL	N/A
Manual	⌐M	N/A
Repeating flash	⌐RPT	N/A
Commander mode	⌐CMD	⌐FP

NOTE: Flash control mode for the built-in flash is selected via CS-e3.

EXTERNAL FLASH	FLASH SYNC	AUTO FP
i-TTL	⌐TTL	⌐FP
Auto Aperture [1]	⌐AA	⌐AA/FP
Non-TTL auto flash	⌐A	⌐A/FP
Distance-priority manual (GN)	⌐GN	⌐GN/FP
Manual	⌐M	⌐M/FP
Repeating flash	⌐RPT	N/A
Advanced wireless lighting	⌐CMD	⌐CMD/FP

[1] SB-900 and SB-800 only

Not to be confused with the flash exposure control modes available on the D7000 (e.g., i-TTL Balanced Fill Flash, Standard i-TTL flash, or Manual flash) described earlier, the flash synchronization (sync) modes determine when the built-in or external Speedlight is fired in relation to the opening and closing of the shutter. The availability of a particular flash sync mode will depend on the selected exposure mode. In turn, the choice of flash sync mode will influence the range of shutter speeds that is available (see Shutter Speed Restrictions chart on page 294).

To set a flash sync mode on the D7000, press and hold the ⚡ button, and rotate the main command dial to scroll through the various options until the icon for the required mode appears in the control panel. In **P**, **S**, **A**, and **M** exposure modes the following options are available:

⬚ **Front-Curtain Sync:** The flash fires as soon as the shutter has fully opened. In **P** and **A** exposure modes, the shutter speed range is restricted to between 1/60 and 1/250 second, unless a lower speed has been selected via CS-e2 [**Flash shutter speed**]. In **S** and **M** exposure modes, the Speedlight synchronizes at shutter speeds between 30 seconds and 1/250 second.

👁 **Red-Eye Reduction:** The AF-Assist lamp on the front right side of the camera body illuminates for approximately one second before the main exposure; the purpose is to induce the pupils in the subject's eyes to constrict and thus reduce the risk of red-eye occurring. Shutter speed synchronization is the same as for Front-Curtain Sync.

HINT: This mode not only alerts your subject that you are about to take a picture but also causes an inordinate delay in the shutter's operation by which time the critical moment has generally passed and you have missed the shot! Personally, I never bother with this feature. You can always fix red-eye in post processing.

👁 **Slow Sync:** Only available in **P** and **A** exposure modes, the flash fires as soon as the shutter has fully opened and at all shutter speeds between 30 seconds and 1/250 second. It is useful for recording low-level ambient light, as well as those areas of the scene or subject illuminated by flash (see pages 294-295).

Slow Sync with Red-Eye: Only available in **P** and **A** exposure modes, the two features operate together, creating a Slow-Sync exposure with Red-Eye Reduction applied.

HINT: The same advice applies—avoid this mode!

Rear-Curtain Sync: Available in **S** and **M** exposure modes, the flash fires just before the shutter closes and at all shutter speeds between 30 seconds and 1/250 second. Any image of a moving subject recorded by the ambient light exposure will appear to be behind the image of the subject illuminated by the flash output.

Rear Curtain with Slow Sync: Available in **P** and **A** exposure modes, the flash fires just before the shutter closes and at all shutter speeds between 30 seconds and 1/250 second. Any image of a moving subject recorded by the ambient light exposure will appear to be behind the image of the subject illuminated by the flash output.

In the **AUTO** and **SCENE** modes that support flash, the operation of the flash is fully automated. There is no ability to apply Flash Compensation or use Custom Settings pertaining to flash control other than adjusting the sync speed under CS-e1. The following options are available:

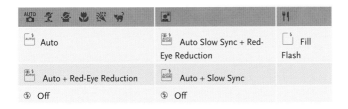

AUTO 🏃 🌄 🌷 🎇 🐾	🖼	🍴
AUTO Auto	Auto Slow Sync + Red-Eye Reduction	Fill Flash
AUTO Auto + Red-Eye Reduction	AUTO Auto + Slow Sync	
Off	Off	

SHUTTER SPEED RESTRICTIONS WITH FLASH

This table summarizes how the shutter speed value is influenced according to the exposure mode that is selected (**P**, **S**, **A**, and **M** modes only), with either the built-in flash or an external Speedlight:

EXPOSURE MODE	SHUTTER SPEED	LENS APERTURE
Programmed Auto (P)	Set automatically by camera (1/250 – 1/60 second) 1, 2	Set automatically by the camera
Shutter Priority (S)	Value selected by user (1/250 – 30-seconds) 2	
Aperture Priority (A)	Set automatically by camera (1/250 – 1/60 second) 1, 2	Value selected by the user
Manual (M)	Value selected by user (1/250 – 30-seconds) 2	

[1] Shutter speed may be set as slow as 30 seconds in Slow Sync, Slow Rear-Curtain Sync, and Slow Sync with Red-Eye Reduction modes.

[2] Speeds as fast as 1/8000 second are available with optional SB-900, SB-800, SB-700 and SB-600 flash units when **[1/320 s (Auto FP)]** or **[1/250 s (Auto FP)]** is selected for CS-e1 **[Flash sync speed]**.

In ⚙ and the **SCENE** modes that support flash, the following shutter speeds are available:

EXPOSURE MODE	SHUTTER SPEED
🔒 🌃 🌆 🏔 🐕	Set automatically by camera (1/250 – 1/60 second)
🌷 🍴	Set automatically by camera (1/250 – 1/125 second)
🌃	Set automatically by camera (1/250 – 1 second)

SLOW SYNCHRONIZATION FLASH

The camera will normally set a shutter speed that is within the restricted range of 1/60 – 1/250 second when using the built-in flash or a compatible external Speedlight, and the camera is in Program (**P**) or Aperture-Priority (**A**) autoexposure mode. The actual speed that is used within this narrow range depends on the level of ambient light (the brighter the conditions, the shorter the shutter speed).

This restriction can have a significant effect on the overall exposure. For example, in situations when you photograph a subject outside at night or in a dark interior, any area of the scene illuminated by ambient light alone will be lit dimly compared with those areas that will be illuminated by the flash. It is more than likely that the level of ambient light will not be sufficient for a proper exposure within this restricted range of shutter speeds; consequently, these areas of the scene will be underexposed. A typical photograph taken under these conditions has a well-exposed subject set against a dark, featureless background.

To prevent this, select the appropriate Slow-Sync mode. This enables the camera to use a wider range of slower shutter speeds, extending from 1/250 second to the longest available shutter speed of 30 seconds. Therefore, the camera will be able to select a more appropriate shutter speed for the low level of ambient light, so the correct exposure can be achieved for the background (remember, the flash output will have little if any effect in this region because the intensity of light from the flash will diminish according to the inverse square law). However, the flash output will be controlled for a proper exposure of the subject and its surroundings.

HINT: Since the shutter speed may be quite slow when using Slow Sync flash mode, consider using a tripod or other camera support to avoid the effects of camera shake.

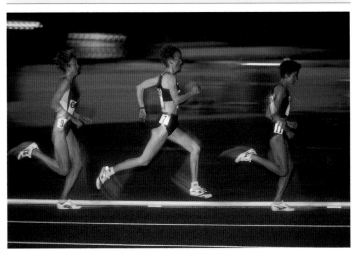

^ Mixing low-level ambient light with flash and a slow shutter speed allows you to create some interesting effects.

REAR-CURTAIN SYNCHRONIZATION

If a subject you want to photograph is moving, it is possible to achieve some interesting effects by using Slow Sync flash mode in combination with a slow shutter speed, as the flash will illuminate the subject briefly to record it as sharp, while the slow shutter speed will record the ambient light resulting in the subject's motion being recorded as a blur. This technique can be achieved using Rear-Curtain Sync flash mode in either Shutter-Priority (S) or Manual (M) exposure mode. Alternatively, in Programmed-Auto (P) or Aperture-Priority (A) exposure modes, use Rear-Curtain with Slow Sync flash mode. In each case, it will cause the blur due to subject movement to appear as though it is following the sharp image of the subject formed by the flash illumination, to produce a more natural appearance of subject movement.

AUTO FOCAL PLANE (FP) HIGH-SPEED SYNC

One of the limitations of using daylight fill-flash is the maximum flash sync speed of the D7000, which is limited to 1/250 second; so, working in bright lighting conditions, it is often not possible to open the lens aperture very far, due to the restriction of the maximum (briefest) shutter speed limit imposed by the use of flash. The Auto FP High-Speed Sync feature allows a compatible external Speedlight to sync at any shutter speed faster than 1/250 second, plus you can adjust the flash output automatically, which makes using Fill Flash far more flexible. If an incompatible flash (anything other than the SB-900, SB-800, SB-700, SB-600, or SB-R200) or the camera's built-in Speedlight is used, the shutter speed defaults to 1/250 second. To use this handy feature, select the [1/250 s (Auto FP)] option at CS-e1 [Flash sync speed].

In order to operate quickly enough to keep up with those faster shutter speeds, the flash emits its output of light as a very rapid series of pulses instead of a single continuous pulse; however, this has the effect of reducing the amount of light emitted by the flash so, as the flash is synchronized with increasingly faster shutter speeds, the flash output is reduced progressively, which in turn reduces the operational range of the Speedlight.

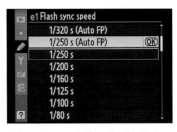

e Bracketing/flash	
e1 Flash sync speed	1/250
e2 Flash shutter speed	1/60
e3 Flash cntrl for built-in flash	TTL⚡
e4 Modeling flash	ON
e5 Auto bracketing set	AE⚡
e6 Bracketing order	Ⓝ
f1 ☀switch	☀
f2 OK button (shooting mode)	RESET

e1 Flash sync speed	
1/320 s (Auto FP)	
1/250 s (Auto FP)	ⓄⓀ
1/250 s	
1/200 s	
1/160 s	
1/125 s	
1/100 s	
1/80 s	

∧ The [Flash sync speed] item in the Custom Settings menu

∧ The options available under the [Flash sync speed] item include the two Auto FP sync options.

For example, at flash sync speeds of 1/250 second or less, the SB-900 has a guide number for the DX format and its Standard lighting pattern of 131/40 (ft/m, ISO 100, 35mm, 20°C/68°F), but selecting the [1/250 s (Auto FP)] option reduces its guide number to 60/18 (ft/m, ISO 100, 35mm, 20°C/68°F). Flash range is calculated by dividing the guide number by the lens aperture value; so using f/5.6, the SB-900 has a maximum range of 23 feet (7.0 m) at flash sync speeds of 1/250 second or slower, but only 10.5 feet (3.2 m) when the [1/250 s (Auto FP)] option is active.

The D7000 also has an additional Auto FP High-Speed Sync option, [1/320 s (Auto FP)], again selected via CS-e1 [Flash sync speed], which works in a slightly different way: It allows any SB-15 or later Speedlight to sync up to 1/320 by emitting a single pulse of light from the flash (rather than the weaker, repeating pulses used with regular high-speed sync), but with a reduced maximum duration compared with the duration of the flash output at the normal maximum flash sync speed of 1/250. This reduced-power firing at 1/320 is standard sync, not high-speed sync, as long as you're using the built-in flash or a compatible accessory flash.

Additionally, any compatible external Speedlight will sync up to the shortest shutter speed available on the camera in exactly the same way as it does using the [1/250 s (Auto FP)] option, and when using the built-in flash or an incompatible accessory flash, the shutter will default to 1/320 second. Like the 1/250 option, the flash unit's guide number is effectively reduced, so use this feature sparingly. The table below sets out the combination of shutter speed ranges and flash sync options.

FLASH SYNC	1/320 S (AUTO FP)		1/250 S (AUTO FP)		1/250 SECOND	
SHUTTER SPEED	BUILT-IN FLASH	EXTERNAL FLASH	BUILT-IN FLASH	EXTERNAL FLASH	BUILT-IN FLASH	EXTERNAL FLASH
1/8000 – 1/320 s	not possible	Auto FP	not possible	Auto FP	not possible	not possible
1/320 – 1/250 s	standard flash synchronization 1		not possible	Auto FP	not possible	not possible
1/250 – 30 s	standard flash synchronization					

1 Effective flash range is reduced when shutter speed is increased from 1/250 second to 1/320 second in standard sync; however, it is still greater than the range achieved at the same shutter speeds with Auto FP sync.

HINT: The very modest increase in shutter speed made available by the [1/320 s (Auto FP)] option is unlikely to be of much use in many situations, unless you only have the built-in Speedlight of the D7000 available to you. Since an external Speedlight (SB-900, SB-800, SB-700 or SB-600) provides far greater flexibility in the control of lighting for Fill Flash, I would recommend using one of these units with the [1/250 s (Auto FP)] option of the Auto FP High-Speed Sync feature.

HINT: Since both of the Auto FP High-Speed Sync options reduce flash shooting range, always check the distance scale displayed in the control panel of the external Speedlight when using the Auto FP feature. "FP" will be displayed in the control panel of the external Speedlight to let you know that this feature is in use.

FLASH COMPENSATION

Flash Compensation is used to modify the level of flash output; it can be set on the D7000 by pressing and holding the ⚡ button while turning the Sub-Command dial (only available in P, S, A, and M shooting modes). Compensation can be set in increments of 0.3 (1/3), 0.5 (1/2), or 1 EV (subject to settings in CS-b2 [EV steps for exposure cntrl]) over a range of +1.0 to –3.0 EV. To restore normal flash output, set the Flash Compensation to ± 0.0.

Flash Compensation can also be applied directly on compatible external Speedlights: SB-900, SB-800, SB-700 and SB-600. If Flash Compensation is applied on the D7000 and on an external Speedlight at the same time, the effect is cumulative. For example, applying a value of +1 EV to both the camera and external Speedlight results in a Flash Compensation of +2 EV.

As discussed earlier in this chapter, the default i-TTL Balanced Fill-Flash mode will automatically set a Flash Compensation based on scene brightness, contrast, focus distance, and a variety of other factors. The level of automatic adjustment applied to flash output by the D7000 will often cancel out any compensation value entered manually. Since there is no way of telling what the camera is doing, you will never have control of the flash exposure. To regain control, set the flash mode to Standard i-TTL by either selecting Spot metering on the camera (this is the only option for setting the built-in Speedlight to Standard i-TTL) or setting the flash control mode on an external Speedlight accordingly; in the latter case, ensure that only TTL is displayed in the control panel of the Speedlight for the flash mode, and not TTL-BL.

FLASH VALUE (FV) LOCK

Flash Value (FV) Lock allows you to use the camera and Speedlight to estimate the required flash output for a subject and then retain this value temporarily, before making the main exposure. This is a very useful feature if you want to compose a picture so that the main subject is located toward the edge of the frame area, particularly if the background is very bright or dark. Under these circumstances, using the normal i-TTL flash exposure control, there is a risk that the camera may calculate an incorrect level of flash output, and cause the main subject to be either under- or overexposed.

On the D7000, the FV Lock feature can be activated via a number of different routes. The following describes how to assign its operation to the **Fn** button. Open CS-f3, and select the following options: **[Assign Fn button]** > **[FV lock]**. Select **FL** FV Lock and press ⊛.

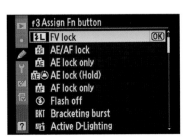

‹ The FV Lock feature can be assigned to one of three buttons on the D7000; here, CS-f3 has been selected for the **Fn** button.

Raise the built-in flash and check that the flash ready light is lit; then, compose the picture with the subject in the center of the viewfinder area, acquire focus by pressing the shutter release halfway, then press the **Fn** button on the camera. The Speedlight will emit monitor pre-flashes, so the D7000 can assess the required amount of flash output. The flash output value is saved by the camera, and 🔒 is displayed in the viewfinder to indicate that the function is active. Now you can recompose the picture and place the subject toward the edge of the frame area. Finally, make the exposure by fully depressing the shutter release button. The flash will fire at the saved, predetermined level. If you alter the focal length of a zoom lens or adjust the lens aperture, the FV Lock function will compensate the flash output automatically. To release FV Lock, press the **Fn** button and ensure that 🔒 is no longer displayed.

NOTE: The FV Lock function can only be used with the D7000's built-in Speedlight when **[TTL]** is selected at CS-e3.

NOTE: The FV Lock feature is very useful when shooting flash pictures of people, because once the flash output level has been established by the initial emission of the monitor pre-flashes, no further pre-flashes are fired, which significantly reduces the risk of causing a blink reflex in your subject.

FV Lock is supported by the following external Speedlights: SB-900, SB-800, SB-700, SB-600, SB-400, and SB-R200. These external Speedlights must be set to perform TTL flash control; the SB-900 and SB-800 can also be used in the Auto Aperture (AA) flash control mode. The FV Lock function is also supported by the SB-900, SB-800, SB-700, SB-600, and SB-R200 when the built-in Speedlight of the D7000 is set to **[Commander]** mode via CS-e3 and any of these Speedlights is used as a wirelessly controlled remote unit, provided TTL is set as the flash mode. If the wireless remote Speedlight group is composed exclusively of one or more SB-900 / SB-800 Speedlights, the FV Lock feature can be used with either TTL or AA flash control modes.

The area of the frame from which the camera takes a light meter reading when the **[FV Lock]** function is active varies according to the number of Speedlights and flash control mode in use, as shown in the following table:

Speedlight	Flash Mode	Metered Area
Single Speedlight connected to the camera	i-TTL	4-mm circle at center of frame
	AA	Area metered by built-in sensor on SB-900 / SB-800
Speedlight used with others as part of wireless flash control system	i-TTL	Entire frame
	AA	Area metered by built-in sensor on SB-900 / SB-800
	A (master flash only)	

NOTE: The camera-to-subject distance must remain unaltered during the use of the FV Lock function. Otherwise, the flash exposure will be inaccurate.

NOTE: The FV Lock function can also be assigned to either the Depth-of-Field Preview button via CS-f4 or to the AE-L/AF-L button via CS-f5.

FLASH COLOR INFORMATION COMMUNICATION

When Automatic White Balance is selected on the D7000 (this feature does not operate with any other White Balance option) and you are using the SB-900, SB-800, SB-700, SB-600, or SB-400 Speedlight, the external flash unit automatically transmits information to the camera about the color temperature of the light it emits. The camera will then use this information to adjust its final White Balance setting, attempting to optimize the color temperature of the light from the flash to compensate for the effects of voltage variation from the Speedlight batteries, duration of the flash output, and influence of other non-flash light sources.

WIDE AREA AF-ASSIST ILLUMINATOR

The purpose of the AF-Assist lamp built into the SB-900, SB-800, SB-700, and SB-600 Speedlights and the SU-800 wireless commander unit is to facilitate autofocus in low-light situations. The AF-Assist lamp on these units is significantly more powerful and covers a much wider area compared with the built-in AF-Assist lamp of the D7000, which has the additional disadvantage of being obstructed by many Nikkor lenses due to its proximity to the lens mount.

The wider coverage provided by the AF-Assist lamp of the external units is particularly useful with the D7000, with its wide array of 39 AF points that cover a large proportion of the frame area. The effective range of the Wide-Area AF-Assist lamp varies according to the focal length of the lens in use. Use of the Wide-Area AF-Assist lamp introduces restrictions on the AF points that are available for autofocus (see charts below).

SB-900: Autofocus is only available with the AF points shown in bold. If other AF points are selected, the AF-Assist lamp may not provide sufficient light for autofocus to work.

FOCAL LENGTH OF AF LENS	AF POINTS SUPPORTED BY AF-ASSIST ILLUMINATION
17 – 19 мм	(AF point diagram)
20 – 105 мм	(AF point diagram)
106 – 135 мм	(AF point diagram)

SB-800, SB-600, and SU-800: Autofocus is only available with the AF points shown in bold.

FOCAL LENGTH OF AF LENS	AF POINTS SUPPORTED BY AF-ASSIST ILLUMINATION
24 – 34 мм	(AF point diagram)
35 – 49 мм	(AF point diagram)
50 – 105 мм	(AF point diagram)

SB-700: Autofocus is only available with the AF points shown in bold. If other AF points are selected, the AF-Assist lamp may not provide sufficient light for autofocus to work.

FOCAL LENGTH OF AF LENS	AF POINTS SUPPORTED BY AF-ASSIST ILLUMINATION
24 – 135 мм	(AF point diagram)

HINT: When a compatible external Speedlight with a Wide-Area AF-Assist illuminator is used off the camera (see below), the light emitted by the lamp may not be reflected with sufficient strength to be effective if it strikes the subject at an oblique angle. In this situation, consider using the Nikon SC-29 TTL flash cord, which has a built-in AF-Assist illuminator in its terminal block that attaches to the camera accessory shoe. This places the AF-Assist illuminator immediately above the central axis of the lens to help improve the accuracy of autofocus.

OFF-CAMERA FLASH WITH A TTL CORD

When you work with a single external Speedlight, it is often desirable to take the flash off the camera. There are several different dedicated Nikon cords for this purpose: the SC-17 (discontinued), SC-28, and SC-29. All three cords are 4.9 feet (1.5 m) long, but up to three SC-17 or SC-28 cords can be connected together if you need a longer cord. Whenever you take a Speedlight off the camera and use any TTL flash mode that will incorporate focus distance information in the flash output computations, take care where you position the flash. If the Speedlight is moved closer or farther away by a significant amount compared with the camera-to-subject distance, the accuracy of the flash output may be

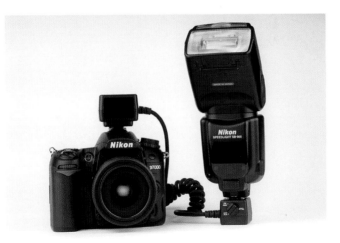

∧ The SC-28 TTL cord is one of three cords that can be used to connect external Speedlights; it is pictured here with the D7000 and SB-900 Speedlight.

compromised, as the TTL flash control system works on the assumption that the flash is located at the same distance from the subject as the camera. Likewise, when using Manual flash exposure control, remember to calculate the lens aperture based on the flash-to-subject distance, not camera-to-subject distance.

○ Increasing the angular separation between the central axis of the lens and the flash head will significantly reduce the risk of the red-eye effect with humans or eye-shine with animals.

○ In situations when it is not practicable to use bounce flash, moving the flash off-camera will usually improve the quality of the lighting, especially the degree of modeling it provides, compared with the typical flat, frontal lighting produced by a flash mounted on the camera.

○ By taking the flash off-camera and directing the light from the Speedlight accordingly, it is often possible to control the position of shadows so that they become less noticeable.

○ When using Fill Flash, it is often desirable to direct light to a specific part of the scene to help reduce the level of contrast locally.

○ An SB-900, SB-800, or SB-700 Speedlight connected to the camera via one of Nikon's dedicated TTL cords can be used as the master / commander flash to control multiple Speedlights off-camera using the Advanced Wireless Lighting system (see next section).

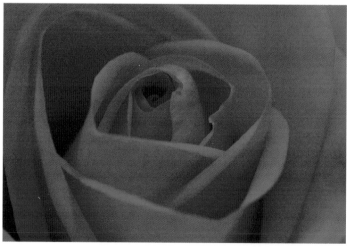

^ Taking an external Speedlight flash off the camera using a TTL flash cord, such as the Nikon SC-28, is the simplest and most effective way of improving the quality and flexibility of your lighting.

This feature is compatible with the Speedlights that support the CLS (SB-900, SB-800, SB-700, SB-600, and SB-R200), together with the SU-800 Wireless Speedlight Commander unit. It allows for one or more remote Speedlight(s) to be operated and controlled wirelessly in up to three autonomous groups, using the **P**, **S**, **A** and **M** exposure modes available on the D7000. The remote Speedlights can be used in a variety of flash modes: TTL, Auto Aperture (with remote SB-900 / SB-800 Speedlights only), or Manual. The remote Speedlights are controlled by pulsed infrared (IR) light (think of it as an optical Morse code), via one of four dedicated communication channels using the SB-900, SB-800, or SU-800 as a commander unit.

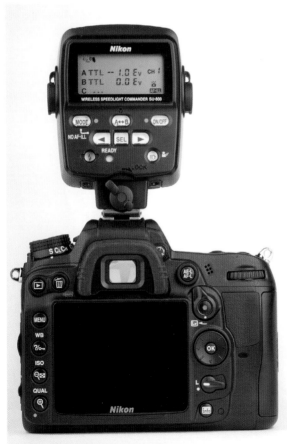

‹ The SU-800 can control up to three groups of compatible Nikon Speedlights.

Alternatively, the built-in Speedlight of the D7000 can be used to control up to two separate groups of remote Speedlights; this option, which is known as its [Commander mode], is selected under CS-e3 [Flash Cntrl for Built-in flash]. To use the built-in Speedlight in [Commander mode], where it can be set to act as either the master flash that will contribute light to the flash exposure and emit the control signals for the remote Speedlights or as a commander unit that will only emit the control signals for the remote Speedlights and not contribute to the exposure:

1. Open the Custom Settings menu and navigate to CS-e3 [Flash cntrl for built-in flash], and then press ▶.

2. Highlight the [Commander mode] option and press ▶ to open a submenu of flash mode and flash compensation options together with flash group and control channel options.

3. Highlight [Built-in flash] to set the required flash mode and use ▲ or ▼ to select [TTL], [M], or [- -] (flash cancelled). If [TTL] or [M] is selected, press ▶ to highlight [Comp] (Flash Compensation) and use ▲ or ▼ to select the required value. In TTL mode, the Flash Compensation can be set over a range of ±3 EV in steps of 0.3 EV; in Manual flash mode, the output can be set to any level between full output and 1/128 of full output. Finally, press ▶ to set and confirm the value, and highlight [Group A].

4. Set the required flash mode for Group A by using ▲ or ▼ to select [TTL], [AA] (SB-900 / SB-800 only), [M], or [- -] (flash cancelled). If [TTL], [AA], or [M] is selected, and you want to set a Flash Compensation level, repeat the procedure from Step 3. Otherwise, press the Multi-Selector to the right to highlight [Group B]. Repeat steps 3 and 4 to set flash mode and Flash Compensation.

5. Highlight [Channel] and use ▲ or ▼ to select the required channel number.

6. Finally, press the ⊛ button to confirm and lock the settings made in steps 3 – 5 above.

7. Check that each remote Speedlight is set to operate as a remote flash unit and that it is also set to the same channel as selected on the camera at Step 5 above.

8. Press the ⚡ flash button to raise the built-in Speedlight of the camera and ensure the ready light of each flash unit is lit. The system is now ready to be used.

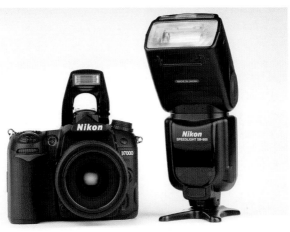

^ The built-in Speedlight of the D7000 can control external CLS compatible
Speedlights wirelessly.

FLASH COMMANDER UNITS' EFFECTIVE RANGE IN AWL

When one of the following units is used as the commander for wireless
control of compatible remote Speedlights (SB-900, SB-800, SB-700, SB-
600, and SB-R200), the effective range of operation is:

O SB-900 / SB-800: When either of these units is used as a commander
   flash, Nikon states that the maximum effective operating range is 33 ft
   (10 m) along the central axis of the lens and 23 ft (7 m) within 30° of
   the central axis of the lens.

O SU-800: This is a dedicated IR transmitter (i.e., unlike the SB-900, SB-
   800, and built-in Speedlights that emit the control signals as part of a
   full spectrum emission when used as a master flash, the SU-800 only
   emits IR light). It is a more powerful unit compared with the SB-900
   or SB-800, so it is capable of controlling remote Speedlights up to a
   distance of 66 ft (20 m).

O SU-800 / SB-R200: When the SU-800 is used as the commander unit,
   Nikon states that the maximum effective operating range between it
   and remote SB-R200 Speedlights is 13 ft (4 m) along the central axis of
   the lens and 9.8 ft (3 m) within 30° of the central axis of the lens.

O D7000 built-in Speedlight: When used as a commander unit, the built-
   in Speedlight of the D7000 can control remote Speedlights up to a
   maximum effective operating range of 33 ft (10 m) within 30° of the
   central axis of the lens and 16 ft (5 m) between 30° and 60° from the
   central axis of the lens.

I have found the quoted maximum operating ranges for the components of the Advanced Wireless Lighting system to be very conservative, particularly indoors, where reflective surfaces can help to bounce the control signals farther. For example, I have used both SB-900 and SB-800 Speedlights as master and remote units at ranges outdoors of 100 feet (30 m) or more, which is three times greater than the suggested maximum range.

However, in bright sunlight, which contains a high level of naturally occurring IR light, you may find that the practical limit of the operating range is reduced, often significantly. In these circumstances, try to shade the IR sensor window of the remote Speedlight units from direct sunlight, as this will improve both effectiveness and reliability of the IR communication system. I have even managed to use remote flash units very successfully without direct line-of-sight between the master flash / commander unit and the sensor on the remote Speedlight(s). Again, I've been able to make this work particularly indoors, by taking an SU-800 unit off-camera using either the SC-28 or SC-29 TTL flash cord to connect it, or alternatively, bouncing the IR command signals off a reflector. However, every shooting situation is different, so my advice is to set up the lighting system to your requirements, and always take test shots to ensure that it works as intended.

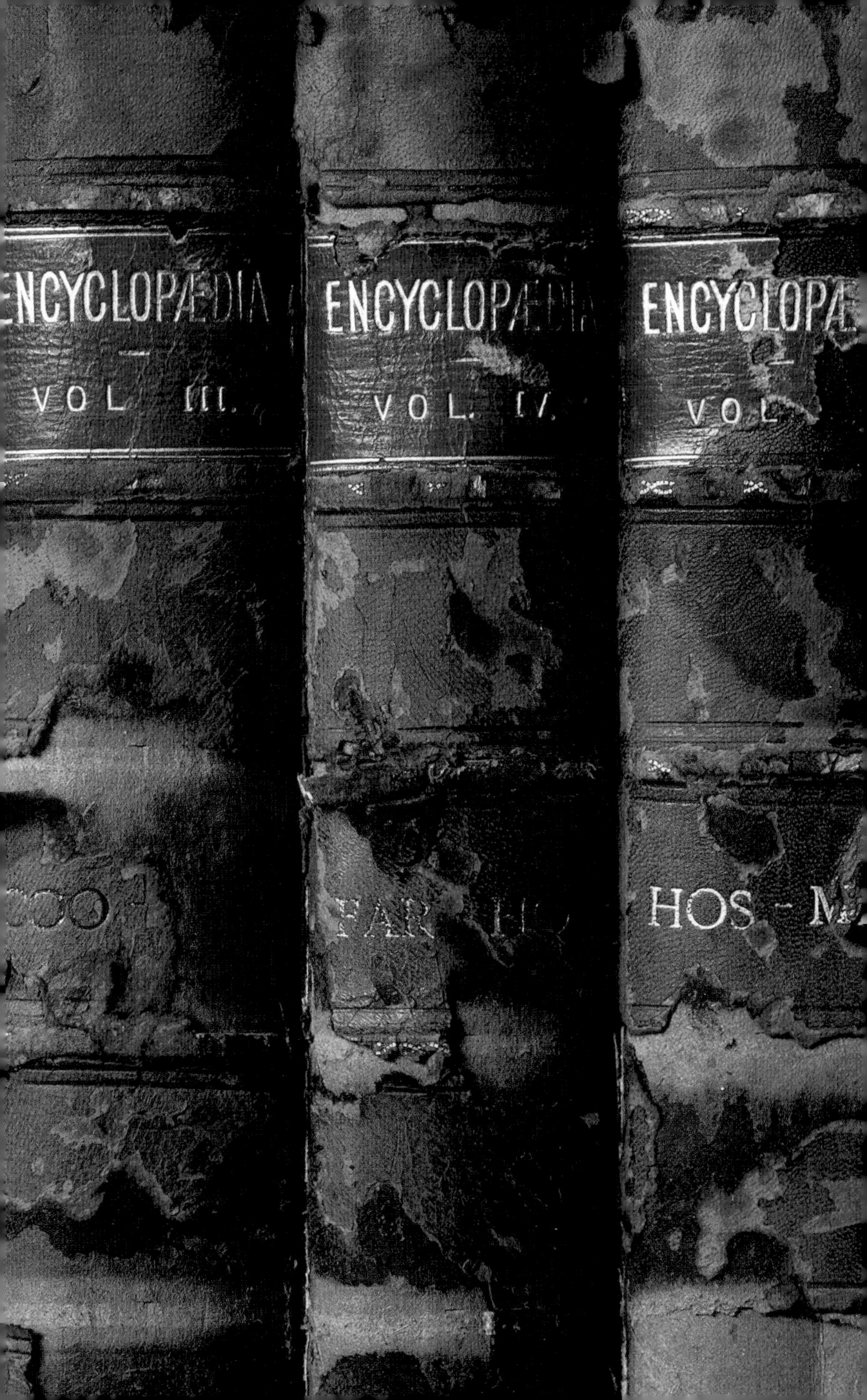

ENCYCLOPÆDIA

VOL. III.

ENCYCLOPÆDIA

VOL. IV.

ENCYCLOPÆ

VOL

OO

FAR — HO

HOS - M

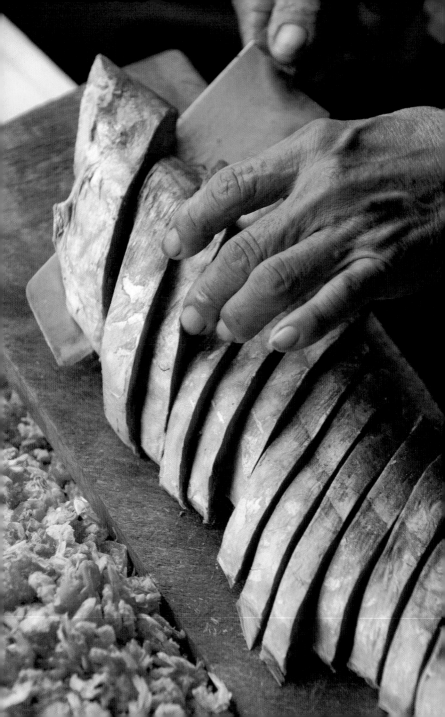

Nikon Lenses & Accessories

Nikon currently makes a range of approximately sixty lenses, known by their proprietary name of Nikkor, for their DSLR and film camera models. The "F" mount used on these Nikkor lenses is legendary; it has been used on all Nikon 35mm film and digital SLR cameras since the introduction of the original Nikon F SLR in 1959. As such, a great many of the lenses Nikon has produced in the past five decades can be mounted on the D7000, including most manual focus lenses that conform to the Ai lens-mount standard (see list on pages 313-314 for definitions of lens acronyms). The fullest level of compatibility is offered by modern AF-S (D-type and G-type) and the earlier AF-I autofocus Nikkor lenses that have an integral motor for driving the focus action. The D7000 has a built-in focusing motor, so it also supports autofocus with earlier AF Nikkor lenses that do not have an integral focusing motor. If a non-CPU type manual focus Nikkor lens is attached to the D7000, the camera can still be used in Aperture-Priority and Manual exposure control with color Matrix metering; however, this requires information about the lens to be stored in the camera (see pages 317-320 for full details).

Nikon also produces a range of software applications and camera accessories for the D7000. A vast amount of information and assistance with these products is available online. In addition, there is a wide range of other useful off-brand accessories available from other sources, some of which are referenced in the Resources section at the end of this book (see pages 368-369).

Whenever you attach or detach a lens from the D7000, make sure the camera is turned off. Identify the mounting index mark (white dot) on the lens and align it with the mounting index mark (white dot) next to the bayonet ring of the camera's lens mount. Enter the lens bayonet into the camera and rotate the lens counter-clockwise until it locks into place with an audible click. To remove a lens from the camera, press and hold the lens release button (located on the front of the camera to the left of the lens mount), and then rotate the lens until the two index marks are aligned before lifting the lens clear of the camera body. If you do not intend to mount another lens immediately, make sure you place the BF-1B body cap (one is supplied with the camera) back on the camera to help prevent unwanted material from getting inside.

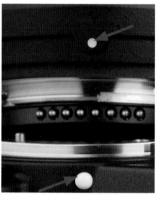

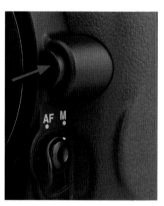

∧ To mount a lens, align the two white index marks on the camera and on the lens (see red arrows) before entering the lens mount flange into the camera body, and then twist the lens counter-clockwise until it locks into place.

∧ The lens release button is located on the front of the camera adjacent to the lens mount.

When using a CPU lens with an aperture ring, ensure it is set and locked to its minimum aperture value (highest f/number). If FE E blinks in the Information Display and viewfinder, the lens has not been set to its minimum aperture value. In this state, the shutter release is disabled and the camera will not operate. The latest G-type Nikkor lenses don't even have a conventional aperture ring.

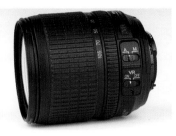

< The AF-S DX 18-105mm f/3.5-5.6G is one of a number of Nikkor lenses designed specifically for the DX-format of the D7000, and it is usually the lens supplied with the camera when it is purchased as a kit.

> A Nikkor CPU-type lens is readily identified by the electrical contact pins set around the lens mount flange; note the AF-S and G (after the maximum aperture value) designations on the lens barrel.

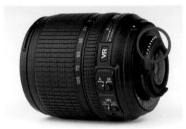

DEMYSTIFYING NIKKOR LENSES

The designations of Nikkor lenses, particularly modern autofocus types, are peppered with initials. Here is an explanation of what some of these stand for:

○ AF-type: These lenses are the predecessors to the later D- and G-type designs. They have a conventional aperture ring but do not communicate focus distance information to the camera.

○ AF D-type: These lenses have a conventional aperture ring and an integral electronic chip that communicates information about lens aperture and focus distance between the lens and the camera body. Nikon refers to this chip as a central processing unit (CPU), but to be strictly accurate, it is an integrated circuit. A "D" appears on the lens barrel after the maximum aperture value.

○ AF G-type: These lenses have no aperture ring and are only compatible with Nikon cameras that allow the aperture value to be set from the camera body. They contain an electronic chip that communicates information about lens aperture and focus distance between the lens and the camera body, similar to the D-type lenses. A "G" appears on the lens barrel after the maximum aperture value.

- AF-I: The predecessor to the AF-S lens type; these lenses also have an internal focusing motor.

- AF-S: These lenses use a silent-wave motor (SWM) for focusing; alternating magnetic fields drive the motor, which moves lens' elements to shift focus. This system offers the fastest autofocusing of all AF Nikkor lenses. Most AF-S lenses have an additional feature that allows you to switch between autofocus and manual focus, without adjusting any camera controls, by simply taking hold of the focus ring. "AF-S" appears on the lens barrel.

- DX: These lenses have been specially designed for use on Nikon small-format DSLR cameras. They project a smaller image circle than lenses designed for 35mm format cameras, and the light exiting their rear element is more collimated (actually parallel) to improve the efficiency of the photo diodes (pixels) on the camera's sensor. "DX" appears on the lens barrel.

- ED: To reduce the effect of chromatic aberration, Nikon developed a special type of glass known as Extra-Low Dispersion to bring various wavelengths of light to a common point of focus.

- IF: To speed up focusing, particularly with long focal length lenses, Nikon developed their Internal Focusing (IF) system. This moves a group of elements within the lens so that it does not alter the length of the lens during focusing and prevents the front filter mount from rotating, facilitating the use of filters such as polarizers.

- Nano Crystal Coat: This is a specialized lens coating that is applied to the surface of some lens elements to help reduce the level of light reflection, improving overall image quality. An "N" appears on the lens barrel.

- Non-CPU: Nikon uses the term "non-CPU" to describe any Nikkor lens lacking the components and electrical connections that enable communication of information between the lens and the camera body. With the exception of the PC-E 24mm f/3.5D, PC-E Micro 45mm f/2.8D, PC-E Micro 85mm f/2.8D, PC-Micro 85mm f/2.8D lens, and Ai-P type Nikkor lenses, all manual focus Nikkor lenses are non-CPU types.

- Micro-Nikkor: "Micro" is the name given to specialized lenses designed specifically for close-up and macro photography; the optical formula of these lenses is optimized for close focusing.

- PC-E: This is a special type of lens that offers the ability to shift and tilt the lens relative to the plane of the sensor in the camera to control perspective and depth of field. "PC-E" appears on the lens barrel.

- VR: Vibration Reduction (VR) is Nikon's name for a sophisticated technology that enables a lens to counter the effects of camera shake and other vibrations. A set of built-in motion sensors that cause micro-motors to shift a dedicated set of lens elements is used to improve the sharpness of pictures. "VR" appears on the lens barrel.

As mentioned previously in this chapter, the D7000 has a built-in electric motor to drive the focus action of those Nikkor AF lenses that lack their own integral AF motor; therefore, autofocus is supported with both the AF-S or the AF-I type Nikkor lenses (which can be identified by the presence of "AF-S" or "AF-I" at the beginning of the lens designation marked on the lens barrel) or any other AF Nikkor lenses. Nikon classifies all AF-S, AF-I, and AF Nikkor lenses, plus manual focus Ai-P Nikkor lenses, as CPU-type lenses; these lenses can be readily identified by the electrical contact pins set around the edge of the lens mount bayonet flange. The following table provides details of the compatibility of CPU-type Nikkor lenses with the D7000:

CAMERA SETTING	Focus mode		Exposure Mode		Metering		
					🔲		ⓞ
LENS/ACCESSORY[1]	S C	M (with electronic rangefinder)	M	P, S	A M	3D	Color	
Type G or D AF Nikkor[2] AF-s, AF-I Nikkor	✔	✔	✔	✔	✔	✔	—	✔[3]
PC-E Nikkor series	—	✔[4]	✔	✔[4]	✔[4]	✔[4]	—	✔[3, 4]
PC Micro 85mm f/2.8[5]	—	✔[4]	✔	—	✔[6]	✔	—	✔[3, 4]
AF-S / AF-I Teleconverter[7]	✔[8]	✔[8]	✔	✔	✔	✔	—	✔[3]
Other AF Nikkor (except lenses for F3AF)	✔[9]	✔[9]	✔	✔	✔	—	✔	✔[3]
AI-P Nikkor	—	✔[10]	✔	✔	✔	—	✔	✔[3]

[1] IX-Nikkor lenses cannot be used.
[2] Vibration Reduction (VR) supported with VR lenses.
[3] Spot metering meters selected focus point.
[4] Cannot be used with shifting or tilting.
[5] The camera's exposure metering and flash control systems do not work properly when shifting and/or tilting the lens or when an aperture other than the maximum aperture is used.
[6] Manual exposure mode only.
[7] Can be used with AF-S and AF-I lenses only.
[8] With maximum effective aperture of f/5.6 or faster.
[9] When focusing at minimum focus distance with AF 80–200mm f/2.8, AF 35–70mm f/2.8, AF 28–85mm f/3.5-4.5, or AF 28–85mm f/3.5-4.5 lens at maximum zoom, in-focus indicator may be displayed when image on matte screen in viewfinder is not in focus. Adjust focus manually until image in viewfinder is in focus.
[10] With maximum aperture of f/5.6 or faster.

The Nikon AF-S / AF-I teleconverters can be used with the following AF-S and AF-I lenses:

- AF-S VR Micro 105mm f/2.8G ED [1]
- AF-S VR 200mm f/2G ED
- AF-S VR II 200mm f/2G ED
- AF-S VR 300mm f/2.8G ED
- AF-S VR II 300mm f/2.8G ED
- AF-S 300mm f/2.8D ED II
- AF-S 300mm f/2.8D ED
- AF-I 300mm f/2.8D ED
- AF-S 300mm f/4D ED [2]
- AF-S 400mm f/2.8D ED II
- AF-S 400mm f/2.8D ED
- AF-I 400mm f/2.8D ED
- AF-S 500mm f/4D ED II [2]
- AF-S 500mm f/4D ED [2]
- AF-I 500mm f/4D ED [2]
- AF-S 600mm f/4D ED II [2]
- AF-S 600mm f/4D ED [2]
- AF-I 600mm f/4D ED [2]
- AF-S VR 70 – 200mm f/2.8G ED
- AF-S VR II 70 – 200mm f/2.8G ED
- AF-S 80 – 200mm f/2.8D ED
- AF-S VR 200 – 400mm f/4G ED [2]
- AF-S VRII 200 – 400mm f/4G ED [2]
- AF-S 400mm f/2.8G ED VR
- AF-S 500mm f/4G ED VR [2]
- AF-S 600mm f/4G ED VR [2]

1 Autofocus is not recommended. At close focusing distances, the maximum effective aperture is likely to be less than f/5.6.

2 Autofocus is not guaranteed when used with the TC-17E II or TC-20 E II teleconverter, as maximum effective aperture is less than f/5.6, although in bright conditions or with good levels of contrast in the subject, it will often work quite well, if a little more slowly.

The D7000 supports the use of manual focus Nikkor lenses that lack the electrical components built in to modern AF and Ai-P type lenses. Nikon defines their lenses in to two broad groups: non-CPU lenses and CPU lenses (strictly speaking, it is not a CPU that is used in these lenses, but an ASIC (Application-Specific Integrated Circuit) that handles lens aperture and focus distance information to control the lens and support functions performed in the camera body, such as Matrix TTL metering).

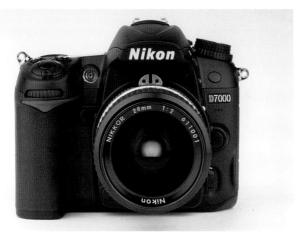

^ The D7000 is shown here with an Ai-S Nikkor 28mm f/2.8 manual focus lens; the semi-circular meter-coupling prong on the top of the lens is found on virtually all manual focus Nikkor lenses.

Compatible non-CPU type lenses include most manual focus lenses manufactured since 1977 and some earlier lenses that have been converted to the Ai lens mount standard (the exceptions are the Ai-P type, PC-Micro 85mm f/2.8D, PC-E 24mm f/3.5D, PC-E 45mm f/2.8D, and PC-E Micro 85mm f/2.8D lenses, all of which are classified as CPU-types). I have several older manual focus Nikkor lenses that I treasure not least for their optical quality, which work very well with the D7000.

If you specify the focal length and maximum aperture (lowest f/number) of a lens to the D7000, many of the features and functions available with the CPU-type lenses will also be supported when a non-CPU lens is used. If non-CPU lens data is specified in the camera using the [Non-CPU lens data] menu item in the Setup menu, the following operations can be performed when using a non-CPU lens:

- The automatic zoom-head function of the SB-900, SB-800, SB-700, and SB-600 Speedlights will function.

- The lens focal length, marked by an asterisk, is listed in image file information.

- The aperture value is displayed in the control panel and viewfinder.

- Flash output is adjusted automatically for changes to the aperture.

- The aperture value, marked by an asterisk, is listed in image file information.

- Color Matrix metering is available (although it may be necessary to use Center-Weighted or Spot metering with some lenses, such as Reflex-Nikkor types).

- The precision of Center-Weighted metering, Spot metering, and i-TTL flash exposure control is improved.

SPECIFYING LENS DATA

The information about a non-CPU type lens can be entered using the [Non-CPU lens data] item in the Setup menu. Highlight the [Non-CPU lens data] option and press ▶ to open a page that displays three parameters: [Lens number], [Focal length (mm)], and [Maximum aperture]. Highlight [Lens number] and press ◀ or ▶ to select a number between 1 and 9; highlight [Focal length (mm)] and press ◀ or ▶ to select a focal length between 6 and 4000mm; highlight [Maximum aperture] and press ◀ or ▶ to select a maximum aperture value between f/1.2 and f/22 (if you use a teleconverter, the maximum aperture is the effective maximum aperture of the lens and teleconverter). Finally, highlight [Done] and press the ⊛ button to store the lens data.

The stored data can be recalled at any time by using the following camera controls: Select [Choose non-CPU lens number] as the option for one of the following in the Custom Settings menu: CS-f3 [Assign Fn button] or CS-f4 [Assign preview button]. Once assigned, press the appropriate button and rotate the Main Command dial to scroll through the list of stored lens numbers.

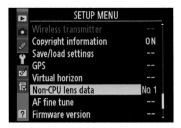

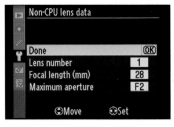

^ This screen shows the [Non-CPU lens data] item in the Setup menu.

^ I've set up my Ai-S 28mm f/2 lens as lens number 1 in the [Non-CPU lens data] submenu.

NOTE: Non-CPU lenses can only be used in the **A** (Aperture-Priority) and **M** (Manual) exposure modes, and the aperture value must be set using the aperture ring on the lens; in all other exposure modes the shutter release is disabled. If the maximum aperture value (lowest f/number) of the lens is not specified under the **[Non-CPU lens data]** menu item in the Setup menu, the D7000 displays the number of f/stops from the maximum aperture; the actual value can be read from the aperture ring.

NOTE: If lens data is not specified, Color Matrix metering is not available, and Center-Weighted metering is used instead.

NOTE: If you attach a non-CPU type zoom lens, the lens data is not adjusted automatically as the focal length / maximum aperture value is altered when operating the zoom function; if these values change, it is necessary to input the new focal length and maximum aperture value accordingly.

The following non-CPU lenses can be used, as described above, with the D7000:

CAMERA SETTING / LENS/ACCESSORY[1]	Focus mode			Exposure Mode		Metering		
	S C	M (with electronic rangefinder)	M	P, S	A M	3D	Color	⊙
AI-, AI-modified Nikkor or Nikon Series E lenses[2]	—	✓[3]	✓	—	✓[4]	—	✓[5]	✓[6]
Medical Nikkor 120mm f/4	—	✓	✓	—	✓[7]	—	—	—
Reflex Nikkor	—	—	✓	—	✓[4]	—	—	✓[6]
PC Nikkor	—	✓[8]	✓	—	✓[9]	—	—	✓
AI-type Teleconverter[10]	—	✓[11]	✓	—	✓[4]	—	✓[5]	✓[6]
PB-6 Bellows Focusing Attachment[12]	—	✓[11]	✓	—	✓[13]	—	—	✓
Auto extension rings (PK-series 11A, 12, or 13; PN-11)	—	✓[11]	✓	—	✓[4]	—	—	✓

[1] Some lenses cannot be used.
[2] Range of rotation for AI 80-200mm f/2.8 ED tripod mount is limited by camera body. Filters cannot be exchanged while AI 200-400mm f/4 ED is mounted on camera.
[3] With maximum aperture of f/5.6 or faster.
[4] If maximum aperture is specified using Non-CPU lens data, aperture value will be displayed in viewfinder and control panel.
[5] Can be used only if lens focal length and maximum aperture are specified using Non-CPU Lens Data. Use Spot or Center-Weighted metering if desired results are not achieved.
[6] For improved precision, specify lens focal length and maximum aperture using Non-CPU Lens Data.
[7] Can be used in Manual exposure mode at shutter speeds slower than flash sync speed by one step or more.
[8] Electronic rangefinder cannot be used with shifting or tilting.
[9] Exposure determined by presetting lens aperture. In Aperture-Priority autoexposure mode, preset aperture using lens aperture ring before performing AE Lock and shifting lens. In Manual exposure mode, preset aperture using lens aperture ring and determine exposure before shifting lens.
[10] Exposure Compensation required when used with AI 28–85mm f/3.5–4.5, AI 35–105mm f/3.5–4.5, AI 35–135mm f/3.5–4.5, or AF-S 80–200mm f/2.8D. See teleconverter manual for details.
[11] With maximum effective aperture of f/5.6 or faster.
[12] Requires PK-12 or PK-13 auto extension ring. PB-6D may be required depending on camera orientation.
[13] Use preset aperture. In Aperture-Priority autoexposure mode, set aperture using focusing attachment before determining exposure and taking photograph.

The following accessories and lenses are incompatible with the D7000. If you attempt to use them it may damage the equipment.

- O TC-16A AF teleconverter
- O Non-AI lenses
- O Lenses that require the AU-1 focusing unit (400mm f/4.5, 600mm f/5.6, 800mm f/8, 1200mm f/11)
- O Fisheye (6mm f/5.6, 7.5mm f/5.6, 8mm f/8, OP 10mm f/5.6)
- O 2.1 cm f/4
- O K2 rings
- O 180–600mm f/8 ED (serial numbers 174041 – 174180)
- O 360–1200mm f/11 ED (serial numbers 174031 – 174127)
- O 200–600mm f/9.5 (serial numbers 280001 – 300490)
- O Lenses for the F3AF (AF80mm f/2.8, AF ED200mm f/3.5, TC-16 teleconverter)
- O PC 28mm f/4 (serial number 180900 or earlier)
- O PC 35mm f/2.8 (serial numbers 851001 – 906200)
- O PC 35mm f/3.5 (old type)
- O 1000mm f/6.3 Reflex (old type)
- O 1000mm f/11 Reflex (serial numbers 142361 – 143000)
- O 2000mm f/11 Reflex (serial numbers 200111 – 200310)

DEPTH-OF-FIELD PREVIEW

In order that the viewfinder image be as bright as possible for composing, focusing, and metering, the D7000 operates with the lens automatically set to its maximum aperture (lowest f/number). The iris in the lens does not close down to the shooting aperture until after the shutter release has been pressed. However, this means that the image you see in the viewfinder appears as it would if the photograph were taken at the maximum aperture of the lens attached to the camera. To assess the depth of field visually, you must close the lens iris down to the shooting aperture.

The D7000 has a Depth-of-Field Preview button between the right hand finger grip and the lens mount which, when pressed, closes the lens down to the selected shooting aperture, allowing you to see the effect the aperture has on the depth of field; the viewfinder image will become darker as less light passes through the lens when the aperture iris in the lens is closed down.

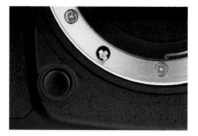

> The (Depth-of-Field) Preview button is located toward the bottom of the front panel close to the lens mount.

HINT: The D7000's Depth-of-Field Preview feature is most effective at aperture values of f/11 or larger since the viewfinder image becomes very dim at smaller aperture values.

DEPTH-OF-FIELD CONSIDERATIONS

When a lens brings light to focus on a camera's sensor, there is only one plane of focus that is critically sharp. However, in the two-dimensional picture produced by the camera, there is a zone in front of and behind the plane of focus that is perceived to be sharp. This area of apparent sharpness is referred to as the depth of field, and its extent is influenced by the camera-to-subject distance together with the focal length and aperture of the lens in use.

If the focal length and camera-to-subject distance are constant, depth of field will be shallower with large apertures (low f/numbers) and deeper with small apertures (high f/numbers). If the aperture and camera-to-subject distance are constant, depth of field will be shallower with a long focal length (telephoto range) and deeper with shorter focal length (wide-angle range). If the focal length and aperture are constant, depth of field will be greater at longer camera-to-subject distances and shallower with closer camera-to-subject distances. Depth of field is an important consideration when deciding on a particular composition, as it has a direct and fundamental effect on the final appearance of the picture.

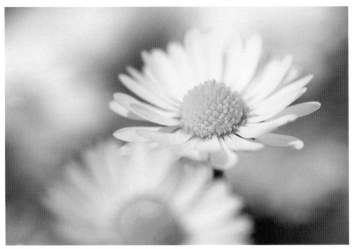

^ Depth of field is a function of subject magnification and lens aperture. In this close-up shot, the depth of field is extremely shallow due to the high degree of magnification and the large lens aperture I used (f/4); this helps to isolate the flower from those around it.

Probably the most important consideration concerning depth of field is that it is slightly less for images shot using the DX format compared with those taken on the FX-format cameras such as the Nikon D700 and D3-series models. This is due to the smaller size of the imaging area of the DX format (23.6 x 15.6 mm) of the D7000 as compared with the FX format (36 x 23.9 mm); the DX-format picture must be magnified by a greater amount compared with the FX-format shot to achieve any given identical print size. Therefore, at normal viewing distances, detail that appears to be sharp in a print made from an FX-format shot may no longer look sharp in a print of the same dimensions made from one recorded in the DX format. If you use the depth of field values given in tables for FX format / 35mm film, you will find they do not correspond to images shot on the DX format, assuming the same camera-to-subject distance and focal length apply. To guarantee that the depth of field in pictures taken on the DX format is sufficiently deep, use the values for the next larger lens aperture. For example, if set your lens to f/11, use the depth of field values for f/8 in the DX format.

Diffraction is an optical effect that, under certain circumstances, will limit the resolution you can achieve in a photograph. Assuming conditions of a uniform atmosphere (i.e., still, clear air), light waves will travel in straight lines. However, if those same light waves have to pass through a small hole, such as the aperture in the iris diaphragm of a camera lens, they become dispersed, or diffracted. At wide apertures (low f/numbers), the number of diffracted light waves is very small compared to the total number that pass through the aperture, hence the diffraction effect is negligible, but the proportion of diffracted waves increases as the size of the aperture is reduced, to a point where it becomes significant. After passing through a small aperture, the previously parallel light waves become diverged (i.e., they spread out in different directions) and consequently travel different distances between the iris diaphragm and the digital sensor, causing some light waves to shift out of phase and interfere with others. This process of interference creates a diffraction pattern that is manifest as a general softening of detail in the image.

At a certain lens aperture, the loss of resolution (softening) that occurs due to the effects of diffraction cancels out any gain in perceived sharpness due to increased depth of field. At this point, the camera lens is said to have become "diffraction limited." It is essential to know the diffraction limit for your lens(es) and different cameras, since there is no point in selecting aperture values beyond the diffraction limit, as image resolution will become increasingly degraded and exposure times extended with the risk of further loss of resolution through camera or subject movement.

I recommend you test each of your lenses with your D7000 to determine the diffraction limit for your own equipment. As a general rule, and in common with other Nikon DX-format camera models, I find that the D7000 diffraction limit is around f/11 to f/13, so bear this in mind when you are looking to maximize depth of field by choice of lens aperture, and avoid using smaller values.

SHUTTER SPEED CONSIDERATIONS

If you handhold your camera, it is worth remembering a rule of thumb concerning the minimum shutter speed that is generally sufficient to prevent a loss of sharpness due to camera shake. For the DX format, multiply the focal length of the lens by 1.5—the approximate magnification factor of the D7000 sensor compared with the FX format—and then take the reciprocal of this value and use it as the slowest shutter speed with that lens while shooting with a handheld camera. For example, a focal length of 300mm would require a minimum shutter speed of 1/450; the closest value available on the D7000 is 1/500.

The shutter speed can be used for creative effect because it controls the way that motion of the subject or camera is depicted in a photograph. Conventionally, a fast shutter speed is used to freeze motion in sports or action photography; however, slower shutter speeds can be used to good effect by introducing a degree of blur that will often evoke a greater sense of movement compared with a subject that is rendered pin-sharp. The panning technique is an example: using a slow shutter speed while moving the camera to track the subject, so that it appears relatively sharp against an increased level of blur in the background.

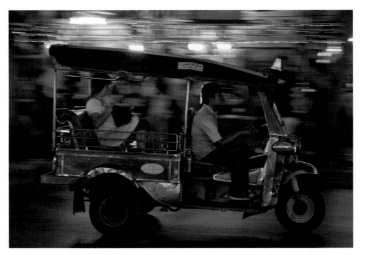

⌃ In low light situations, it is possible to mitigate the restriction of a relatively slow shutter speed when shooting a moving subject by panning the camera.

It is beyond the scope of this book to describe fully the features and functions of Nikon's dedicated software, but details can easily be obtained from the technical support sections of the websites maintained by the Nikon Corporation. The D7000 is supplied with a copy of Nikon View NX2, which incorporates the Nikon Transfer 2 application. The following section is intended to provide a brief overview of the three principal Nikon software applications in their current versions at the time of this writing:

O Nikon Transfer (version 2.0.2) / Nikon View NX2 (version 2.0.3)
O Nikon Capture NX2 (version 2.2.6)
O Nikon Camera Control Pro 2 (version 2.8.0)

For Windows, the following operating systems are supported:

O Microsoft Windows XP Professional (Service Pack 3, 32-bit versions)
O Microsoft Windows XP Home Edition (Service Pack 3, 32-bit versions)
O Microsoft Windows Vista (Service Pack 2, 32- and 64-bit versions)
O Microsoft Windows 7 (32- and 64-bit versions)

NOTE: Nikon Capture NX2 and Camera Control Pro 2 software is compatible with both 32- and 64-bit versions of Windows 7 and Vista; however, under 64-bit versions of these two operating systems, they operate as 32-bit applications.

For Macintosh, the following operating systems are supported:

O Mac OSX 10.4.11
O Mac OSX 10.5.8
O Mac OSX 10.6.4

NOTE: For information about Nikon software and to download updates to existing applications, I recommend you visit the various technical support websites maintained by Nikon, which can be accessed via: www.nikon.com.

NIKON TRANSFER 2

Nikon Transfer 2 is Nikon's updated utility for downloading images from the camera or memory card to your computer. Nikon Transfer provides a simple, intuitive workflow suitable for all users, from beginners to professionals. It is included as part of Nikon Viw NX2, a copy of which is supplied with the D7000, and can also be downloaded for free from any of Nikon's technical support websites. Features include:

- O Automatic recognition / auto-start after camera connection or inserting a memory card into a card reading device
- O Transfers images from CD, external HD, other removal media
- O Transfers images to computer's hard drive, with options to create dedicated folders and / or rename picture files
- O Easy selection and viewing of images on up to five external devices before transfer
- O Transfers image data to a primary destination and to a backup location simultaneously
- O Add metadata during transfer; both XMP and IPTC standards are supported
- O Select the application the images are displayed in after transfer

NIKON VIEW NX2

View NX2 offers photographers a fast solution to the organization and classification of their digital images. This software uses your computer's file directory to display and browse images. Nikon View NX2 is included with the latest Nikon DSLR cameras, such as the D7000, and can also be downloaded for free from Nikon's website. Features include:

- O High-speed thumbnail and preview display
- O Three customizable workspaces that are selected according to the images being worked on: Browser, GeoTag, and Edit
- O D-Movie editing tools that allow selection of start and stop point of individual movie clips, frame grab, merge of movie and JPEG files with transition effects, and the ability to add audio tracks
- O A simple way to choose images, operation similar to Explorer / Finder
- O Fast sorting using image-rating and labeling classification systems, plus integration with GPS data recorded by the camera
- O Image enhancement tools, such as Sharpness, Contrast, and Brightness controls, along with tools such as Highlight and Shadow protection, D-Lighting, and Color Booster

- Adjustment tools such as Crop, Straighten, and Auto Red-Eye Reduction
- Includes Picture Control Utility (including sharpening, contrast, saturation, hue, brightness, black-and-white conversion)
- Batch processing to convert file format, resize, rename, change settings, and save to multiple destinations
- Integration with Capture NX2
- Printing and email transmission
- IPTC / XMP data compatible (user settings retained when image opened in other supported applications)
- Quick Adjustment features for NEF (RAW) images, including White Balance, exposure adjustment, correction for axial chromatic aberration, and creating custom curves
- Full integration with Nikon Picturetown—Nikon's online image storage and sharing service—images can be uploaded directly from Nikon View NX2 via a simple drag and drop action, or stored images can be browsed directly from Nikon View NX2

NIKON CAPTURE NX2

In mid-2008, Nikon released an updated version of Capture NX, Capture NX 2; while not an extensive reworking of the program, it does introduce some key improvements. As a general purpose image-editing application, Nikon Capture NX 2 is really quite good, since all the adjustment features work with JPEG and TIFF files as they do with NEF files. It incorporates the same unique U-Point technology that permits complex selections of an area (or areas) within an image to be made with accuracy and speed that is far greater than can be achieved using other digital imaging software currently available. The program offers an extensive toolbox to enhance and modify any image file, regardless of whether it was saved in the NEF RAW, TIFF, or JPEG format.

Capture NX 2 applies non-destructive image processing to NEF RAW files, which means that the original image data is never compromised. Each enhancement made is saved in an edit list with the original data and thumbnail. However, changes made to JPEG or TIFF files will alter the data of the original image. To avoid this from occurring, the image can be saved using a different file name or converted into Nikon's NEF format. Parameters set on any Nikon camera-produced NEF RAW file, such as White Balance, sharpening, color mode, and saturation, are applied to the image when it is opened in Nikon Capture NX 2 for editing, so the camera settings are preserved. Key features in the latest iteration include:

o A new Workspaces option provides four pre-defined palette and toolbar configurations (Browser, Metadata, Multi-Purpose, and Edit) with support for two monitors, plus you can create your own custom Workspace (desktop layout), which can be supported across one or two displays. The pre-defined and custom Workspaces can be assigned a keyboard shortcut to help improve efficiency (Option / Alt keys + keys 1 through 9 are assignable for this purpose).

o An improved image browser palette with an extended feature set that should lessen the need to switch between Capture NX and View NX for thumbnail viewing. There is also a new Favorite Folders option, which makes accessing frequently used folders very quick. The time to open an image from the image browser has been improved significantly.

o New Quick Fix and Adjust sections of the Edit List improve the general layout and access to key tools such as Exposure Compensation, levels and curves adjustments, contrast, saturation, and the new Highlight Protection and Shadow Protection controls.

o The U-Point technology of Capture NX, which is the key to its image-editing simplicity, has been extended to almost all photo adjustment tools, including Noise Reduction and Unsharp Mask, to enhance an already powerful feature for applying local changes to an image.

o Separate controls for the correction of both axial and lateral chromatic aberration

o There is a new Auto Retouch Brush that provides a one-click tool to remove the effects of dust spots and other blemishes in an image.

o Enhanced batch-processing speeds

o Advanced White Balance control with the ability to select a specific color temperature or sample from a gray point

o Advanced NEF file control that permits attributes such as Exposure Compensation, sharpening, contrast, color mode, saturation, and hue to be modified after the exposure has been made, without affecting the original image data

o The Image Dust Off feature, which compares an NEF file with a reference image taken with the same camera to help reduce the effects of any dust particles on the low-pass filter

o A D-Lighting tool that emulates the dodge and burn techniques of traditional photographic printing to control highlight and shadow areas, producing a more balanced exposure

o A Color Noise Reduction tool, which minimizes the effect of random electronic noise that can occur, especially at high ISO settings

o An Edge Noise Reduction tool that accentuates the boundary between areas of an image to make them more distinct

- The Color Moiré Reduction feature, which helps to remove the effects of moiré, which can occur when an image contains areas with a very fine repeating pattern
- The LCH Editor, which allows for control of luminosity (overall lightness), chroma (color saturation), and hue in separate channels
- Lens Vignette control to correct for uneven illumination across an image, particularly near the corners
- The Fisheye Lens tool, which converts images taken with the AF Fisheye-Nikkor DX 10.5mm f/2.8G lens so they appear as though they were taken using a conventional rectilinear lens with a diagonal angle-of-view equivalent to approximately 120°

NOTE: If you are not familiar with Nikon Capture NX2 and need some help to understand its tools, there is a lot of useful information available here: http://www.capturenx.com/en/lessons/lessons/index.html.

CAMERA CONTROL PRO 2

Camera Control Pro 2 enables remote control of most functions of Nikon DSLR cameras including the D7000, from a computer that is connected via USB cable, or through wired (Ethernet) or wireless LAN using a wireless transmitter (the WT-4 / WT-4a is required for the D7000). Features and functions of the camera, such as the Picture Control System, operation of Live View, and video recording are supported. The significant change between the latest version of Camera Control Pro 2 and previous iterations is the removal of the built-in viewer; now it is necessary to use Nikon View NX2 in conjunction with Camera Control Pro 2 to view pictures, Live View, and recording video. For example, when the [Show images captured by Camera Control Pro 2] option in View NX2 is selected in the [File] menu, pictures taken via Camera Control Pro 2 are displayed in View NX2 as they are taken. Key features include:

- Most settings of Nikon DSLR cameras, such as exposure mode, shutter speed, aperture, and White Balance can be controlled remotely.
- Full control of the 39-Point AF system, including display of the selected AF point on a computer monitor
- Support for the Picture Control System of the camera; Picture Control parameters can be selected and adjusted on a computer, and custom curves (to modify contrast) can be created and saved.

- Images in a camera buffer can be confirmed with thumbnail or preview display on a computer prior to transferring, which enables deletion of unwanted images.

- Support of the Live View of the D7000, including control for the contrast-detect AF system from a computer monitor

- Keyboard shortcuts can be assigned to the control buttons for **[Shoot]** and **[AF and shoot]**.

- Video recording can be managed from a computer; video files are saved to the memory card installed in the camera and can then be downloaded to the computer once recording has ended.

- Pictures taken with the D7000 can now be saved to just the memory card installed in the camera (in previous versions of the software all images were saved to the hard drive of the computer only).

NOTE: The WT-4 wireless transmitter supports image transfer and printing options via IEEE 802.11b/g/a wireless connections and comes in a number of different configurations; for example the WT-4 is sold in countries that approve the use of 13 frequency channels, while the WT-4a version is sold in countries that limit use to eleven frequency channels (for example, the USA). Image transfer via wired 10BASE-T and 100BASE-TX Ethernet connections is also supported. The D7000 is not compatible for use with previous variants of the Nikon Wireless Transmitter, the WT-1, WT-2, or WT-3.

GENERAL NIKON ACCESSORIES

- AS-15: An accessory shoe adapter that has a standard PC sync socket for connecting the D7000 to a non-dedicated flash unit via a PC sync cable

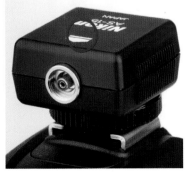

‹ The D7000 can be used to trigger flash units via a standard PC (Prontor-Compur) sync terminal, but this requires the optional AS-15 accessory.

- BF-1B: Supplied with the D7000, a body cap that will help prevent dust from entering the camera; keep it in place at all times when a lens is not mounted on the camera

---

NOTE: The earlier BF-1 body cap cannot be used, as it may damage the lens mount of the D7000; however, the BF-1A cap is also compatible with the D7000.

- DK-20C: Supplementary eyepiece correction lenses for use when the built-in diopter adjustment is insufficient
- DK-21: The standard viewfinder eyecup for the D7000; one is supplied with the camera
- DK-21M: A magnifying viewfinder eyepiece lens for the D7000; it increases magnification of the viewfinder by approximately 1.17x
- DR-6: Right-angle viewfinder attachment
- EG-D2: The video cable to connect the D7000 to a TV set; one is supplied with the camera
- EH-5a: The multi-voltage AC adapter used to power the D7000
- EN-EL15: The dedicated Lithium-ion battery for the D7000; one is supplied with the camera
- EP-5B: The adapter required to connect the D7000 to the EH-5a multi-voltage AC adapter
- GP-1: GPS unit for the D7000; it connects to the remote accessory terminal of the camera

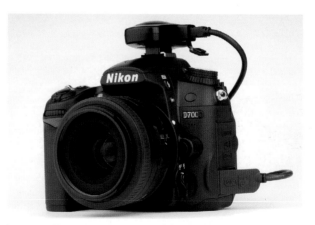

^ The camera will record GPS data when the Nikon GP-1 GPS unit is attached the D7000 and embed the information in the EXIF data of image files. Nikon View NX2 software supports GPS data for GeoTagging of image files.

- MB-D11: Optional multi-power battery pack for the D7000
- MC-DC2: Remote shutter release cord with lockable shutter release button

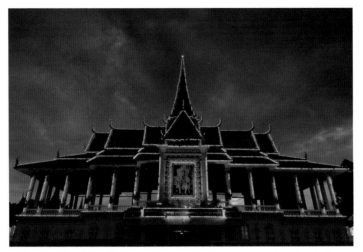

∧ When shooting at slow shutter speeds, supporting the camera on a tripod or similar stable platform is essential. Using a remote shutter release, such as the MC-DC2 or ML-L3, will further prevent image blur due to inadvertent camera vibration.

- MH-25: The multi-voltage AC charger for a single EN-EL15 battery; the MH-25 is supplied with the D7000
- ML-L3: Optional infrared wireless remote shutter release; it requires a 3V CR2025 button-type battery
- SB-400: An external Speedlight (flash unit) for the D7000; it can be attached to the camera's accessory shoe or via the SC-28 / SC-29 TTL flash cord
- SB-600: An external Speedlight (flash unit) for the D7000; it can be attached to the camera's accessory shoe or via the SC-28 / SC-29 TTL flash cord
- SB-700: An external Speedlight (flash unit) for the D7000; it can be attached to the camera's accessory shoe or via the SC-28 / SC-29 TTL flash cord
- SB-800: An external Speedlight (flash unit) for the D7000; it can be attached to the camera's accessory shoe or via the SC-28 / SC-29 TTL flash cord

o SB-900: An external Speedlight (flash unit) for the D7000; it can be attached to the camera's accessory shoe or via the SC-28 / SC-29 TTL flash cord

o SB-R200: An external Speedlight (flash unit) for the D7000 intended for close-up and macro photography; it cannot be attached to camera's accessory shoe but is fitted to an adapter ring that is attached to the front of the lens

NOTE: Triggering the SB-R200 requires the use of either the D7000's built-in Speedlight, the optional SU-800 Speedlight Commander unit, or an SB-800 / SB-900 Speedlight used in its Commander mode.

o SC-28: A TTL flash cord that maintains full functionality between a compatible external Speedlight and a D7000

o SC-29: A TTL flash cord that maintains full functionality between a compatible external Speedlight and a D7000; the terminal unit that attaches to the camera has a built-in AF-Assist lamp

o SD-8a: An external battery pack for SB-900 or SB-800 Speedlights

o SD-9: An external battery pack for SB-900 Speedlights

o SK-6 / SK-6a: A power bracket for SB-900 or SB-800 Speedlight; it attaches to the base of the D7000, allowing the flash to be mounted farther away from the central axis of the lens

o UC-E4: A USB cable for connecting the D7000 to another USB-compliant device

o WT-4: Wireless transmitter for connecting the D7000 to wireless or Ethernet computer networks; it requires an independent power source, preferably the Nikon EH-6 AC adapter or the Nikon rechargeable Li-ion EN-EL3e battery; it is important to ensure the use of the correct version of the WT-4 to comply with the laws / regulations pertaining to radio transmissions at your location

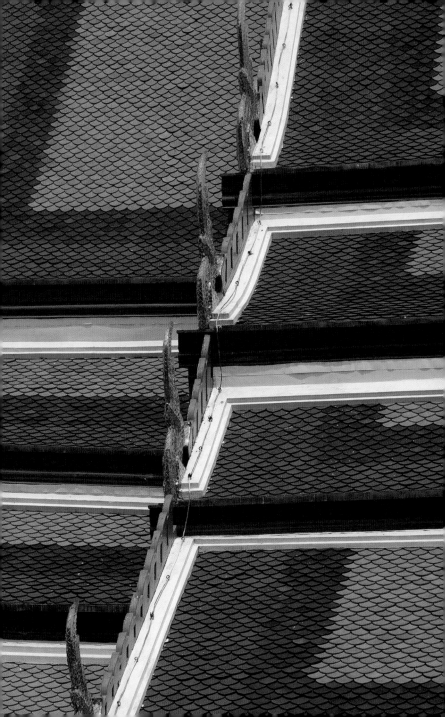

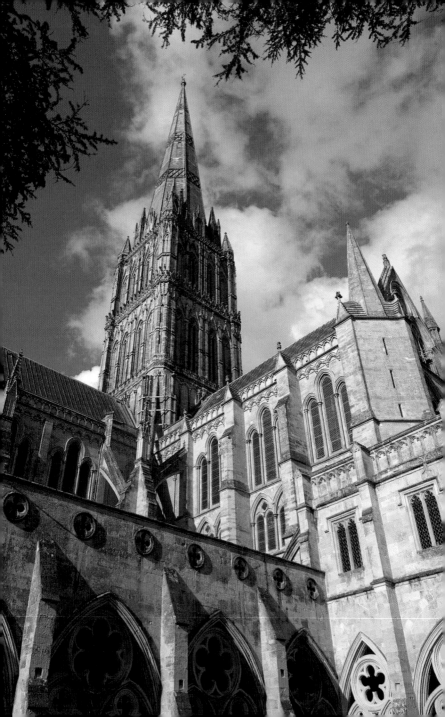

Digital Workflow

You may be surprised to learn that, apart from image data, the picture files generated by the D7000 contain a wealth of other information, including the shooting parameters and instructions about printing pictures. This information is tagged to the image file using a number of common standards, depending on the sort of information to be saved with the file. The supported standards are:

O DCF (v 2.0): Design Rule for Camera File System (DCF) is a widely used standard in the digital imaging industry to ensure compatibility across different makes of cameras.

O DPOF: Digital Print Order Format (DPOF) is a standard used to enable pictures to be printed from a print order created and saved on a memory card.

O EXIF (v 2.3): The D7000 supports Exchangeable Image File Format for Digital Still Cameras (EXIF); this standard allows information stored with image files to be read by software and it ensures image quality when printed on an EXIF-compliant printer.

O PictBridge: A standard that permits an image file stored on a memory card to be output directly to a printer without the need to connect the camera to a computer or download the image file from a memory card to a computer.

Metadata is any data that helps to describe the content or characteristics of a file. You may be familiar with viewing and perhaps adding some basic metadata through the File Info or Document Properties box found in many software applications and some operating systems. You may also use a digital image management application that can search some image file properties, such as date recorded, and display all the images taken on a specified date.

EXIF DATA

The D7000 uses the EXIF (Exchangeable Image File Format) version 2.3 standard to tag additional information to each still image file it records. Most popular digital imaging software is able to read and interpret the EXIF tags, so the information can be displayed; but other software is not as capable, in which case, some or all of the EXIF data values may not be available. The information recorded includes:

- Nikon (the name of the camera manufacturer)
- D7000 (the model number)
- Camera firmware version number
- Exposure information including shutter speed, aperture, exposure mode, ISO, EV value, date / time, Exposure Compensation, flash mode, Flash Compensation, and focal length
- Thumbnail of the main image

Examining EXIF data by either viewing the image information pages on the camera's monitor or accessing the shooting data in appropriate software is a great teaching aid, as you can see exactly what the camera settings were for each shot. By comparing pictures and the shooting data, you can quickly learn about the technical aspects of exposure, focusing, metering, and flash exposure control.

NOTE: There is no equivalent standard to EXIF data across the wide range of video file formats; therefore, only limited information is available, such as camera model, lens specification and date / time of recording.

Other metadata that can be tagged to an image file includes the use of a standard developed by the International Press Telecommunications Council (IPTC). Known as Digital Newsphoto Parameter Record (DNPR), it can append image information to include details of the origin, authorship, copyright, caption details, and keywords for searching purposes. Any application that is DNPR compliant will show this information and allow you to edit it. If you are considering submitting any pictures you shoot with the D7000 for publication, you should make use of DNPR (IPTC) metadata, as most publishing organizations require it to be present before accepting a submission.

Adobe's Extensible Metadata Platform (XMP) is an open standard, digital labeling technology that allows metadata to be embedded into an image file. Any XMP-enabled software application allows descriptions and titles, searchable keywords, plus author and copyright information to be stored in a format that is easily understood by other software applications, hardware devices, and even file formats. Since XMP is extensible, it can accommodate existing metadata schemes.

The EXIF metadata recorded by the D7000 is not saved as standard IPTC / XMP metadata; however, standard IPTC / XMP metadata can be embedded automatically in images recorded by the D7000 during transfer by completing the appropriate data fields in the **[IPTC / XMP preset]** option under the **[Preferences]** tab in Nikon Transfer software. Nikon View NX2 and Nikon Capture NX2 also support the EXIF, IPTC, and XMP standards.

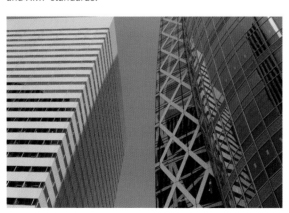

‹ If you expect to sell any of your pictures, it is essential to include details of the subject and location in the relevant IPTC / XMP metadata fields.

The D7000 can be connected to many different devices for the purpose of image display and transfer. This section outlines the processes for doing so.

> The external connection ports for the D7000 are located under the two rubber covers on the left side of the camera.

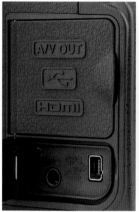
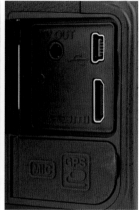

AUDIO / VIDEO (A/V)

The D7000 can be connected to a television set or LCD screen for Playback, or alternatively, to a VCR or DVD player for recording of saved images. In many countries, the camera is supplied with the EG-D2 A/V cable for this purpose. First, you need to select the appropriate video standard. To do this, open the Setup menu; navigate to the [Video Mode] item, and press ▶. Highlight the required option: **[NTSC]** or **[PAL]**, and then press ▶ again to confirm the selection. NTSC is the video standard used in the USA, Canada, and Japan, while PAL is used in most European countries.

Before connecting the camera to the video cord, make sure the camera's power is switched off. Open the top rubber cover on the left end of the camera body to reveal the A/V-out port. Connect the narrow jack pin of the EG-D2 to the camera and the other end to the TV, LCD screen, VCR, or DVD player (the yellow plug goes to the video input and the white plug to the audio input). Tune the TV to the video channel, then turn on the camera and press the ▶ button. The image is displayed on the camera monitor and on the television screen and can now be recorded to video or DVD. The menus and all other camera operations will function normally, which means that you can take pictures with the camera connected to a TV set and carry out Review / Playback functions using the TV screen as though it were the camera's LCD screen. It is probably best to use the EH-5a AC adapter (also requires the EP-5B adapter) to power the camera if you intend to use the camera for an extended period for image Playback via a television screen.

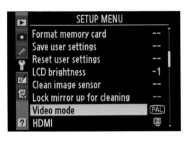

< Make sure you select the correct video standard for your geographical location.

CONNECTING VIA HDMI

The D7000 can be connected to an HDMI device using a type-C mini-pin HDMI cable. Check the HDMI format options in the Setup menu under the [HDMI] item; the [Auto] option is the default (see page 241 for more information). Then, switch the camera off and connect the HDMI cable to the HDMI port (it is located immediately below the A/V-out port under the top rubber cover on the left side of the camera body). Tune the device to the HDMI channel. Now, turn the camera on and press the ▶ button. The camera monitor will remain blank, as the display of an image or menus on the camera's LCD monitor is not supported when the camera is connected via the HDMI output; however, all other camera operations will function normally.

CONNECTING TO A COMPUTER

The D7000 can be connected directly to a computer via the supplied UC-E4 USB cable. The camera supports the high-speed USB (2.0) interface that offers a maximum transfer rate of 480 MB/s. You can download images from the camera using the supplied Nikon Transfer software. Images can be viewed and organized using the supplied Nikon View NX2 software, while the optional Nikon Capture NX2 can be used to enhance images. The D7000 can also be controlled from the computer using the optional Nikon Camera Control Pro 2 software (see pages 330-331 for further details).

HINT: If you use the D7000 tethered to a computer for any function, ensure that the installed camera battery is fully charged. For protracted periods of tethered shooting, I recommend using the EH-5a AC adapter with EP-5B connector to prevent interruptions to data transfer by loss of power.

Before connecting the D7000 to a computer, check that one of the following operating systems is running:

O Windows 7 (Home basic / Home Premium / Professional / Enterprise / Ultimate)

O Windows Vista Service Pack 2 (Home basic / Home Premium / Business / Enterprise / Ultimate)

O Windows XP Service Pack 3 (Home Edition, or Professional).

NOTE: View NX2 runs as a 32-bit application in 64-bit editions of Windows 7 and Vista.

O Macintosh OS X 10.4.11

O Macintosh OS X 10.5.8

O Macintosh OS X 10.6.4

Also, make sure that the appropriate version of Nikon software (e.g., Nikon View NX2) is installed (for details of software compatibility, see page 326).

DIRECT USB CONNECTION

To connect the camera to a computer, start by turning the camera off, and then turn the computer on and wait for it to start up. Connect the UC-E4 USB cable to the USB port of the camera (it's located under the large rubber cover on the left side) and to the computer. Turn the camera on.

Nikon Transfer should start automatically. The first time you use the application, I recommend you set the preferences by clicking on the **[Preferences]** tab before clicking on the **[Transfer]** button to initiate data transfer. The camera can be turned off as soon as the data transfer is complete.

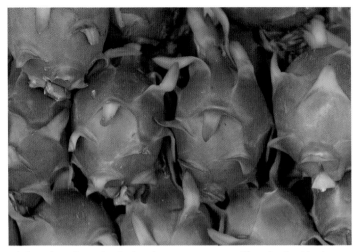

^ It is good practice to download any images as soon as possible and make at least one backup copy before you format any card.

MEMORY CARD READERS

Although the D7000 can be tethered directly to a computer for transferring image data, there are several reasons why you should consider using a dedicated memory card reader as an alternative:

O If you use the tethered camera method, you will drain battery power and risk data being lost or corrupted if the power fails during the data transfer process.

O Using a card reader allows you to run software to recover lost or corrupted image files, as well as diagnose problems with the memory card.

O You can leave a card reader permanently attached to your computer, which further reduces the risk of losing or corrupting files as a result of a poor connection due to the wear and tear caused by constantly connecting a USB cable to the camera.

If the optional WT-4 wireless transmitter is attached to the camera, photographs can be transferred or printed over a wireless or Ethernet network. Video recordings can also be transferred. Furthermore, the camera can be controlled from any network computer running Nikon Camera Control Pro 2 software. For full information, see the instruction manual supplied with the WT-4.

To configure the D7000 / WT-4, use the [Wireless transmitter] item in the Setup menu. When a WT-4 is connected to the D7000 and powered on, highlight [Wireless transmitter] and press ▶ to display the operating modes. The WT-4 can be used in any of the following modes:

MODE	FUNCTION
Transfer mode	Upload new or existing image files to a computer or FTP server.
Thumbnail select mode	Preview photographs on a computer monitor before upload.
PC mode	Control the D7000 from a computer using Camera Control Pro 2 software.
Print mode	Print JPEG image files on a printer connected to a network computer.

DIRECT PRINTING

As mentioned previously, the D7000 supports a standard that allows either individual or multiple pictures to be printed directly from the camera via a USB connection without the aid of a computer. This feature is only compatible with JPEG image files and a printer that supports the PictBridge standard.

NOTE: Nikon recommends images destined for direct printing should be recorded in the sRGB color space (use the [Color Space] item in the Shooting menu).

The D7000 can be connected to a PictBridge compatible printer to print pictures directly from the camera. Start by turning the camera off, and then turn the printer on before connecting the printer to the camera via the supplied UC-E4 USB cord; do not connect the camera and printer via a USB hub. Turn the camera on, and a welcome message will appear on the camera monitor, followed by the PictBridge Playback display.

> **HINT:** Printing directly from the D7000 is likely to require powering the camera for an extended period, so at the very least, ensure that the installed camera battery is fully charged; and consider using the EH-5a AC adapter with the EP-5B connecter if you make regular use of this feature.

PRINTING A SINGLE PICTURE

To select a picture for printing from the PictBridge Playback display, scroll through the images saved on the memory card using ◄ and ►; use ▲ and ▼ to display photo information. To view an enlarged section of the image, press the ⊕ button. To view up to six thumbnail images at a time, press ⊕. Use the Multi Selector button to highlight an individual thumbnail picture. Again, you can press ⊕ to display the selected thumbnail image in full frame. To print a single image selected in the PictBridge Playback display, press and release the ⊗ button. The PictBridge printing menu will appear. Use ▲ or ▼ to select the required option and press ► to select it:

O [Page Size]: Press ▲ and ▼ to select the appropriate paper size from [Printer Default] (uses default setting of current printer), [3.5 x 5in], [5 x 7in], or [A4]. Then press ⊗ to select the option and return to the main print menu.

O [Number of Copies]: Press ▲ and ▼ to select the number of copies of the highlighted image to be printed (maximum 99), and then press ⊗ to select the option and return to the main print menu.

O [Border]: Press ▲ and ▼ to select [Printer Default] (uses default setting of current printer), [Print with Border] (white border), or [No Border]. Then press ⊗ to select the option and return to the main print menu. Note that this item is only available if supported by the selected printer.

O [Time Stamp]: Press ▲ and ▼ to select [Printer Default] (uses default setting of current printer), [Print Time Stamp] (date and time image was recorded printed on picture), or [No Time Stamp]. Use ⊗ to select the option and return to the main print menu.

- ○ **[Cropping]**: Press ▲ and ▼ to select **[Crop]** (picture can be cropped in-camera), or **[No Cropping]** (printed full frame). Selecting **[No Cropping]** and pressing ⊛ returns you to the main print menu. Selecting **[Crop]** and then pressing ▶ displays a dialog box; press ⊕ to increase the degree of cropping, and press ⊞ to reduce the crop. Use the Multi Selector button to position the crop frame. Press ⊛ to return to the main print menu. Note that this item is only available if supported by the selected printer.
- ○ **[Start Printing]**: Select **[Start printing]** and press ⊛ to print the image highlighted in the PictBridge display. To cancel the process before all copies have been printed, press the ⊛ button.

PRINTING MULTIPLE PICTURES

Multiple pictures can be printed either directly from the camera by connecting it to a compatible printer, or using the DPOF feature. In the case of the latter option, either the camera or the memory card can be connected directly to a printer.

To print directly from the camera, connect it to a compatible printer as described above, and make sure the PictBridge Playback display is shown on the monitor. Now, press the MENU button to display the available options (a description of these four options is set out below), highlight the required option and press ▶:

- ○ **[Print Select]**: The selected images are printed.
- ○ **[Select date]**: Print one copy of all pictures taken on a specific date.
- ○ **[Print (DPOF)]**: Print an existing print order created in the Playback menu using the **[Print set (DPOF)]** item.
- ○ **[Index Print]**: Creates an index print of all images saved in the JPEG format. (If the memory card contains more than 256 JPEG images, only the first 256 will be printed.)

Print Select: If you select the **[Print Select]** option from the PictBridge menu and press ▶, six thumbnail images will be displayed on the monitor. Use the Multi Selector button to scroll through the images and to scroll to other pages of thumbnails, and then press and hold ⊕ to see the highlighted image full frame. To select the currently highlighted image for printing, hold down the ⊞ button and press ▲; the image is marked with 凸, and the number of copies to be printed is set to one **[1]**. To specify the number of copies of each image selected for printing, keep the ⊕ button pressed, and then use ▲ and ▼ to increase or decrease the number, respectively. Repeat this process for each image to be printed. To deselect a picture for printing, press ▼ when the number of prints is set to [1]. Press ⊗ to display printing options and set [Page size], [Border], and [Time stamp] options as required, according to the instructions on pages 345-346 under "Printing a Single Picture." To print the images you selected, highlight [Start Printing] and press ⊗. To cancel the printing process before all the selected images have been printed, press ⊗.

NOTE: There is no option for cropping images when printing multiple pictures, as there is for printing a single picture.

NOTE: Images saved in the NEF RAW format will be displayed in the Print Select menu, but it is not possible to select them for printing. However, it is possible to create a JPEG copy of an NEF file using the [NEF (RAW) processing] item in the Retouch menu.

Select Date: To print all the pictures taken on a specific date, highlight the [Select date] option from the PictBridge menu and press ▶; a list of the dates for images recorded on the installed memory card will be displayed. Press ▲ or ▼ to highlight the desired date, and then press ▶ to select it. To view the pictures taken on a specific date, highlight the date and press ⊕; use the Multi Selector buttons to scroll through the pictures, or press and hold the ⊕ button to view the highlighted picture at full screen. Once a specific date is selected, press ⊗ to display the printing options and set [Page size], [Border type], and [Time stamp] as described in the instructions above under Printing a Single Picture.

DPOF PRINTING

The D7000 supports the Digital Print Order Format (DPOF) standard that embeds an instruction set in the appropriate EXIF data fields of an image file. This allows you to insert the memory card directly into any DPOF-compatible home printer or commercial mini-lab printer and automatically get a set of prints of only those images you wish to print (JPEGs only). Apart from the fact that you do not have to attach the camera to a compatible printer through a USB connection as described above (although you can do it that way, too), this feature can be particularly useful if, for example, you are away from home on vacation, as you can still produce prints from your digital files even if you do not have access to your own printer; DPOF prints can be made by any DPOF-compatible printer.

To print the current DPOF Print Set saved to the installed memory card (see pages 390-350 for details of how create a DPOF Print Set) when the camera is connected to a compatible PictBridge printer, highlight [Print (DPOF)] from the PictBridge Playback display and press ▶ to select it.

The camera will display thumbnails of all the images in the current DPOF Print Set in groups of up to six at a time. If desired, the current Print Set can be modified using the same procedure as described in the "Print Multiple Pictures" section to change the number of copies of each picture to be printed and set [Page size], [Border type], and [Time stamp] under the printing options as required. To print the existing Print Set without modification, and / or to print once any modifications have been completed, highlight [Start Printing] and press ⊛. Or, alternatively, remove the memory card from the camera, insert it into a DPOF-compatible printer, and follow the instructions for the printer to make prints from the memory card instead of from the camera.

NOTE: If you delete images from the current Print Set using a computer or other device after the Print Set has been created and saved, it may not print correctly.

NOTE: Print Set selections can only be made from JPEG format images stored on the memory card; if an image was shot using the NEF+JPEG option, only the JPEG image can be selected for printing. However, it is possible to create a JPEG copy of an NEF (RAW) file using the [NEF (RAW) processing] item in the Retouch menu.

NOTE: There are subtle differences in the functionality between the direct printing routes. For example, direct printing of a single image with the D7000 connected to a PictBridge compatible printer allows you to perform cropping before printing. On the other hand, in multiple printing from the camera or memory card, with the latter using a Print Set created using the DPOF standard, the images can only be printed full-frame.

CREATING A DPOF PRINT ORDER SET

To select images for printing using the DPOF feature, it is necessary to create a DPOF print order. Start by highlighting **[Print set (DPOF)]** from the Playback menu of the D7000; the **[Select/Set]** option will be highlighted. Press ▶ to select it, and the camera will display a thumbnail view of all the images stored on the inserted memory card, in groups of up to six. To view images on another memory card installed in the camera or in a different folder, hold the **BKT** button and press ▲. Highlight the required card slot and press ▶ to display a list of folders; next, highlight the required folder and press ⊛ to view the pictures in that folder.

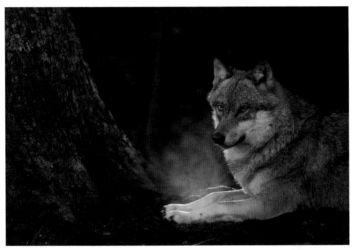

∧ Printing direct from the D7000 can be very convenient, but it is not as flexible as using digital imaging software on a computer.

Use the same procedure as described under the "Print Select" section on pages 346-347 to view and select the required pictures and the number of copies to be printed. Once you've selected all the images you want to print, press the ⊛ button to save the selected group of images and display the options for data imprinting.

To imprint shooting data on the image, highlight **[Data imprint]** and press ▶ to switch the option on or off. To print the date and time the image was recorded onto the image, highlight **[Imprint date]** and press ▶ to switch the option on or off. In both cases, a check mark will appear in the box to the left of the item in the menu screen to indicate the option is set to [On]. To finish, save the Print Set order by highlighting [Done] and pressing ⊛.

NOTE: Information entered via the [Data Imprint] and [Imprint Date] options is not printed when the DPOF Print Set is printed using a direct USB connection between the camera and printer, but only when the memory card is inserted directly into a PictBridge compatible printer.

To deselect the entire Print Set, highlight [Print Set (DPOF)] from the Playback menu and press ▶, then highlight [Deselect all?]. Press ▶ and highlight [Yes], and press ⊛ to confirm the selection.

INDEX PRINT

To make an index print (multiple images on the same page), connect the camera to a compatible printer as described above. Once the PictBridge Playback display is open, it is possible create an index print of all the JPEG files on the memory card. Start by pressing the MENU button, select the [Index print] option, and then press ⊛. Next, press ⊛ to display the PictBridge printing options and set [Page size], [Border type], and [Time stamp] as required according to the instructions under "Printing a Single Picture." (Note that if the selected page size is too small, a warning will be displayed.) To print, highlight [Start Printing] and press ⊛. To cancel the operation before printing is complete, press ⊛.

DIGITAL WORKFLOW

For many photographers who shoot with film, their direct involvement in the production of their pictures ends when they hand over the exposed film to be processed and printed by someone else. The digital photographer can exercise a far greater level of control over every stage of image processing, from initial capture in the camera to the output of an image as a print or for electronic display.

It is essential to develop a routine to make sure you work in an efficient and effective manner. You may wish to consider the following seven-stage workflow as a starting point for establishing one of your own, built around your specific requirements.

- Familiarize yourself with your camera. The more intuitive you become with your equipment, the more time you are able to spend concentrating on the scene / subject being photographed.

- Make sure the camera battery is charged, and always carry a spare.

- Rather than saving all your pictures to a single, high-capacity memory card, reduce the risk of a catastrophic loss due to card failure or loss by spreading your images over several memory cards.

- Always clean the low-pass filter array in front of the sensor before you begin a shoot to reduce the amount of post-processing work.

- Always format the memory card in the camera each time you insert the card.

SHOOTING

- Adjust camera settings to match the requirements of your shoot. Choose an appropriate Image Quality, Image Size, ISO, color space, and White Balance.

- Set other camera controls such as metering and autofocus according to the shooting conditions.

- Use the [Copyright information] item in the Setup menu; assign a note about the authorship / copyright of the images you shoot.

- Review images and make any adjustments you deem necessary. Use the histogram display to check the exposure level and use the magnification feature to check image sharpness. However, do not rely on this display to assess color, contrast, or hue; remember, even if you shoot NEF (RAW), only a JPEG version of the image is displayed on the camera monitor.

- Do not be in too much of a hurry to delete pictures unless they are obvious failures. It is often better to edit after shooting is completed, rather than "on the fly." Memory cards are relatively cheap; so do not skimp on memory capacity.

TRANSFER

- Before transferring images to your computer, designate a specific folder or folders in which the images will be stored so you know where to find them.

- Rather than connecting the camera directly to the computer, use a card reader. It is much faster, more reliable, and reduces the wear and tear on the camera.

- If the application used to transfer the image files from the memory card to a computer permits you to assign general information to the image files during transfer (e.g., XMP or DNPR (IPTC) metadata) make sure you at least complete appropriate fields for image authorship and copyright.
- Consider renaming files and assigning further information and key words to facilitate searching and retrieving images at a later date.

EDIT AND FILE

- Use a browsing application to sort through your pictures. Again, do not be in too much of a hurry to delete pictures. It is often best to take a second look at images a few days or even weeks after they were shot—your opinions about images will often change.
- Print a contact sheet of small thumbnail images to help you decide which images to retain.

PROCESSING

- Make copies of RAW files and save them to a working file format such as TIFF (RGB) or PSD (Adobe Photoshop).
- Do not use the JPEG format for processing. Each time you modify file data and resave as a JPEG, compression will be applied to the altered data. The effect of such repeated compression is cumulative and will reduce image quality progressively.
- Make adjustments in an orderly and logical sequence starting with overall brightness, contrast, and color. Then, make more local adjustments to correct problems or enhance images.
- Save your adjusted file as a master copy to which you can then apply cropping, resizing, unsharp mask, and any other finishing touches appropriate to your output requirements. The maxim to follow here is: process once, output many times.

ARCHIVE

- Data can become lost or corrupted at any time for a variety of reasons—always make multiple backup copies of your original files and the edited master copies.
- If you shoot in the NEF format, consider creating copies of all your NEF files in Adobe's open Digital Negative (DNG) format to help ensure compatibility with future iterations of software.
- CDs have a limited capacity, so consider using DVDs or an external hard disk drive. No electronic storage media is guaranteed 100% safe, nor does it have an infinite lifespan, so check your backup copies regularly and repeat the backup process as required.

O We all shoot pictures to share with others. Digital technology has expanded the possibilities of image display considerably: we can e-mail pictures to family, friends, colleagues, and clients; prepare digital "slide shows," or post images to websites for fun or for profit.

O Home printing in full color is now reliable and cost effective. Spend some time to set up your system properly and work methodically: Calibrate your monitor and printer to ensure accurate display and consistent reproduction of color, use an appropriate resolution for the print size you require, and choose paper type and finish accordingly.

O Once you have a high-quality print, ensure you present it in a manner befitting its status; make sure to frame or mount it securely. This will also help to protect it from the effects of light and atmospheric pollutants.

CARING FOR YOUR D7000

Obviously, keeping your camera and lens(es) in a clean and dry environment is very important. But, regardless of how scrupulous you are about doing this, dust and dirt will eventually accumulate on or inside your equipment. Since prevention is better than a cure, always keep the body and lens caps in place when not using your equipment. Always switch the D7000 off before attaching or detaching a lens to prevent particles being attracted into the camera by the electrical charge in its electronic components (this also helps prevent any malfunction of the electronic systems).

Remember—in this case, gravity is your friend! Whenever you change lenses, get in to the habit of holding the camera body with the lens mount facing downwards. For the same reason, do not carry or store your D7000 on its back, as particles already inside the camera will settle on the optical low-pass filter. Periodically, vacuum-clean the interior of your camera bag or case; it is amazing how much debris can collect there! Sealing you camera body in a clear plastic bag, which you then keep within your camera case will add another valuable layer of protection in very dusty or damp conditions. In the latter situation, keep some sachets of silica gel inside the bag to absorb any moisture. Putting together a basic cleaning kit is straightforward. You should consider the following:

- 1/2-inch (12mm) artist's paintbrush made from soft sable hair for general cleaning
- Micro-fiber lens cloth for cleaning lens elements
- Micro-fiber towel (available from any camera store or good outdoors store) for absorbing moisture when working in damp conditions. (I find these towels invaluable in all sorts of conditions, and they are soft enough to use for cleaning lenses and filters.)
- Rubber bulb blower made for cleaning lenses and the low-pass filter

Always brush or blow as much material off your equipment as possible before wiping it with a cloth. For lens elements and filters, use a micro-fiber cloth and wipe surfaces in short strokes, not a sweeping circular motion. Turn the cloth frequently to prevent depositing the dirt you have just removed back onto the same surface! For any residue that cannot be removed with a dry cloth, you will need a lens cleaning fluid suitable for photographic lenses. Apply a small amount of fluid to the cloth, not directly to the lens, as it may seep inside and cause damage. Wipe the residue away, and then buff the glass with a dry area of the cloth. Any lens cloth should be washed on a regular basis to keep it clean.

CLEANING THE LOW PASS FILTER

Unwanted material such as dust or particles of lint can accumulate inside the D7000 and may settle on the surface of the optical low-pass filter (OLPF). This is an unfortunate problem that can afflict any digital camera, especially those with interchangeable lenses, as foreign matter can enter the camera when a lens is removed or changed. Focusing or adjusting the zoom ring of a lens causes groups of lens elements to be shifted inside the lens barrel, creating very slight changes in air pressure. This can cause dust in the atmosphere to be drawn through the lens into the camera. Furthermore, the operation of internal camera mechanisms such as the shutter and reflex mirror can generate minute particles due to the wear and tear of the moving parts. During the manufacture of the D7000, Nikon has attempted to reduce the incidence of such problems by cycling the shutter mechanism many hundreds of times before it is installed in the camera.

Any dust or other material that settles on the low-pass filter will often appear as dark spots in your pictures; they cast shadows on the camera's sensor that is located behind this filter. The exact nature of

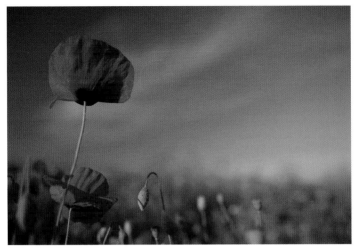

^ Cleaning your D7000 and any lenses you use should be a regular part of your photographic routine before and after every shoot.

the appearance of these shadows will depend on the size of the particle and the lens aperture you use. At very large apertures (f/1.4), it is likely that most very small dust specks will not be visible. However, at small apertures (f/22), they will probably show up with well-defined edges.

Self-Cleaning: The D7000 incorporates a self-cleaning function that vibrates OLPF at four different frequencies using a piezoelectric oscillator; this is exactly the same system as used in the D90 and D300s camera models. The cleaning process can be set to activate automatically when the camera is turned on, turned off, or both. Alternatively, it can be activated at any time you deem necessary.

Whenever you use the self-cleaning feature, make sure the camera is placed base-down on a solid surface. There are two good reasons for this; first, the effect of vibrating the low-pass filter will be most efficient when the camera is supported firmly; and second, there is a strip of highly adhesive material located along the bottom edge of the low-pass filter that is designed to capture and retain any dislodged material.

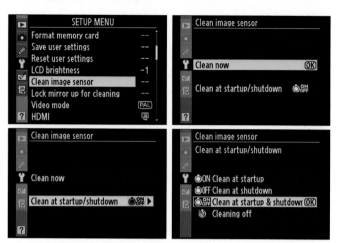

Select [Clean image sensor] in the Setup menu to see the self-cleaning options: [Clean now] and [Clean at startup / shutdown]. Choose [Clean at startup / shutdown] to display the list of options shown in the bottom right screen above.

To configure the self-cleaning feature, open the Setup menu and navigate to the [Clean image sensor] item and press ▶ to display two options: [Clean now] and [Clean at startup / shutdown]. [Clean now] is highlighted by default and pressing the ⊛ button will initiate the process during which the message, "Cleaning image sensor" is displayed on the monitor. This option can be used anytime during camera operation.

HINT: It worth getting into the habit of checking images periodically for any telltale particle shadows, using the zoom function in image Playback (🔍 button). I keep the [Clean image sensor] item listed under [My Menu] on my D7000, so I can access it quickly and effectively anytime, should the need to use it arise.

To have the cleaning process commence automatically, open the Setup menu and navigate to the [Clean image sensor] item and press ▶, then highlight the [Clean at startup / shutdown] option and press ▶ to display four options:

- ⊚ON [Clean at startup]: Cleaning is only performed at startup.
- ⊚OFF [Clean at shutdown]: Cleaning is only performed at shutdown.
- ⊚ON/OFF [Clean at startup and shutdown] (default): Cleaning is performed at startup and shutdown.
- [Cleaning off]: Automatic cleaning function is off.

[Clean at startup] would appear to be the most logical selection, as it will help remove any unwanted material before you start shooting. Having the function operate at camera shutdown will bring no benefit to images that have already been recorded and will have no effect on any material that settles on the low-pass filter while the camera is dormant; therefore, I can see little advantage in running the process at this point.

NOTE: Using any other camera control or function will interrupt the sensor cleaning process. If the built-in flash is raised, the sensor cleaning process may not operate when the camera starts up.

NOTE: If the sensor cleaning process is repeated several times in rapid succession, the D7000 may disable the function to protect the camera's electrical circuitry. If this occurs, wait a few minutes before attempting to use the function again.

NOTE: While the sensor cleaning function is operating, you may hear a short sequence of very faint high-pitched squeaks; this is normal and not an indication of malfunction.

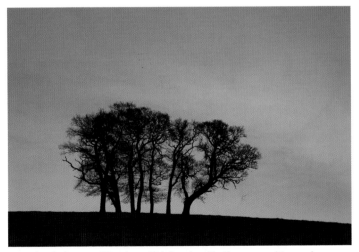

∧ Keeping the low-pass filter clean will help reduce the time you need to spend retouching dust spots, which will be particularly obvious in areas of continuous tone, such as a clear sky.

Manual Cleaning: Nikon expressly recommends that you should leave manual cleaning of the optical low-pass filter to an authorized service center. However, in recognition of the fact that this is likely to be impractical for a variety of reasons, the D7000 has a feature that enables the reflex mirror to be locked up in its raised position and the shutter opened, to provide access to the front surface of the OLPF.

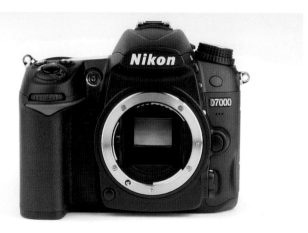

^ Access to the OLPF for the cleaning is via the lens mount opening; here, the reflex mirror is shown in its lowered position, it must be raised and the shutter opened to reveal the front surface of the OLPF (using the [Lock mirror up for cleaning] item in the Setup menu), shown above.

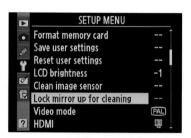

CAUTION: Nikon states that under no circumstances should you touch or wipe the surface of the OLPF, as it is extremely delicate. Any manual cleaning process you perform is done entirely at your own risk; any damage caused to the low-pass filter, or any other part of your camera, as a result of manual cleaning by the user will not be covered by warranties provided by Nikon.

To inspect and / or clean the low-pass filter, you need to perform a few preparatory steps. First, ensure the camera has a fully charged battery installed or is powered by the optional EH-5a AC adapter. Second, remove the lens or body cap, and keep the camera facing downward. Now, switch the camera on, navigate to the [Lock mirror up for cleaning] item in the Setup menu, and press ▶ to display [Start]. Press ⊛ and a dialog box will appear with the following instruction: "When shutter button is pressed, the mirror lifts and shutter opens. To lower mirror, turn camera off." When shutter release is pressed all the way down, the mirror will lift and remain in its raised position, and the monitor display and viewfinder will go blank. Keeping the camera facing down so that any debris falls away from the filter, look up into the lens mount to inspect the low-pass filter surface (it is probably helpful to shine a light onto it).

NOTE: The [Lock mirror up for cleaning] item in the Setup menu is not available if the battery level is at ⚡▥▥ (60%), or less; it will be grayed out.

NOTE: The photosites on the CMOS sensor of the D7000 are just **4.78** microns (μm) square (one micron = 1/1000 of a millimeter); therefore, offending particles are often very, very small, and it is unlikely you will be able to resolve all of them by eye.

To clean the low-pass filter, keep the camera facing down and use a rubber bulb blower to gently puff air toward the low-pass filter surface. Take care that you do not enter any part of the blower into the camera. Never use an ordinary blower brush with bristles, which can damage the surface of the low-pass filter, or an aerosol-type blower, which might emit propellant agent or cause condensation and leave a residue. Once you have finished cleaning, switch the camera off to return the mirror to its lowered position. If the blower bulb method fails to remove any stubborn material, I recommend you have the sensor cleaned professionally.

CAUTION: If the power supply fails during the cleaning process, the shutter will close and the mirror will return to its down position. This has potentially dire consequences if you have any cleaning utensils in the camera at the moment! Therefore, always use a fully charged EN-EL15 battery, or the EH-5a AC adapter with EP-5B power adapter.

NOTE: If power from the installed battery begins to run low while the mirror is locked up for cleaning, the camera will emit an audible warning and the Self-Timer lamp will begin to flash, indicating the mirror will be automatically lowered in approximately two minutes.

For users with plenty of confidence, there is a range of proprietary sensor cleaning materials that can be used to clean stubborn material from the low-pass filter. These include brushes, swabs, and fluids and are available from a number of manufacturers (see the list of resources on pages 368-369). It must be stressed that if you use any such materials or implements, it is done entirely at your own risk.

CAUTION: If you decide to clean the low pass filter of your D7000 with a wet process, make sure you NEVER use any alcohol-based (e.g., ethanol, methanol) cleaning fluid. The low-pass filter of the D7000 has a special anti-static coating made from indium tin oxide that can be damaged by such chemical compounds.

Finally, if you have Nikon Capture NX2 software, you can use the [Image Dust Off ref photo] item in the Setup menu with NEF files shot using the D7000 to help remove the effects of dust particles on the low-pass filter by masking their shadows electronically (see pages 244-245 for more details).

TROUBLESHOOTING

On occasion, the D7000 camera may not operate as you expect. This may be due to an alternate setting that has been made (often inadvertently), or for some other reason. Many of the reasons for these problems are straightforward and possible solutions are set out in the table below:

PROBLEM	SOLUTION
Viewfinder appears out of focus	• Adjust viewfinder focus. • Use diopter adjustment lens.
Viewfinder is dark	Insert a fully charged EN-EL15 battery.
Displays turn off unexpectedly	Set longer delay under [Auto off timers] in the Setup menu.
Camera does not respond to controls	See page 367 for information about electrostatic interference.
Displays in LCD screen and viewfinder appear slow to react and / or are dimmed	This is probably due to the effect of high or low ambient temperature.
Fine lines visible around AF point, or display turns red when AF point is highlighted	This is normal operation and not a sign of malfunction.
Camera takes longer than expected to turn on	Delete files / folders.
Shutter release disabled	• Focus not acquired. • CPU lens aperture ring not set to minimum value. • Memory card full, locked, or not installed. • Non-CPU lens attached but camera not in Manual exposure mode. • Flash is charging.
No image taken when remote control shutter release is pressed	Replace battery in remote control. Choose Remote Control release mode. Flash is charging. Delay selected for CS-5 [Remote on duration] has elapsed. Bright light is interfering with IR signal from remote.
Pictures out of focus	• AF-S or AF-I lens not attached. • Camera set to Manual focus. • AF unable to operate; use Manual focus.
Focus does not lock when shutter release is depressed halfway	Camera in AF-C focus mode: Use 🔒 button to lock focus.
Cannot select focus point	• AF-A set as AF-Area mode. • Shutter release half depressed to turn LCD screen off or activate exposure meter.
Subject-Tracking AF not available	Select non-Monochrome Picture Control.
Cannot select AF-Area mode	Manual focus selected.
Image Size cannot be altered	NEF (RAW) selected for Image Quality.

PROBLEM	SOLUTION
Camera is slow to record photos	Turn Noise Reduction off in Shooting menu.
Randomly-spaced bright pixels appear in photos ("noise")	• Select lower ISO setting or use Noise Reduction. • Shutter speed exceeds 8 seconds; use Long Exposure Noise Reduction.
Banding appears in Live View and D-Movie recording	Choose option under [Flicker reduction] that matches local AC power supply.
Sound not recorded in D-Movie mode	[Microphone off] selected in Movie Settings in the Shooting menu.
Photos are blotched or smeared	• Clean lens. • Clean low-pass filter.
Date is not imprinted on picture	Image Quality set to NEF (RAW), or NEF + JPEG.
Menu item cannot be selected	Some menu items not available in all exposure modes.
Shutter-release disabled	• Flash charging. • Non-CPU lens attached: Select M mode. • buLb selected in M mode and then Mode dial set to S mode: Choose new shutter speed.
Full range of shutter speeds is not available	Flash in use. Use CS-e1 [Flash sync speed] to set required sync speed; 1/320s (Auto FP) or 1/250s (Auto FP) enables full range of shutter speeds. [On] is selected for [Manual movie settings].
Colors appear unnatural	• Adjust White Balance. • Adjust [Set Picture Control] settings in the Shooting menu.
Cannot measure Preset White Balance	Test target too dark or too bright.
Image cannot be selected as source for Preset White Balance	Image not created with D7000.
Results with Picture Control vary from image to image	Avoid A (auto) for sharpening, contrast, or saturation when shooting a sequence of pictures.
Unable to adjust contrast for selected Picture Control	Switch off Active D-Lighting in the Shooting menu.
Metering cannot be changed	Autoexposure Lock is active.
Exposure Compensation cannot be used	Select P, A, or S exposure mode.

PROBLEM	SOLUTION
Only one shot taken when shutter release button is pressed in Continuous shooting mode	Lower the built-in flash.
Reddish areas and / or uneven textures appear in photos	May occur with long exposures; use Noise Reduction when shooting with shutter speed set to bu Ꮭ b.
• Flashing areas appear in images • Shooting data appear on images • A graph appears during Playback	Press ▲ or ▼ to select what photo information is displayed, or change settings for [Display mode] in the Setup menu.
NEF (RAW) image is not played back	Photo taken at NEF + JPEG Image Quality.
Some photos not displayed in Playback mode	Select [All] for [Playback Folder].
"Tall" (portrait) orientation photos are displayed in "Wide" (landscape) orientation	• Select [On] for [Rotate tall]. • [Off] selected for [Auto image rotation]. • Camera orientation was altered while shooting in Continuous mode, or camera was pointed up / down when shooting. • Picture is already displayed in Image Review.
Cannot delete a photo	• Photo is protected: Remove protection. • Memory card is locked.
Cannot retouch picture	• Picture cannot be edited any further within the D7000. • Image file is a video; these cannot be retouched in camera.
Cannot change print order	• Memory card is full: Delete images. • Memory card is locked.
Cannot select image for direct printing	• Photo saved in NEF (RAW) format. • Create JPEG copy using [NEF Raw processing] item. • Transfer to computer and print using Nikon View NX2 or Capture NX2.
Photos not displayed on TV	Select correct video mode in the Setup menu. Ensure A/V or HDMI cable is connected properly.
Cannot transfer photos to a computer	Computer operating system incompatible with D7000 or transfer software.

PROBLEM	SOLUTION
NEF (RAW) photos not displayed in Capture NX2	Update software to Capture NX 2 version 2.2.6 or later.
Image Dust Off option in Nikon Capture NX2 is ineffective	Image sensor cleaning alters the position of dust and other material on the low-pass filter. The Dust Off reference data recorded before image sensor cleaning is performed cannot be used with images recorded after image sensor cleaning is performed. Dust Off reference data recorded after image sensor cleaning is performed cannot be used with photographs taken before image sensor cleaning is performed.
Computer displays NEF (RAW) images differently than camera display	Off-brand software does not display effects of Picture Controls or Active D-Lighting; use Capture NX.
Date of recording is not correct	Reset camera clock.
Menu item cannot be selected	Some options are not available at certain combinations of settings or when no memory card is inserted.

ERROR MESSAGES AND DISPLAYS

The D7000 is a sophisticated electronic device, capable of reporting a range of malfunctions and problems through indicators and error messages that appear in the displays of the viewfinder, control panel, and LCD monitor. The following table will assist you in finding a solution, should one of these indicators or messages be displayed.

PROBLEM	INDICATOR		SOLUTION
	CONTROL PANEL	VIEW-FINDER	
Lens aperture ring is at a setting other than the minimum aperture (largest f/number).	FE E (blinks)	FE E (blinks)	Set lens aperture ring to minimum aperture (largest f/number).
Low battery	▭	▭	Prepare a fully-charged spare battery.
• Battery exhausted • Battery cannot be used • Heavily discharged battery is inserted in the camera or MB-D11 battery pack	▭ (blinks)	▭ (blinks)	• Recharge or replace battery. • Contact Nikon-authorized service representative. • Replace battery or recharge the battery.

| PROBLEM | INDICATOR | | SOLUTION |
	CONTROL PANEL	VIEW-FINDER	
Camera clock not set	CLOCK (blinks)	—	Set camera clock.
No lens attached, or non-CPU lens attached without specifying maximum aperture value	m	m	Aperture will be displayed if maximum aperture is specified.
Camera unable to focus using autofocus	—	● (blinks)	Focus manually or change composition.
Lens not attached. Non-CPU lens attached	F-- (blinks)	F-- (blinks)	• Attach non-IX NIKKOR lens. • If non-CPU lens is attached, select mode A or M.
Subject is too bright	Hi	Hi	• Use a lower ISO Sensitivity. • Use a commercial ND filter. • In mode: S Increase shutter speed. A Choose a smaller aperture (larger f/number).
Subject is too dark.	Lo	Lo	• Use a higher ISO Sensitivity. • Use flash. • In mode: S Choose a slower shutter speed. A Choose a larger aperture (smaller f/number).
bulb selected in S mode.	bulb (blinks)	bulb (blinks)	• Change shutter speed or select Manual exposure mode.
- - selected in S mode.	- - (blinks)	- - (blinks)	• Change shutter speed or select Manual exposure mode.
Optional flash unit that does not support i-TTL flash control attached and set to TTL	▯ (blinks)	ϟ (blinks)	Change flash mode settings on flash unit.
If icon blinks for more than 3s after flash fires, picture maybe underexposed	—	ϟ (blinks)	Check picture in LCD monitor, and adjust exposure settings if required.
Insufficient memory to record additional pictures at current settings, or camera has run out of file / folder numbers	Full (blinks	Ful (blinks	• Reduce Image Quality or Size. • Delete photographs. • Insert new memory card.
Camera malfunction	Err (blinks)	Err (blinks)	Release shutter. If error persists consult Nikon-authorized service representative.

PROBLEM	INDICATOR		SOLUTION
	CONTROL PANEL	VIEW-FINDER	
Camera cannot detect a memory card	No memory card.	(-E-)	• Turn camera off and confirm that card is correctly inserted.
Error accessing memory card Unable to create new folder	This memory card cannot be used. Card may be damaged. Insert another card.	Err (blinks)	• Use approved card. • Format card. If problem persists, card may be damaged. Contact Nikon-authorized service representative. • Delete files or insert new memory card.
Camera cannot control Eye-fi card	📶	Err (blinks)	Check that Eye-fi card firmware is up to date. Copy files on Eye-fi card to computer or other device and format card, or insert alternative card.
Memory card is locked – write protected	Memory card is locked. Slide lock to "write" position.	Cd (blinks)	Slide write-protect switch to "write" position.
Memory cad has not been formatted for use in camera	This card is not formatted. Format card?	For (blinks)	Format card or turn camera off and insert new memory card.
Firmware for flash unit not updated correctly	Failed to update flash unit firmware. Flash cannot be used. Contact Nikon	—	Contact Nikon-authorized service representative.
No images on memory card or in folder(s) selected for Playback	Folder contains no images.	—	Folder selected for Playback contains no images. Insert another memory card or select a different folder.

PROBLEM	INDICATOR		SOLUTION
	CONTROL PANEL	VIEW-FINDER	
All pictures are hidden	All pictures in current folder are hidden.	—	No pictures can be played back until another folder is selected, or [Hide image] is used to allow at least one picture to be displayed.
File has been created / modified using a computer or different make of camera	Cannot display this file.	—	File cannot be played back on camera.
Selected image cannot be retouched	Cannot select this file.	—	Pictures created with other devices cannot be retouched.
Selected movie file cannot be edited	This movie cannot be edited	—	Movies created with other devices cannot be edited. Movie clip must be at least 2 seconds long.
Printer error	Check printer.	—	Check printer. To resume, select [Continue] (if available).
Paper in printer is not of selected size	Check paper.	—	Insert paper of correct size and select [Continue].
Paper is jammed in printer	Paper jam.	—	Clear jam and select [Continue].
Printer is out of paper	Out of paper.	—	Insert paper of selected size and select [Continue].
Ink error	Check ink supply.	—	Check ink. To resume, select [Continue]. [1]
Printer is out of ink	Out of ink.	—	Replace ink and select [Continue].

[1] See printer manual for more information.

DIGITAL WORKFLOW

367

ELECTROSTATIC INTERFERENCE

Operation of the D7000 is totally dependent on electrical power. Occasionally, the camera may stop functioning properly or display unusual characters or unexpected messages in the viewfinder, control panel, and monitor displays. Such behavior is often due to the effects of a strong external electrostatic charge. If this occurs, try switching the camera off, disconnecting it from its power supply (remove the installed EN-EL15 battery or unplug the EH-5a AC adapter), and then reconnecting the power and switching the camera back on. If this does not resolve the problem and the symptoms persist, the camera will require inspection by an authorized technician.

A number of other manufacturers and suppliers provide equipment to compliment and enhance the performance of the cameras and flash accessories produced by Nikon. The following is a list of some that you may find useful:

○ Adobe: Authors of popular digital imaging software including Photoshop CS5, Photoshop Elements 9, and Lightroom 3, all of which are compatible with files from the D7000; www.adobe.com

○ Audio-Technica: Manufacturers of external microphones suitable for use with the D7000; www.audio-technica.com

○ B&W: Manufacturers of filters and accessories; www.schneideroptics.com

○ Gitzo: Manufacturers of tripods, monopods, and general camera support accessories; www.gitzo.com

○ HDRsoft: Authors of the popular Photomatix high-dynamic range software; www.hdrsoft.com

○ Hoodman: Manufacturers of viewfinder and LCD monitor screen accessories, such as the Hoodman Loupe; www.**hoodmanusa.com**

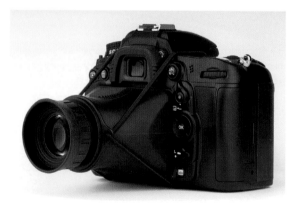

> Hoodman Hoodloupe 3 makes viewing the D7000's monitor that much easier, which is especially useful when recording video with the camera.

○ Kirk Enterprises: Manufacturers of camera and flash accessories, including flash brackets; www.kirkphoto.com

○ Lastolite: Manufacturers of lighting accessories for portable flash units and a wide range of reflectors, diffusers, and other light modifying devices; www.lastolite.com

○ Lee Filters: Manufacturers of both lens and lighting filters, including graduated filters; www.leefilters.com

- Lexar Media: Manufacturers of flash memory cards, including Secure Digital (SD), Secure Digital High Capacity (SDHC), and Secure Digital Extended Capacity (SDXC) cards compatible with the D7000; www.lexar.com
- Lightshpere: A range of flash diffusion devices designed by photographer Gary Fong; www.garyfong.com
- Lumiquest: Manufacturers of flash modifiers and diffusers; www.lumiquest.com
- Manfrotto: Manufacturers of tripods, lighting stands, and flash support accessories; www.manfrotto.com
- Rode: Manufacturers of external microphones suitable for use with the D7000; www.rodemic.com
- Really Right Stuff: Manufacturers of an extensive range of camera, flash, close-up, and panoramic photography accessories; www.reallyrightstuff.com
- SanDisk: Manufacturers of flash memory cards, including SD, SDHC and SDXC cards compatible with the D7000; www.sandisk.com
- Singh-Ray: Manufacturers of camera lens filters, including graduated filter types; www.singh-ray.com

WEB SUPPORT

Nikon maintains product support and provides further information online at the following sites:

- www.nikon.com – Global gateway to Nikon Corporation
- www.nikonusa.com – Continental North America
- www.europe-nikon.com – Most European countries
- www.nikon-asia.com – Asia, Oceania, Middle East, and Africa

Glossary

AI
Automatic Indexing.

angle of view
The area that can be recorded by a lens, usually measured in degrees across the diagonal of the film frame. Angle of view depends on both the focal length of the lens and the size of its image area.

anti-aliasing
A technique that reduces or eliminates the jagged appearance of lines or edges in an image by filling in nearby pixels with intermediate values.

aperture
The opening in the lens that allows light to enter the camera. Aperture is usually described as an f/number. The higher the f/number, the smaller the aperture; the lower the f/number, the larger the aperture.

bit depth
The number of bits per pixel that determines the number of colors the image can display. Eight bits per pixel is the minimum requirement for a photo-quality color image.

buffer
Temporarily stores data so that other programs, on the camera or the computer, can continue to run while data is in transition. Also called a memory buffer.

card reader
A device that connects to your computer and enables the quick and easy download of images from memory card to computer.

CMOS
Complementary Metal-Oxide Semiconductor. Like CCD sensors, this sensor type converts light into an electrical impulse. Unlike CCDs, CMOS sensors allow individual processing of pixels, are less expensive to produce, and use less power. See also, CCD.

color cast
A colored hue over the image often caused by improper lighting or incorrect white balance settings. Can be produced intentionally for creative effect.

color space
A mapped relationship between colors and computer data about the colors.

compression
A method of reducing file size through removal of redundant data. Comes in two forms: lossy (i.e., JPEG) and lossless (i.e., TIFF).

contrast
The difference between two or more tones in terms of luminance, density, or darkness.

depth of field (DOF)
The image space in front of and behind the plane of focus that appears acceptably sharp in the photograph. Determined by aperture, focal length, and camera-to-subject distance.

EV
Exposure value. A number that quantifies the amount of light within a scene, allowing you to determine the relative combinations of aperture and shutter speed to accurately reproduce the light levels of that exposure.

firmware
Software that is permanently incorporated into a hardware chip. All computer-based equipment, including digital cameras, uses firmware of some kind.

focal length

When the lens is focused on infinity, it is the distance from the optical center of the lens to the film or sensor plane.

focal plane

The plane perpendicular to the axis of the lens that is the sharpest point of focus. Also, it may be the film plane or sensor plane.

FP High-Speed sync

Focal Plane high-speed sync. An FP mode in which the output of an electronic flash unit is pulsed to match the small opening of the shutter as it moves across the sensor, so that the flash unit can be used with higher shutter speeds than the normal flash sync limit of the camera. In this flash mode, the level of flash output is reduced and, consequently, the shooting range is reduced.

f/stop

The size of the aperture or diaphragm opening of a lens, also referred to as f/number or stop. The term stands for the ratio of the focal length (f) of the lens to the width of its aperture opening. (f/1.4 = wide opening, and f/22 = narrow opening.) Each stop up (lower f/number) doubles the amount of light reaching the sensitized medium. Each stop down (higher f/number) halves the amount of light reaching the sensitized medium.

gray card

A card used to take accurate exposure readings. It typically has a white side that reflects 90% of the light and a gray side that reflects 18%.

grayscale

A successive series of tones ranging between black and white, which have no color. Also, an image with purely luminance data and no chroma information.

guide number (GN)

A number used to quantify the output of a flash unit. It is derived by using this formula: GN = aperture x distance. Guide numbers are expressed for a given ISO film speed in either feet or meters.

histogram

A two-dimensional graphic representation of image tones. Histograms plot brightness along the horizontal axis and number of pixels along the vertical axis, and are useful for determining if an image will be under- or overexposed.

infinity

In photographic terms, the theoretical most distant point of focus.

ISO

From ISOS (Greek for equal), a term for industry standards from the International Organization for Standardization. When an ISO number is applied to film, it indicates the relative light sensitivity of the recording medium. Digital sensors use film ISO equivalents, which are based on enhancing the data stream or boosting the signal.

JPEG

Joint Photographic Experts Group. This is a lossy compression file format that works with any computer and photo software. JPEG examines an image for redundant information and then removes it. It is a variable compression format because the amount of leftover data depends on the detail in the photo and the amount of compression. At low compression/high quality, the loss of data has a negligible effect on the photo. However, JPEG should not be used as a working format—the file should be reopened and saved in a format such as TIFF, which does not compress the image.

latitude

The acceptable range of exposure (from under to over) determined by observed loss of image quality.

lithium-ion (Li-ion)

A popular battery technology that is not prone to the charge memory effects of nickel-cadmium (Ni-Cd) batteries, or the low temperature performance problems of alkaline batteries.

Manual exposure mode

A camera operating mode that requires the user to determine and set both the aperture and shutter speed. This is the opposite of automatic exposure.

middle gray

Halfway between black and white, it is an average gray tone with 18% reflectance. See also, gray card.

midtone

The tone that appears as medium brightness, or medium gray tone, in a photographic print.

overexposed

When too much light is recorded in the image, causing the photo to be too light in tone.

pan

Moving the camera to follow a moving subject. When a slow shutter speed is used, this creates an image in which the subject appears sharp and the background is blurred.

plugin

Third-party software created to augment an existing software program.

pre-flashes

A series of short duration, low intensity flash pulses emitted by a flash unit immediately prior to the shutter opening. These flashes help the TTL light meter assess the reflectivity of the subject. See also, TTL.

Program mode

In Program exposure mode, the camera selects a combination of shutter speed and aperture automatically.

RAW

An image file format that has little internal processing applied by the camera. It contains 12-bit color information, a wider range of data than 8-bit formats such as JPEG.

RAW+JPEG

An image file format that records two files per capture; one RAW file and one JPEG file.

rear-curtain sync

A feature that causes the flash unit to fire just prior to the shutter closing. It is used for creative effect when mixing flash and ambient light.

RGB mode

Red, Green, and Blue. This is the color model most commonly used to display color images on video systems, film recorders, and computer monitors. It displays all visible colors as combinations of red, green, and blue. RGB mode is the most common color mode for viewing and working with digital files onscreen.

S

See Shutter-priority mode.

saturation

The degree to which a color of fixed tone varies from the neutral, grey tone; low saturation produces pastel shades whereas high saturation gives pure color.

Shutter-priority mode

An automatic exposure mode in which you manually select the shutter speed and the camera automatically selects the aperture.

slow sync

A flash mode in which a slow shutter speed is used with the flash in order to allow low-level ambient light to be recorded by the sensitized medium.

synchronize

Causing a flash unit to fire simultaneously with the complete opening of the camera's shutter.

thumbnail

A small representation of an image file used principally for identification purposes.

TIFF

Tagged Image File Format. This popular digital format uses lossless compression.

TTL

Through-the-Lens, i.e., TTL metering. Any metering system – ambient exposure or flash – which works through the lens. Such systems require sensors built into the camera bodies with beam splitters to transfer incoming light to the sensor systems.

vignetting

A reduction in light at the edge of an image due to use of a filter or an inappropriate lens hood for the particular lens.

VR

Vibration Reduction. This technology is used in such photographic accessories as a VR lens and reduces camera shake and vibration.

Index

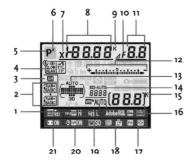

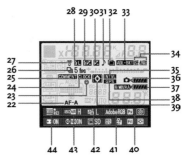

1. WB White Balance / WB Fine-Tuning indicator
2. Image Quality / role played by card in slot 2
3. Image Size
4. Flash mode
5. Shooting mode
6. P* Flexible Program indicator
7. Flash Sync indicator
8. Shutter speed / Exposure Compensation / Flash Compensation / number of shots in bracketing sequence / Focal length non-CPU lenses / color temperature
9. Color temperature indicator
10. Aperture stop indictor
11. f/number / number of stops / bracketing increment / max aperture for non-CPU lenses
12. Exposure indicator / Exposure Compensation display / bracketing progress / Exposure, Flash, WB Bracketing
13. Auto-Area AF / focus points / AF-Area mode / 3D-Tracking indicator
14. ISO / Auto ISO indicator
15. "K" displays when over 1000 exposures remain in memory
16. Number of exposures remaining / manual lens number
17. Fn button assignment
18. AE-L/AF-L button assignment
19. Picture Control indicator
20. Long Exposure Noise Reduction indicator
21. Auto Distortion Control
22. Autofocus mode
23. Copyright Information
24. Clock not set indicator
25. Image comment indicator
26. Release mode / Continuous shooting speed
27. Eye-Fi connection indicator
28. FV-Lock indicator
29. Flash Compensation indicator
30. Exposure Compensation indicator
31. Beep indicator
32. Multiple Exposure indicator
33. Exposure / Flash / WB / ADL Bracketing indicator
34. ADL Bracketing amount
35. Interval Timer indicator
36. Battery level indicator
37. MB-D11 battery type display / MB-D11 battery indictor
38. GPS connection indicator
39. Metering
40. Depth-of-Field Preview button assignment
41. Color space
42. Active D-Lighting indicator
43. High ISO Noise Reduction indicator
44. Movie quality

VIEWFINDER

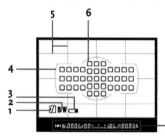

1. No memory card indicator
2. Black-and-white indicator
3. Low-battery warning
4. AF-Area brackets
5. Framing Grid
6. Focus points
7. Focus indicator
8. Autoexposure (AE) Lock
9. Shutter speed / AF mode
10. Aperture f/number / aperture number of stops
11. Low-battery indicator
12. Exposure / Flash / WB / ADL Bracketing indicator

13. ISO
14. K displays when over 1000 exposures remain in memory
15. Flash-Ready indicator
16. Number of exposures remaining / ISO / Preset WB recording indicator / ☒ Exposure Compensation value / 🕮 Flash Compensation value / Active D-Lighting amount / AF-Area mode
17. Auto ISO indicator

18. ☒ Exposure Compensation indicator
19. 🕮 Flash compensation indicator
20. Exposure indicator / ☒ Exposure Compensation display / Tilt indicator
21. Aperture stop indicator
22. Flash Sync indicator
23. FV-Lock indicator

CONTROL PANEL

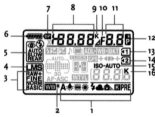

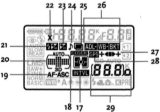

1. White Balance
2. White Balance Fine-Tuning indictor
3. Image Quality
4. Image Size
5. ⚡ Flash mode
6. Battery level indicator
7. MB-D11 battery pack indicator
8. Shutter speed / ☒ Exposure Compensation value / 🕮 Flash Compensation value / WB Fine-Tuning / color temperature / WB Preset number / Number of shots in bracketing sequence / Number of intervals for Interval Timer / Focal length (non-CPU lenses)
9. Color temperature indicator
10. Aperture stop indicator (non-CPU lenses)

11. Aperture f/number / number of stops / bracket increment / number of shots per interval / Max aperture (non-CPU lenses) / PC mode indicator
12. Flexible Program indicator
13. Memory card indicator (slot 1)
14. Memory card indicator (slot 2)
15. ISO / Auto ISO indicator
16. K displays when over 1000 exposures remain in memory
17. Interval Timer indicator
18. Clock not set
19. Autofocus mode
20. Auto-Area AF / AF-Area / 3D-Tracking indicator
21. 🕮 Flash Compensation indicator

22. Flash Sync indicator
23. ☒ Exposure Compensation indicator
24. Beep indicator
25. Multiple Exposure indicator
26. Exposure and Flash Bracketing / WB Bracketing / ADL Bracketing indicator
27. Bracketing progress indicator
28. GPS connection indicator
29. Metering
30. Number of exposures remaining / capture mode indicator / ISO / Preset WB recording Indicator / Active D-Lighting amount / manual lens number / HDMI-CED connection indicator